# Learning ACT! Pro Made Easy

## By Indera E. Murphy

Tolana Publishing
Teaneck, New Jersey

**Learning ACT! Pro Made Easy**

Tolana Publishing
PO Box 719
Teaneck, NJ 07666  USA

Find us online at www.tolanapublishing.com
Inquiries may be sent to the publisher: tolanapub@yahoo.com

Our books are available online at www.barnesandnoble.com. They can also be ordered from Ingram.

ISBN-13: 978-1-935208-39-6
ISBN-10: 1-935208-39-X

Library of Congress Control Number: 2018901195

Printed and bound in the United States Of America

Notice of Liability
The information in this book is distributed on as "as is" basis, without warranty. Every effort has been made to ensure that this book contains accurate and current information. However, the publisher and author shall not be liable to any person or entity with respect to any loss or damage caused or alleged to be caused directly or indirectly, as a result of any information contained herein or by the computer software and hardware products described in it.

Trademarks
All companies and product names are trademarks or registered trademarks of their respective companies. They are used in this book in an editorial fashion only. No use of any trademark is intended to convey endorsement or other affiliation with this book.

# About The Tools And Techniques Series

Learning ACT! Pro Made Easy, is part of a growing series of computer software books that cover a variety of software tools that provide the ability to create a variety of reports and visualizations, to aid in the analysis and decision making process. This book has been designed to be used as a self-paced learning tool, in a classroom setting or in an online class. All of the books contain an abundance of step-by-step instructions and screen shots to help reduce the "stress" often associated with learning new software. Some of the titles are shown below.

ISBN: 978-1-935208-36-5

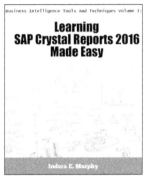

ISBN: 978-1-935208-35-8

ISBN: 978-1-935208-18-1

ISBN: 978-1-935208-34-1

ISBN: 978-1-935208-29-7

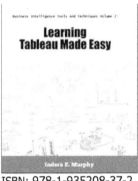

ISBN: 978-1-935208-37-2

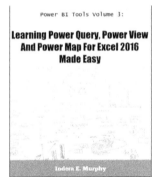

ISBN: 978-1-935208-28-0

ISBN: 978-1-935208-38-9

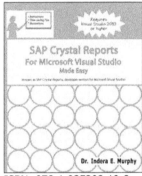

ISBN: 978-1-935208-19-8

ISBN: 978-1-935208-27-3

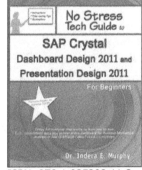

ISBN: 978-1-935208-11-2

ISBN: 978-1-935208-26-6

**Visit us online at www.tolanapublishing.com for more titles and information**

## Why A Book On ACT! Pro?

I felt that readers, especially people new to ACT! Pro, would prefer to have more assistance in learning how to get the most out of the software. I do not feel that flipping between a web site and the software's help file is the most ideal way to learn how to use software.

In general, there are very few books with hands-on exercises for this software. I know that many books claim to have "step-by-step instructions". If you have tried to follow books that make this claim and you got lost or could not complete a task as instructed, it may not have been your fault. When I decided to write computer books, I vowed to really have step-by-step instructions that actually included every step. This includes steps like which file to open, which menu option to select and more. In my opinion, it is this level of detail that makes a computer book easy to follow. I hope that you feel the same way.

Over the years, I have come to realize that many people only use a small percent of the features that software has to offer. One of my goals in all of the books that I write, is to point out as many features as possible. My theory is that if more people knew about more than 10% of the features that a software package has, at the very least, they would try a few of them.

## About The Author

Dr. Indera E. Murphy is an author, educator and IT professional that has over 25 years of experience in the Information Technology field. She has held a variety of positions including technical writer, programmer, consultant, web designer, course developer and project leader. Indera has designed and developed software applications and web sites, as well as, manage technology driven projects in several industries. In addition to being an Executive Director and consultant, as an online adjunct professor, she has taught courses in a variety of areas including project management, technical writing, information processing, Access, HTML, Windows, Excel, Dreamweaver and critical thinking.

**Thank you for purchasing this book!**

# CONTENTS

# GETTING STARTED WITH ACT! PRO

Overview

The fastest and easiest way to overcome an obstacle is to have someone that has been there, to be by your side every step of the way. That is the goal of this book, to be by your side, while you learn ACT! Pro.

This book is a visual guide that shows you how to create and modify contact, company, group and opportunity records. There are over 500 illustrations in this book that practically eliminate the guess work and let you know that you are doing the steps correctly. Real world examples are provided to help give you an idea of when to use certain features. There is more to ACT! than knowing how to enter contact information. ACT! is robust and has a lot of features.

Learning new tips and shortcuts will allow you to work faster and smarter. The more that you know about ACT!, the easier your day to day contact and customer relationship management experiences will be.

By the time that you complete all of the exercises in this book, you will know more than the basics of ACT!. While you can jump from one section of the book to another, mainly because you paid for the book and can do as you please, I hope that you complete all of the exercises in the order that they are presented, because that will help you gain a better understanding of the features and functionality that ACT! offers. You will also gain more insight into how the features work together.

**Sit back and lets get started!**

CHAPTER 1

## What Is ACT! And What Can It Do For Me?

ACT! is a very popular Contact and Customer Relationship Management (CRM) database software package that is used by individuals and companies. In the beginning, ACT! was primarily used by sales people, but over the years the user base and types of companies that use ACT! has expanded. There are millions of ACT! users. CRM software provides a way to keep your contacts, which can be business associates, customers, friends, family, vendors, potential customers and any type of contacts that you have, organized. More importantly to many users, ACT! has the ability to create an audit trail and history for each contact. This makes it easier to remember your relationship with each contact.

ACT! is used to store information like addresses, contact type, to-do lists, meeting and sales information, as well as, other information that will help you maintain existing contacts and develop new contacts. ACT! also has built in applications that allow you to do word processing, send faxes, create and send email. One feature that you may find very useful is the variety of ways that you can look up contact information. Additionally, you can put contacts into groups like friends, sales reps and territory. You can also design and run reports. One of the best features of ACT! is that you can customize it to better meet your needs.

There are two editions of ACT!: ACT! Pro and ACT! Premium. The biggest difference between these two editions is that the latter can be used to access the database on the web and via a mobile device.

The list of features that ACT! has for managing contacts is extensive. There are over 40 fields that can be used to store general contact information like name, company, email and address. Not only can you keep your contact information organized, you can attach documents that you create in other software packages to the contacts and activities in the database. That is just the beginning of what ACT! offers. The list below explains some of the functionality that ACT! has.

- ☑ Over 50 pre-built reports that present the data in an easy to understand format.
- ☑ The ability to customize existing reports and create your own reports.
- ☑ Automate the creation of a series of tasks that you have to complete for contacts on a regular basis.
- ☑ Put a copy of the database on your laptop to work remotely. When you return to the office, you can sync the copy on your laptop with the live copy of the database that is on a server.
- ☑ Use dashboards, graphs and pipelines to help make business decisions and discover new opportunities.

ACT! is relatively easy to learn. One reason that ACT! is easy to learn is because it has many of the same options that are in other software packages that you may have already used. This includes options on menus and keyboard shortcuts. When you first start using ACT!, you may think that there are not a lot of features, but there are more features then meets the eye. The majority of people that use ACT!, use it to manage contacts, but there is nothing stopping you from using it to keep track of your book, movie or music collection. If you already know that you need a custom contact management database, you may find it helpful to take notes, while reading this book, on the features that you will need to create a database that meets your needs.

If you have read any reviews of ACT!, you have probably read that using the software will make you more efficient and will save you time when it comes to managing your contacts. That is true. What the reviews do not point out or make obvious is that to get the most out of ACT! or any software package for that matter, one has to know more than the basics of the software.

## Overall Objectives

This book is written to accommodate a variety of learning styles. While there are no prerequisites to successfully complete the exercises in this book, having a general knowledge of any of the following would be helpful.

- ☑ Prior version of ACT!
- ☑ Windows environment
- ☑ Database structures, if you want to create fields or reports

Step-by-step instructions are included throughout this book. This book takes a hands-on, performance based approach to teaching you how to use ACT! and provides the skills required to use the software efficiently. After reading and completing the exercises in this book, you will be able to perform the following tasks and more:

- ☑ Customize ACT!
- ☑ Create, edit and duplicate contact, company, group and opportunity records
- ☑ Use the Lookup command

☑ Sort contact records
☑ Link company and contact records
☑ Run reports
☑ Schedule activities and create opportunities
☑ Perform database maintenance tasks

## Chapter 1 Objectives

In this chapter you will learn about the following:

☑ What ACT! can do for you
☑ The ACT! demo database
☑ The My Record
☑ Creating and copying databases
☑ Sharing a database

## Conventions Used In This Book

I designed the following conventions to make it easier for you to follow the instructions in this book.

☑ The `Courier font` is used to indicate what you should type.
☑ **Drag** means to press and hold down the left mouse button while moving the mouse.
☑ **Click** means to press the left mouse button once, then release it immediately.
☑ **Double-click** means to quickly press the left mouse button twice, then release the mouse button.
☑ **Right-click** means to press the right mouse button once, which will open a shortcut menu.
☑ Press CTRL+SHIFT means to press and hold down the Ctrl (Control) key, then press the Shift key.
☑ Click **OK** means to click the OK button on the dialog box.
☑ Press **Enter** means to press the Enter key on your keyboard.
☑ Press **Tab** means to press the Tab key on your keyboard.
☑ Click **Save** means to click the Save button in the software.
☑ Click **Finish** means to click the Finish button on the dialog box.
☑ SMALL CAPS are used to indicate an option to click on or to bring something to your attention.
☑ This icon indicates a shortcut or another way to complete the task that is being explained. It can also indicate a tip or additional information about the topic being explained.
☑ This icon indicates a warning, like a feature that has been removed or information that you need to be aware of.
☑ This symbol indicates that some of the screen shot/figure is not displayed, because it does not provide any value.
☑ When you see "YOUR SCREEN SHOULD HAVE THE OPTIONS SHOWN IN FIGURE X-X", or something similar in the exercises, check to make sure that your screen does look like the figure. If it does, continue with the next set of instructions. If your screen does not look like the figure, redo the steps that you just completed so that your screen does match the figure. Not doing so may cause you problems when trying to complete exercises later in the book.
☑ "Clear the (name of option)" means to remove the check mark from the option specified in the instruction.
☑ The section heading EXERCISE X.Y: (where X equals the chapter number and Y equals the exercise number) represents exercises that have step-by-step instructions that you should complete. You will also see sections that have step-by-step instructions that are not an exercise. Completing them as you go through the book is optional, but recommended.
☑ [See Chapter 2, Contact Fields] refers to a section in a chapter that you can use as a reference for the topic that is being explained.
☑ [See Chapter 2, Figure 2-8] refers to an illustration (screen shot) that you can use as a reference for the topic that is being explained.
☑ Many of the dialog boxes in ACT! have OK and Cancel buttons. Viewing these buttons on all of the figures adds no value, so for the most part, these buttons are not shown.

☑ **VIEW** ⇒ **CALENDAR** ⇒ **DAILY**, means to open the **VIEW** menu, select **CALENDAR**, then select **DAILY**, as shown in Figure 1-1.

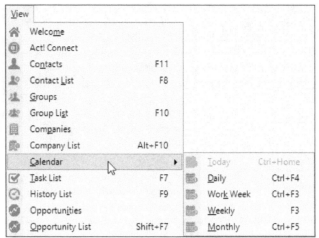

**Figure 1-1** Menu navigation technique

## Assumptions

Yes, I know one should never assume anything, but the following assumptions have been made. It is assumed that . . . .

☑ You know that the operating system used to write this book is Windows 8.1. If you are using a different version of Windows, any or all of the following can apply:

① Some of the screen shots may have a slightly different look.

② Some of the instructions for Windows tasks may be different.

③ The path to folders and files (for the software) on your computer may be different then the paths listed in this book.

☑ You already have installed ACT! v20 or higher.

☑ You understand that references to files or folders are files or folders on your computers hard drive and not a server. If your ACT! database is on a server, that is where the default ACT! folders should be located.

☑ You will have the My_ACT_Demo database open at the beginning of each chapter, starting with Chapter 2, unless instructed otherwise. You will create this database later in this chapter.

☑ You understand that many of the dates in the figures will be different then what you see on your computer screen.

☑ You understand that if you had a previous version of ACT! installed, before installing the latest version of ACT!, that some settings are automatically copied from the older version to the newer version. For the purposes of this book, that means that some of the default options that you see on your computer, will be different from the options displayed in this book.

☑ You have access to the Internet to download any updates that may be available for ACT! and to download the practice files needed to complete some of the exercises in this book.

☑ When you see <smile>, that signifies my attempt of adding humor to the learning process.

☑ You understand that from time to time, I will point out functionality that may not work as expected. When I do this, I am not complaining, merely pointing out things that you should be aware of.

☑ Optional: That you have access to a printer, if you want to print any of the reports that you run or create.

☑ Optional: You have Microsoft Word and Excel, version 2003 or higher installed, if you want to view output files created by some of the exercises in this book.

## What's Not Covered

Rarely does any one book cover all of the features that a software package has. I cannot speak for every author, but I did not omit features or topics to cheat or mislead you. It is often a question of time and importance of the topic in relation to what the most used features are of the software. The reason that the following features are not covered in this book is two-fold: They will not prevent you from using over 95% of the features in ACT! and some of the features listed below require additional software, hardware or both. Another reason they are not covered is because there are as many different set-ups for the additional software and hardware, as there are people using it.

For example, I may use Brand X PDA and you use Brand Y PDA. What works for me may not work for you. If I wrote instructions that you could not follow, you would think that there is something really wrong with me and even worse, you may think that I did not know what I was doing.

☑ Features only found in the Premium edition of ACT!, which aren't many.
☑ Sending broadcast faxes.
☑ Using ACT! with your PDA or with Microsoft Outlook.
☑ Synchronizing databases.
☑ Google integration.

## What Is A Database?

A **DATABASE** is a repository used to store a collection of related information. An ACT! database is used to store contacts and all of the information for each contact that you have. It seems to be human nature to want to enter as little data as possible, often to save time. <smile> ACT!, is more useful in the long run, if it has more data. A database has records and fields.

A **FIELD** holds one piece of information, like the contact name or title.

A **RECORD** is a collection of fields about one entity like a contact, company or opportunity.

## Exercise 1.1: First Time Opening ACT!

1.  Open ACT!. The first time that you open ACT! you will see the window shown in Figure 1-2. If you had a previous version of ACT! installed, you will also see the Open/Share Database dialog box.

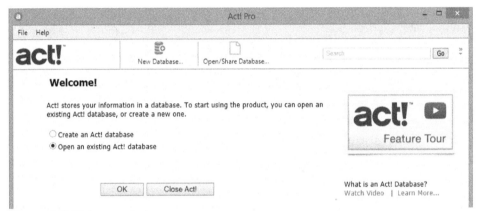

**Figure 1-2** Welcome window

The Welcome window has two options for selecting a database, as explained below.

    ① **CREATE AN ACT! DATABASE** This option is used to create a new ACT! database.
    ② **OPEN AN EXISTING ACT! DATABASE** Select this option when you want to open an existing database.

2.  If you do not see the Open/Share Database dialog box, click the Open/Share Database button ⇒ Select the ACT2018 Demo database ⇒ Click the Open Database button. If this is the first time that you are opening the demo database, it will take a few seconds to open.

## Welcome View

When you open an ACT! database you will see the view shown in Figure 1-3. The options on the window provide quick access to features that may be helpful to new users. The links in the Related Tasks section on the left of the window are explained below.

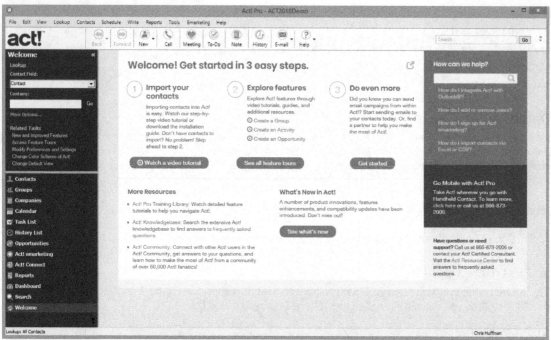

**Figure 1-3** Welcome view with a database open

## Welcome View Related Tasks

**NEW AND IMPROVED FEATURES** Opens the New and Improved Features topic page, in the online help file.

**ACCESS FEATURE TOURS** Opens the Video Feature Tours topic page, in the online help file.

**MODIFY PREFERENCES AND SETTINGS** Opens the Preferences dialog box. [See Chapter 2, Preferences Overview]

**CHANGE COLOR SCHEME OF ACT!** Opens the Colors & Fonts tab on the Preferences dialog box.
[See Chapter 2, Colors & Fonts Tab Preferences]

**CHANGE DEFAULT VIEW** Opens the Startup tab on the Preferences dialog box. [See Chapter 2, Startup Tab Preferences]

## ACT! Demo Database

ACT! comes with a fully functional demo database that you can use to learn how to use the software. This is the database that you will use to complete the exercises in this book. If you have made changes to the data in the demo database prior to using this book, you should copy the original database to your hard drive (or server, if the demo database is on a network). That way your data and results will match the exercises in this book.

## Getting Help

As explained below, there are four primary ways to get help if you have a question on how to use a feature or option in ACT!.

① Read this book from cover to cover and complete the exercises. Many of the basic questions that you may have are probably covered in this book.
② The Online Help file. This is an electronic version of the Users Guide. It is helpful for basic definitions.
③ If you have a question about ACT!, you can post a message in the community forum.
Help ⇒ Online Support ⇒ ACT! Online Community, will display the forum in your web browser.
You can view messages, but not post questions without an account. The account is free. Swiftpage does have staff to answer questions in the forum. The questions are also answered by other ACT! users.
④ Hire an ACT! consultant. Need I say that this is the most expensive option and you probably will not get an answer to your question as fast as you would like.

## Feature Tours

This option is on the Help menu shown in Figure 1-4. It contains tutorials for some of the popular features in ACT!.

Your computer has to be connected to the Internet to view the video tours.

Follow the steps below to run the Activities tour.

1. Help ⇒ Feature Tours ⇒ Activities.

2. When you are finished viewing the video, close the browser.

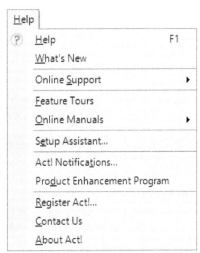

**Figure 1-4** Help menu options

## Online Manuals

The manuals that come with the software are installed when ACT! is installed. You can open them from the Help menu shown above in Figure 1-4. To view them, you need to have the free Adobe Acrobat Reader installed. The reader is probably already installed on your computer. If it is not, the Adobe Reader software can be downloaded from http://get.adobe.com/reader/. You do not have to download and install any of the other software that is on the web page for the Acrobat Reader software to work. You can also use the full version of Adobe Acrobat or another software package that can open and view PDF files.

## Request A Feature

As you go through this book and think of a feature that you wish ACT! had, or a feature that you think needs to be improved, it is probably a good idea to post a message explaining the addition or change that you would like to see in future versions of the software.

They do read the messages, but sadly, it may take a few version releases before a suggestion is implemented, depending on when they receive the request. On the link below, click on the Share Your Ideas forum link, to post your request. http://community.act.com/

## Setup Assistant Wizard

The Setup Assistant option on the Help menu, shown above in Figure 1-4, can be used to help you with the following:

① Creating a new database.
② Converting an existing database to work with the current version of ACT!.
③ Use an existing database with ACT!.

While the wizard will complete all of the tasks listed above, you can pick and choose the options that you want to set up.

## How To Check For Updates

From time to time, it is a good idea to check to see if there are updates for ACT!. Updates provide changes to the software. Sometimes the updates are improvements to existing functionality and sometimes they are fixes to features that are not working correctly. This type of update is sometimes called a **HOT FIX** or **PATCH**.

Your computer needs to be connected to the Internet to check for updates. In a multi-user environment, you probably will not have to check for or install updates because this is usually handled by tech support or a Database Administrator. Before installing any update, you should back up any existing databases that you use. The steps below show you how to check for updates.

1. Help ⇒ ACT! Notifications, is used to check for software updates.

If an update is available, you will see the message shown in Figure 1-5, in the lower right corner of your computer screen.

**Figure 1-5** Update available message

2.  To install the update, click on the message shown above in Figure 1-5 ⇒ If you have existing ACT! databases that you want to back up, click Yes, when prompted, otherwise, click No.

3.  On the ACT! Update Details dialog box, if you want to read about the update, click on the link, otherwise, click the **DOWNLOAD** button to install the update.

## Exercise 1.2: Create A Folder For Your Files

You will create and modify databases in this book. You will also download files. It would be a good idea to store all of the files for this book in the same folder on your computers hard drive so that you can find them easily. You will create a folder at the root of the C drive. If you want to create the folder in another location or under an existing folder, navigate to that location prior to starting step 2 below. This exercise also covers how to obtain and download the practice files that are used in this book.

1.  All of the files that are used in this book are in a zip file. To have the link for the zip file sent to you, send an email to actv20@tolanapublishing.com. If you do not receive an email in a few minutes with the subject line ACT! v20 (2018) Files, check the spam folder in your email software.

2.  Once you receive the email with the link to the files, open Windows Explorer ⇒ Right-click on the C drive ⇒ New ⇒ Folder.

3.  Type `ACT Book` as the folder name, then press Enter. Leave Windows Explorer open.

 Unless stated otherwise, all of the databases and files that you create in this book should be saved in the folder that you just created. I will refer to this folder as "your folder" through out the book.

4.  Go to the web page listed in the email that you received and download the zip file into the folder that you just created.

5.  In Windows Explorer, click on the folder that you created. You should see the zip file on the right side of the window.

    Right-click on the zip file and select **EXTRACT TO HERE**, as illustrated in Figure 1-6. The files will be copied to your folder.

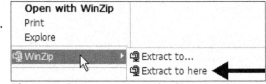

**Figure 1-6** How to extract the files

## What Is The "My Record"?

The My Record is the contact record that is displayed when you first open a database in ACT!. This record contains information about you and is used when you create documents like letters that require information about you, like your name and address. This saves you a lot of time because you do not have to enter this information for every document that you create that needs this information. Each person that uses the database should have their own My Record in the database.

If the database that you use is also used by other people, your My Record may have already been created for you by the administrator of the database. The first time that you use a database you should make sure that the information on your My Record is accurate and as complete as possible. Having the information filled in is really important if you plan to use the templates that come with ACT!. If the information is not filled in on the My Record, a lot of your information that would automatically be filled in, in a mail merge document or template for example, will be missing or inaccurate.

The My Record information is also used to track who created a record, who last modified a record and who deleted a record. This is how different users are designated as the owner (which ACT! calls the Record Manager) of a (contact, company, group or opportunity) record in the database. If the database will be used by more than one person, each person should create a My Record, otherwise they will have to log on as someone else. Logging on as someone else is not the best solution, in my opinion, because the other persons name will automatically be filled in when information is added, changed or deleted. This will make it difficult to know which user added or changed information in the database.

If by chance when the database opens and you do not see your contact record, something may be wrong. The things that come to mind are the following:

① The database could be corrupt.
② You did not log on as yourself.
③ Your contact information has been changed by someone else.

Look at the data on the contact record closely, to see if your name has been changed and all of the other information is correct. If you are sure that the record is not yours, you should review the maintenance options, to see if any of them will resolve the issue. If not, call the help desk at your company or post a message in the forum.

## Database Naming Conventions

At some point, you may have the need to create a database. Like many other things in life, there are rules that you have to follow. Below are the rules for database names.

① The name cannot be more than 32 characters.
② The name cannot contain spaces or any of the following characters:
~ ! @ # $ % ^ & * ( ) + { } | : " < > ? ` - = [ ] \ ; ' , . /
③ The name can have a combination of letters, numbers and the under score. The underscore is often used in place of a space in the database name.

## Exercise 1.3: Create A Database

During the process of creating a database you will create a My Record. The person that creates a database is automatically given administrator security rights to the database. In this exercise you will learn how to create a database from scratch, opposed to using the Setup Assistant Wizard to create the database.

1. Open ACT!, if it is not already open ⇒ Click the **NEW DATABASE** button on the Welcome window, shown earlier in Figure 1-2 or File ⇒ New Database.

2. Type My_ACT_Database in the **DATABASE NAME** field on the New Database dialog box.

3. Click the **BROWSE** button, then navigate to your folder. Click on the folder illustrated in Figure 1-7.

   (**Hint**: If necessary, click on the plus sign or arrow in front of the This PC option at the top of the options on the dialog box.)

   Click OK. This is the folder that the database will be saved in.

**Figure 1-7** Browse For Folder dialog box

4. If the Currency field is not set to USD - US Dollar, select it from the drop-down list.

5. Check the **SHARE THIS DATABASE WITH OTHER USERS** option.

**Tips For Sharing A Database**

① If the Share this database option is not enabled, it usually means that you did not open ACT! as an administrator. To run ACT! as an administrator, right-click on the ACT! shortcut icon, on your desktop and select **RUN AS ADMINISTRATOR**, as illustrated in Figure 1-8. If you want to set this option permanently, at the bottom of the shortcut menu, select Properties ⇒ Advanced ⇒ Check Run as administrator, as shown in Figure 1-9 ⇒ Click OK ⇒ Click Apply ⇒ Click OK.

② When designing a database, one thing that you need to consider is whether or not the database will be used by more than one person. If so, when the database is created, you should put it on a server or shared drive. Creating a database on your computers hard drive and then trying to move it, is more work then it is worth. You would have to back up and restore the database and all associated files to put them on the server.

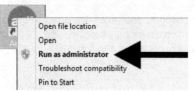

**Figure 1-8** Desktop icon shortcut menu

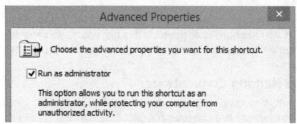

**Figure 1-9** Advanced Properties dialog box

Anyone that you plan to share the database with must be using the same version of ACT! that the database was created with. If you (the creator of the database) are using ACT! Pro v20, other people that want to use your database have to use that version also. For example, they cannot use an older version of ACT! with a database that was created in ACT! Pro v20.

6. Type your first and last name in the **USER NAME** field.

   Other then your name, you should have the same options filled in that are shown in Figure 1-10.

   If you wanted the database to be password protected, you would enter the password in the last two fields on the dialog box.

   It is not a requirement for ACT! databases to have a password.

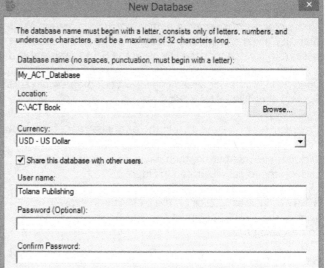

**Figure 1-10** Information for a new database

User names are not case sensitive, but passwords are.

7. Click OK. The database will now be created. When it is finished, there will be one contact record in the database, which is the My Record. It is automatically created for the user name on the New Database dialog box, shown above in Figure 1-10. You would add your information to the contact record when you see it on the screen.

8. If you see the message shown in Figure 1-11, that says that you have successfully shared this database, click OK.

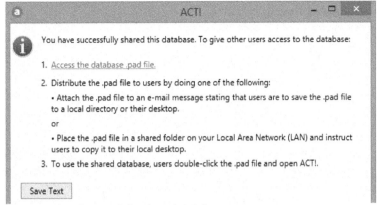

**Figure 1-11** Successfully shared database message

## Password Protected Databases

If the database has a password, you will see the dialog box shown in Figure 1-12 when you open the database.

You would have to enter your user name and password exactly as it was entered on the New Database dialog box, shown earlier in Figure 1-10, or how it was set up by the Database Administrator (by default, that is the person that created the database).

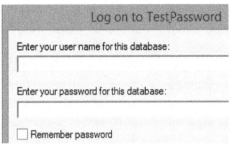

**Figure 1-12** Log on dialog box

## Viewing A Database Structure

Earlier you created a database. You may find it helpful to view the structure and folders of databases in ACT!, so that you will know where files are located.

1. Open Windows Explorer, then navigate to and click on your folder. You should see the files and folders shown in Figure 1-13.

   You will also see the files in the zip file that you downloaded, even though they are not shown in the figure.

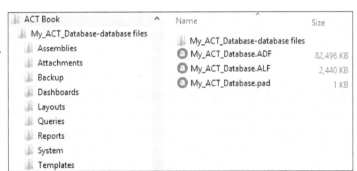

**Figure 1-13** Contents of the ACT Book folder

2. Close Windows Explorer.

**Database Tips**

Below are some tips that you should know about ACT! databases.

① The folders shown on the left side of Figure 1-13 above, are automatically created when a new database is created. They are used to store files that are created or used by ACT!.

② The **.ADF** file is the database file.

③ The **.ALF** file is the log file for the database. This file should be backed up. If this file becomes corrupt and you do not have a copy of it, the last time that I checked, you will need to contact Swiftpage in order to be able to use the database again.

④ The **.PAD** file is used to open the database. It is a shortcut that points to the database. If you want to share a database that is on a shared server with other people, give them a copy of this file. .PAD stands for Pointer to ACT! database.

⑤ ACT! databases store three types of files, as explained in Table 1-1.

| File Type | Description |
|---|---|
| Database | This is the database file that contains the contact records, notes, activities and all of the data that you see when you use ACT!. |
| Database Supplemental | These files are automatically created when ACT! is installed. Reports and templates are supplemental files. (1) |
| Personal Supplemental | These are files that you create and save, like letters or spreadsheets. (1) |

**Table 1-1** ACT! file types explained

(1) Supplemental files are covered in Chapter 9.

### Open/Share Database Dialog Box

The dialog box shown in Figure 1-14 displays the databases that you have access to. If you are the Administrator of the database, you will see a Share or Unshare button next to the database.

Clicking a **SHARE** button opens the dialog box shown in Figure 1-15. This dialog box is used to log onto the database that you want to share with other users.

Clicking an **UNSHARE** button also displays the Log on dialog box. Once your log on information is verified, the database will open. If the Unshare button is clicked after verification, you will see the message shown in Figure 1-16. It lets you know that the database will no longer be shared.

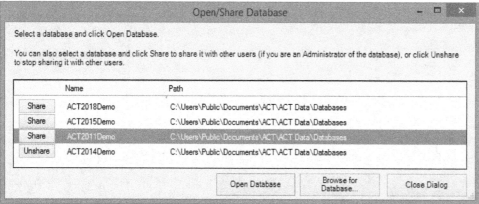

**Figure 1-14** Open/Share Database dialog box

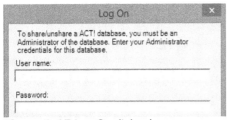

Figure 1-15 Log On dialog box

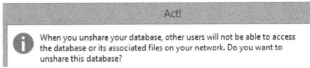

**Figure 1-16** Stop sharing database message

## Exercise 1.4: How To Make A Copy Of A Database

The exercises that you will complete in this book will modify the demo database that comes with ACT!. Therefore, it is a good idea to make a copy of the demo database and use the copy to complete the exercises.

1. File ⇒ Open/Share Database. You will see the dialog box shown earlier in Figure 1-13.

2. Select the ACT2018 Demo database ⇒ Click the Open Database button ⇒ If you see a message stating that the database needs to be updated, click Yes to create a back up ⇒ Click OK on the Back Up Database dialog box. The update process could take a few minutes.

3. When the database opens, File ⇒ Save Copy As, then type My_ACTDemo in the **DATABASE NAME** field.

4. If your folder is not in the Database Location field, click the Browse button ⇒ Double-click on your folder, then click OK.

   Check the **SHARE THIS DATABASE WITH OTHER USERS** option.

   You should have the options shown in Figure 1-17.

   Click OK.

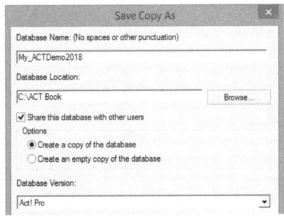

**Figure 1-17** Save Copy As dialog box

**Database Copy Failed Message**
If after completing the steps above, you get the Database copy failed error message, follow the steps below.

1. Close ACT!.
2. Open ACT! as an administrator [See Figure 1-8]
3. Repeat all of the steps in Exercise 1.4.

5. Click OK when you see the "Save As was successful" message. You now have your own copy of the demo database, which you will use in the next chapter.

6. If you see the Alarms dialog box, click the **CLEAR ALARM** button.

A copy of the database does not make your My Record the default My Record. This means that when you open the My_ACTDemo database that you just created, the default My Record will be the creator of the original database, which in this case is Chris Huffman. Do not change the owner to yourself. The exercises in this book are based on Chris Huffman being the default My Record owner. This is especially important because about 135 of the contact records in the demo database are marked as private for Chris Huffman.

# ACT! WORKSPACE

In this chapter, you will learn about the ACT! workspace. You will also learn the following:

☑ Setting default preferences
☑ Changing layouts
☑ The views in ACT!
☑ Detail view tabs

**Name Changes**
From time to time, the name of some options and features can get renamed in new releases. Throughout the book I point out these name changes and include the version of ACT! that the name change first appeared in. I do this because I know that everyone does not buy every upgrade version of the software. Neither do I. <smile> Hopefully, this will keep you from spending a lot of time looking for a feature or option by a name, not realizing that the name has changed.

CHAPTER 2

## Workspace Overview

When you open a database you will see the modified Welcome screen view unless the **STARTUP VIEW** preference option has been changed. The goal of this chapter is to help you learn the various sections of the workspace.

Clicking the Contacts option on the left side of the workspace will display the Contacts detail view, shown in Figure 2-1. Table 2-1 explains the sections of the workspace. Parts of the workspace will change, based on the view that is selected.

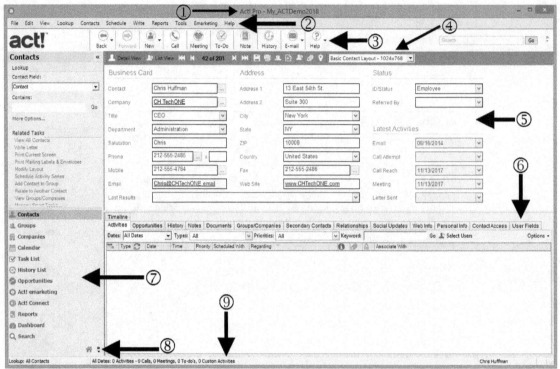

**Figure 2-1** ACT! workspace

| | Section | Description |
|---|---|---|
| ① | Title bar | Displays the name of the database that is open. The icon in the left corner of this section opens the Control menu, shown in Figure 2-2. The options on this menu are used to close, restore, move, size, minimize or maximize the ACT! workspace. |
| ② | Menu bar | Contains the default menus and commands for the current view. The menu options are explained in Table 2-2. (1) |
| ③ | Global toolbar | Contains buttons for the options that you will probably use the most. The buttons are shortcuts to items on the menu bar. The Global toolbar buttons are explained in Table 2-3. |
| ④ | Detail or List view toolbar | The options on this toolbar change, depending on the type of records that are displayed. (1) |
| ⑤ | Detail | Contains basic information for the contact, company, group or opportunity. Many of these fields are used in templates and reports, which means that the information should be as accurate as possible. (1) |
| ⑥ | Tabs | The fields on each tab contain information for the contact, company, group or opportunity record that is displayed in the top half of the window. The information that you see on the tabs depends on the access rights and security that you have. This means that different people that use the database will see different information. (1) |
| ⑦ | Navigation Pane | The buttons in this section are used to display a different view, lookup records and access tasks related to the view. (1) |
| ⑧ | Layout button | The options on this button are used to customize the Navigation Pane. |
| ⑨ | Status bar | This section is primarily used to provide additional information about the record or view that is currently displayed. On the Opportunity list view, total dollar amounts are displayed in this section. |

**Table 2-1** Sections of the ACT! workspace explained

(1)    This section can be customized.

**Figure 2-2** Control menu

## Menu Bar

The majority of options on the menu are the same for each view. The menu options are explained in Table 2-2.

| Menu | Description |
|------|-------------|
| File | The options are used to open, close, save, import, export, backup and print data. |
| Edit | The options are used to modify data in the view. The options on this menu change, based on the view that is selected. |
| View | Is used to select a different view, display the mini calendar, select a tab or refresh data. |
| Lookup | The options are used to find records. For example, some options are used to select the field to use to search for records in the database and create queries. |
| Contacts | The name of this menu option changes based on the view that is selected. The options displayed are for the view that is displayed. For example, if the Opportunity view is displayed, this menu name changes to Opportunities and the options on the menu are for opportunity records. |
| Schedule | The options are used to create an activity, activity series, manage smart tasks, as well as, granting calendar access. |
| Write | The options are used to create emails, letters and other types of documents. |
| Reports | The options are used to select a report to run, create new reports and edit existing reports. |
| Tools | This menu contains options for creating new fields, creating and modifying view layouts, database maintenance, converting old databases, synchronizing databases, customizing menus and toolbars and selecting preferences. |
| Emarketing | This option is used to create, send and manage email marketing campaigns in ACT!, using the Swiftpage Emarketing tools. |
| Help | The options on this menu are primarily used to learn about ACT!. There are also options for updating the software and getting support. |

**Table 2-2** Menu bar options explained

## Global Toolbar

Figure 2-3 shows the Global toolbar.

The buttons are explained in Table 2-3.

**Figure 2-3** Global toolbar

| Button | This Button Is Used To . . . |
|--------|------------------------------|
| 1 | Display a previous record or view. Clicking on the arrow on this button displays the last nine items that were displayed, as shown in Figure 2-4. |
| 2 | Display the previous record or view in the list shown in Figure 2-4. For example, in the figure, the Activities dashboard is the current view (it's in bold). When you click the Forward button, the Task List view would be displayed. |
| 3 | Select the type of new record that you want to create, as shown in Figure 2-5. |
| 4 | Schedule a telephone call activity. (2) |
| 5 | Schedule a meeting activity. (2) |

**Table 2-3** Global toolbar buttons explained

| Button | This Button Is Used To . . . |
|--------|------------------------------|
| 6 | Schedule a To-Do activity. (2) |
| 7 | Create a note. |
| 8 | Create a history record. |
| 9 | Compose and view emails, as well as, select email preferences, as shown in Figure 2-6. |
| 10 | Open the Help system. |

**Table 2-3** Global toolbar buttons explained (Continued)

(2) This option is for the current record on the detail view. It can be used with multiple records on the list view, if the records are selected or tagged.

**Figure 2-4** Back button list

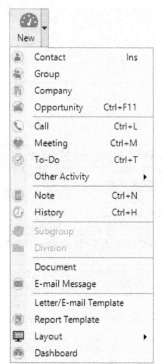

**Figure 2-5** New button options

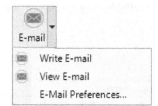

**Figure 2-6** E-mail button options

## Navigation Pane

Table 2-4 explains the buttons on the Navigation Pane. Figures 2-7 to 2-15 show some of the views.

| Button | Displays The . . . |
|--------|---------------------|
| Contacts | Contacts detail view shown earlier in Figure 2-1. |
| Groups | Groups detail view shown in Figure 2-7. |
| Companies | Companies detail view shown in Figure 2-8. |
| Calendar | Calendar view shown in Figure 2-9. |
| Task List | Task List view shown in Figure 2-10. |
| History List | History List view shown in Figure 2-11. |
| Opportunities | Opportunity list view shown in Figure 2-12. |
| ACT! Emarketing | Emarketing options shown in Figure 2-13. |
| ACT! Contact | Products and services for ACT! that are provided by third party vendors. This button displayed the Marketplace view in ACT! v17. |
| Reports | Reports view shown in Figure 2-14. |
| Dashboard | Dashboard view shown in Figure 2-15. |
| Search | Search view shown in Figure 2-16. |
| Welcome | View shown in Chapter 1, Figure 1-3. |

**Table 2-4** Navigation Pane buttons explained

**Figure 2-7** Groups detail view

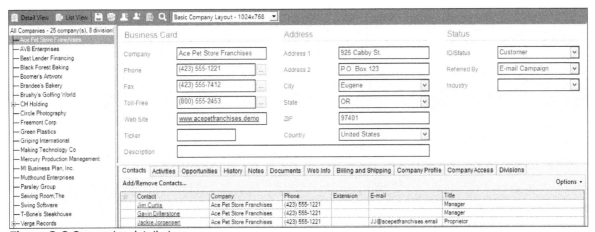

**Figure 2-8** Companies detail view

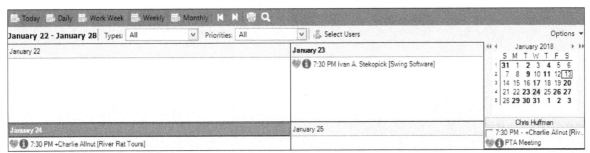

**Figure 2-9** Calendar (weekly) view

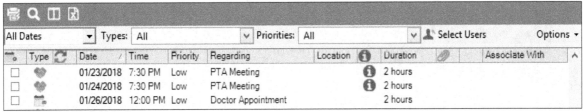

**Figure 2-10** Task List view

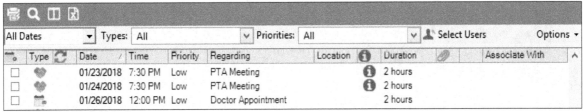

**Figure 2-11** History List view

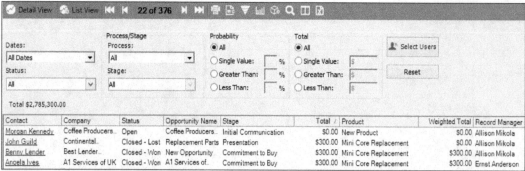

**Figure 2-12** Opportunity list view

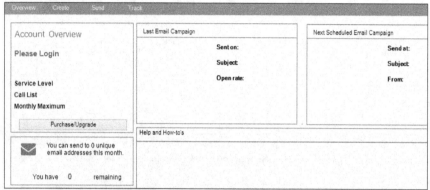

**Figure 2-13** Emarketing options

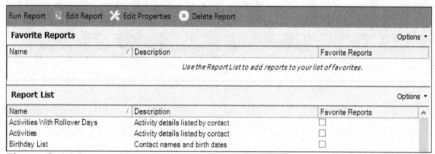

**Figure 2-14** Reports view

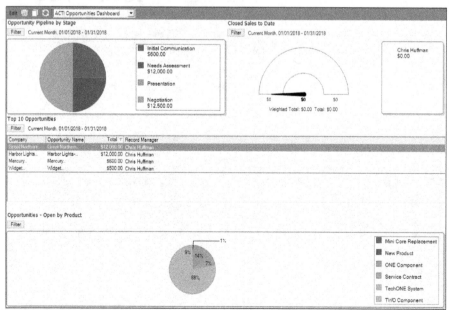

**Figure 2-15** Dashboard view

**Figure 2-16** Search view

## Minimize And Restore The Navigation Pane

If you need more space in the workspace, you can minimize the Navigation Pane by clicking on the arrow shown in the upper right corner of Figure 2-17.

**Figure 2-17** Minimize Navigation Pane button

When you click this button, the Navigation Pane is reduced, as shown in Figure 2-18. If you click on any of the buttons, that view will be displayed.

If you click in the Contacts section of the Navigation Pane toolbar shown in Figure 2-18, the **LOOKUP** and **RELATED TASKS** sections of the Navigation Pane are displayed, as shown in Figure 2-19.

Click on the arrow button at the top of the Navigation Pane toolbar to restore it.

> **Lookup Section**
> If you do not see this section on the Navigation Pane (shown at the top of Figure 2-19), see Startup Tab Preferences, later in this chapter.

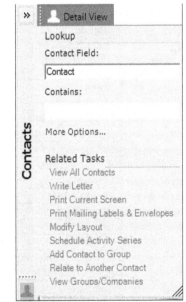

**Figure 2-19** Lookup and Related Tasks sections of the Navigation Pane restored

**Figure 2-18** Navigation Pane minimized to a toolbar

## Related Tasks

The links in this section of the Navigation Pane are shortcuts to tasks that are on menus. The options change, depending on the view that is currently displayed. The Related Tasks options are explained at the end of the chapter that the view is covered in.

## Resizing The Top And Bottom Sections Of Detail Views

The DETAIL views have two sections, which are sometimes referred to as primary and secondary sections. These sections can be resized as needed. The primary section is at the top of the view and contains basic information like the name and address for the contact, company or group. The top section of a detail view contains fields that you will probably enter a lot of information in. The secondary section is at the bottom of the window and displays the tabs.

As you scroll through the records, the data in both sections will change. This is known as RELATIONAL DATA because the data on the tabs is related to the record displayed at the top of the window. You may need to make the bottom half (the Tabs section) longer or shorter. If this is the case, follow the steps below.

1.  Place the mouse pointer on the bar illustrated in Figure 2-20.

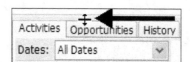

**Figure 2-20** Mouse pointer in position to resize a section of the detail view

2.  Press and hold down the left mouse button, then drag the bar up or down as needed.

## Detail View Tabs

The tabs for each detail view are shown in Table 2-5. The fields on each of these tabs is used to enter more information for each contact.

Click on each of these tabs now to become familiar with the types of data that can be entered for a contact.

When using the ACT Demo layout (which is only available in the sample ACT! Demo database), the tabs are displayed in a different order then the other two layouts.

Table 2-6 explains the type of information that is stored on each tab.

| Tab | Contacts | Company | Group | Opportunity |
|-----|:--------:|:-------:|:-----:|:-----------:|
| Activities | X | X | X | X |
| Opportunities | X | X | X | |
| History | X | X | X | X |
| Notes | X | X | X | X |
| Documents | X | X | X | X |
| Groups/Companies | X | | | X |
| Secondary Contacts | X | | | |
| Relationships | X | | | |
| Social Updates | X | | | |
| Web Info | X | X | | |
| Personal Info | X | | | |
| Contact Access | X | | | |
| User Fields | X | | | X |
| Timeline | X | | | |
| Billing and Shipping | | X | | |
| Company Profile (3) | | X | | |
| Company Access | | X | | |
| Divisions | | X | | |
| Contacts | | X | X | X |
| Group Address (3) | | | X | |
| Group Access (3) | | | X | |
| Subgroups | | | X | |
| Web Forms (4) | | | X | |
| Products/Services | | | | X |
| Opportunity Info | | | | X |
| Opportunity Access | | | | X |

**Table 2-5** Detail view tabs

(3)   This tab has a different name on the ACT Demo layout.
(4)   This tab was formerly named LEAD CAPTURE.

| Tab | Contains This Type Of Information . . . |
|---|---|
| Activities | Scheduled activities. (5) |
| Billing and Shipping | Billing and shipping addresses for the company. |
| Company Access | The name of the person that created and last edited the company record. (6) |
| Company Profile | Tracks the region, revenue, SIC Code and more for each company. |
| Contact Access | The name of the person that created and last edited the contact record. (6) |
| Contacts | List of contacts in the company or group. |
| Divisions | List of the divisions that are associated to the company. |
| Documents | List of files that have been attached to the record currently displayed. (5) |
| Group Access | The name of the person that created and edited the group record. (6) |
| Group Address | Address for the group. |
| Groups/Companies | Groups that the contact or opportunity are a member of. |
| History | Completed and deleted activities, as well as, changes to other types of records. (5) |
| Web Forms | Displays the groups web forms. They are used to pull contact information from the Internet. This requires an emarketing account. |
| Notes | Notes that have been created for a contact, opportunity, company or group. (6) |
| Opportunities | Open, inactive and closed sales. (5) |
| Opportunity Access | The name of the person that created and edited the opportunity record. (6) |
| Opportunity Info | Competitor, Referred by and Reason fields. |
| Personal Info | Home address information, birthday and alternate phone numbers for the contact. |
| Products/Services | Create, edit and delete the items for the opportunity. |
| Relationships | Relationships that the contact has with other contacts in the database. |
| Secondary Contacts | Names of people associated with the contact. |
| Social Updates | The most recent updates (from Facebook® and Linkedin®) by the associated friend or follower. |
| Subgroups | List of the subgroups for the group. |
| Timeline | View contact activity on a timeline, as shown in Figure 2-21. |
| User Fields | Fields that can be customized, so that you can enter any information that does not fit in any other field in the database. |
| Web Info | Social networking web sites for the record currently displayed at the top of the workspace. |

**Table 2-6** Information stored on the tabs explained

(5) Depending on the view, the data displayed on this tab is for a contact, company, group or activity. In some instances, the data on this tab displays data from multiple detail views.

(6) Stores the Public/Private status of the contact, company or group. **PUBLIC STATUS** (the default status) means that anyone that opens the database can view the record. **PRIVATE STATUS** means that only the person that created the record can view it.

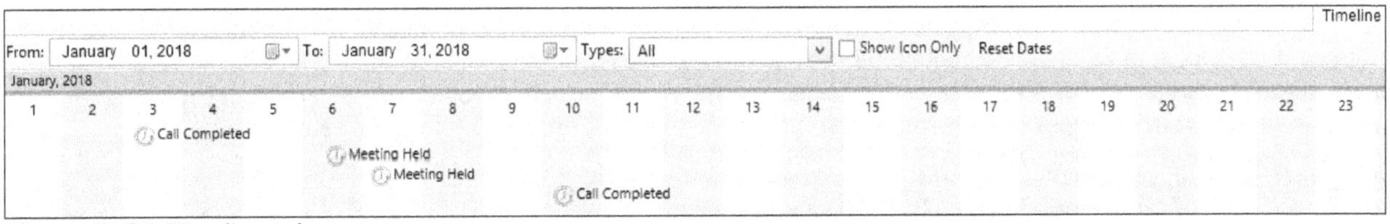

**Figure 2-21** Timeline tab

## Preferences Overview

Preferences are used to modify ACT! to work the way that you want or need it to. Some of the preferences require administrator rights. As you go through the preferences in this chapter, try to think about how you will use ACT!, in terms of how the preferences can be modified to work best for you. It may be a good idea to write down the options that you want to change and what you want to change them to. That way, after you have completed this book, you can make the changes in your database.

For example, if you plan to keep most of the databases that you use in one folder, you could set that folder as the one that ACT! looks in first. The default folder for databases is the My Documents or Documents folder in Windows. I have watched many people lose work that was stored in the My Documents folder because they were not aware of the pitfalls of storing work in a folder that Windows creates. ACT! allows you to change the default location for databases, documents, reports, queries and any other type of file that you can create or use in ACT!.

### Exercise 2.1: View And Modify The Preferences

In this exercise you will learn about the preferences in ACT!. You will also modify some of the preferences for the My_ACTDemo database.

1. Open the My_ACTDemo database. If prompted that the database will be verified, click OK. The update process takes a minute or so. When it is complete, click OK.

2. Tools ⇒ Preferences.

### Notifications Tab Preferences

The options shown in Figure 2-22 are used to select the types of notifications that you want to receive.

If checked, the **AUTOMATICALLY CHECK FOR UPDATES EVERY** option is used to let ACT! know how frequently you want to check for software updates.

If your database is on a server, you should not select this option because the administrator needs to update the copy of ACT! and the database that is on the server before the desktop copies of ACT! (the copy that is installed on your computer) are updated.

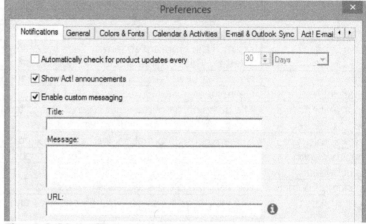

**Figure 2-22** Notifications tab preferences

I disable automatic update checking in all software, because the software will open faster, when it does not have to check for updates each time it is opened.

If checked, the **SHOW ACT! ANNOUNCEMENTS** option will display the popup shown in Chapter 1, Figure 1-5, when an update is available.

The **ENABLE CUSTOM MESSAGING** option enables the fields below it. When enabled, the host computer (the one that has the database, which in this book, is your computer) sends custom notifications, like XML files to the local computer (yours) and stores them in a notification folder on the local computer.

### General Tab Preferences

The options shown in Figure 2-23 are used to select general preferences for the database. The options in the **FILE TYPE** drop-down list shown in Figure 2-24 contain the types of **PERSONAL FILES** that you can set a folder location for. This means that you can store the databases in one folder and the documents that you create in a different folder. If you want to save different file types in the same folder, you have to select the same folder for each file type.

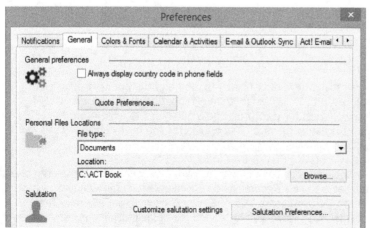

**Figure 2-23** General tab preferences

Personal Files Locations

File type:

Databases

Databases
Documents
Internet Links
Dictionaries
Backup Location

**Figure 2-24** File type options

The **FILE TYPE** and **LOCATION** options are something that you will want to change after you complete the exercises in this book. That is because these options should reflect the location of the database that you use the most.

1.  Click the **BROWSE** button shown above in Figure 2-23 ⇒ Navigate to and click on your folder ⇒ Click OK to close the Browse For Folder dialog box. The **LOCATION** field should have changed to the folder that you just selected.

2.  Select your folder as the location for the Documents file type. You should have the options shown earlier in Figure 2-23.

3.  Click the **SALUTATION PREFERENCES** button ⇒ Select the **USE CONTACT'S FIRST NAME** option, if it is not already selected.

### Colors & Fonts Tab Preferences

The options on this tab are used to change the default font, style, text and background colors that are displayed in the workspace. The options on the right side of the tab shown in Figure 2-25 are used to customize all of the views (lists), tabs, calendar and compositions (the dialog box that you enter notes on) in the **VIEWS** list. Click on the object that you want to modify in the Views list, then change the options on the right side of the dialog box as needed.

 **Changing Multiple Views At The Same Time**
If you want to make the same change to more than one view, click on the first view that you want to change. Press and hold the Ctrl key down, then click on the other views, as shown in Figure 2-26. Once you have selected all of the views that you want to customize, select the options that you want. There is no global change option available, so this is the work around that I came up with. This will provide a consistent look when you go from one part of ACT! to another. This means that you will not have the top half of the Contact detail view with a green background and the background color of the tabs on the Contact detail view purple, unless that is what you want.

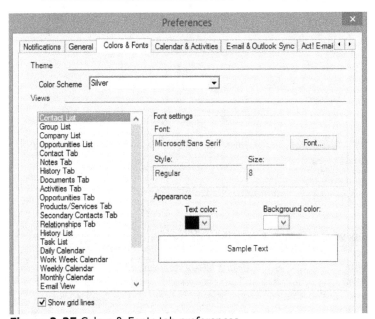

**Figure 2-26** Multiple views selected to be customized at the same time

**Figure 2-25** Colors & Fonts tab preferences

Currently, there are only two **COLOR SCHEMES**, black and silver. You can change the color scheme whenever you want. The **THEMES** are used to make global color changes to the workspace.

If available and checked, the **SHOW GRID LINES** option, on the Colors & Fonts tab, will change the layout of data on a tab to look like a spreadsheet, as shown in Figure 2-27.

You may want to change the colors and fonts or add grid lines to the Notes and History tabs, because over time, they will contain more data than the other tabs and having color or gridlines may make the entries easier to read.

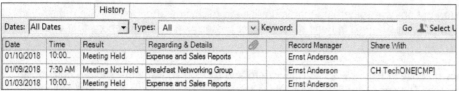

**Figure 2-27** Show grid lines option enabled for the History tab

## Calendar & Activities Tab Preferences

Each of the buttons shown in Figure 2-28 are used to open a dialog box that has options for a specific preference.

The **CALENDAR PREFERENCES** options are used to set the work days and time period increments for the calendars.

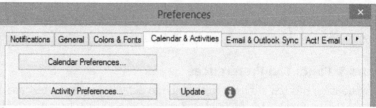

**Figure 2-28** Calendar & Activities tab preferences

The **ACTIVITY PREFERENCES** options are used to set the default values for each of the activity types.

The **UPDATE BUTTON** applies the activity changes to all of the users, currently in the database.

## E-mail & Outlook Sync Tab Preferences

This tab has options that provide more functionality between ACT! and Outlook. The options shown in Figure 2-29 are the settings for the e-mail software that you want to use with ACT!.

It is not a requirement to configure email software because you can use the Email Editor that comes with ACT!.

These settings do not change the options that you currently have set in your e-mail software.

If you do not see any settings on this tab, it means that you have not set up an email package to use with ACT!.

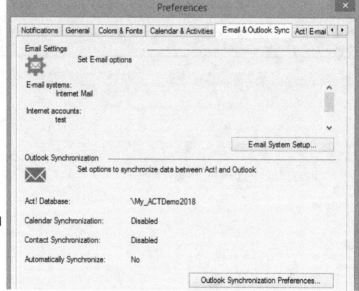

**Figure 2-29** E-mail & Outlook Sync tab preferences

The **E-MAIL SYSTEM SETUP** button shown above in Figure 2-29, opens the **E-MAIL SETUP WIZARD**, which is used to configure Internet Mail or Outlook as the email software that you want ACT! to recognize. The email choices that you see may be different, because the choices depend on the email software that ACT! finds and recognizes on your computers hard drive.

**Removing A Database**
What I discovered while testing this functionality, is that once a database is selected at the top of Figure 2-30, it cannot be removed. It can only be replaced with another database.

The **OUTLOOK SYNCHRONIZATION PREFERENCES** options are used to configure how data will be copied between ACT! and Outlook calendars and contacts.

Clicking this button displays the options shown in Figure 2-30.

The options are used to configure ACT! to work with your contacts in Outlook.

**Figure 2-30** Outlook Synchronization Preferences dialog box

## ACT! E-mail Editor Tab Preferences

The options shown in Figure 2-31 are used to configure the ACT! Email Editor. You will only see this tab when there is at least one email software package configured.

The options on this tab are used to select the incoming and outgoing e-mail settings.

You can even set an option to notify you when you receive e-mail.

If the **CHECK SPELLING BEFORE SENDING E-MAIL** option is selected, emails that you compose will be spell checked automatically before they are sent.

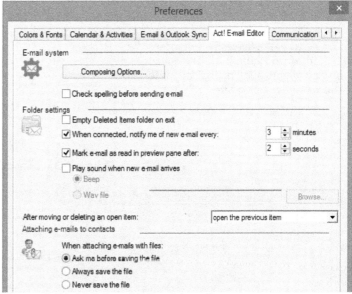

**Figure 2-31** ACT! E-mail Editor tab preferences

The **COMPOSING OPTIONS** button on the ACT! Email Editor tab opens the dialog box shown in Figure 2-32.

This dialog box contains additional e-mail options that can be selected.

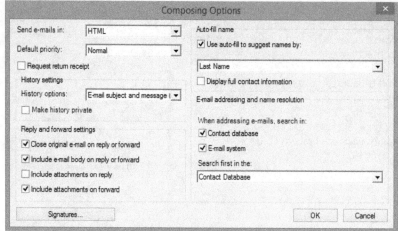

**Figure 2-32** Composing Options dialog box

## Communication Tab Preferences

The options shown in Figure 2-33 are used to select the default word processor, spell check, fax software and print options that you will use.

The **DIALER PREFERENCES** option requires your computer to be connected to a phone line, similar to using dial-up Internet service. These options allow ACT! to dial phone numbers for you.

The **QUICK PRINT PREFERENCES** button, opens the dialog box shown in Figure 2-34. The options are used to select the default printing options for the views shown on the dialog box.

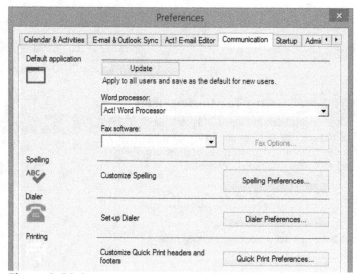

**Figure 2-33** Communication tab preferences

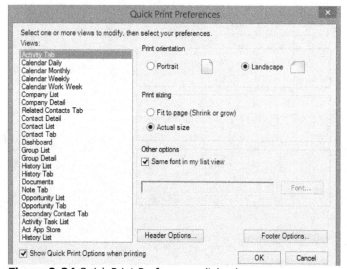

**Figure 2-34** Quick Print Preferences dialog box

1. If the ACT! Word Processor option is not selected, as shown earlier in Figure 2-33, select it now, then click the **SPELLING PREFERENCES** button.

The options in the **UPON SAVING, CHECK SPELLING FOR THE FOLLOWING** section, shown in Figure 2-35, are used to select which tabs on the detail views will have spell checking enabled automatically.

If you have a custom dictionary from another application that you want to use in ACT!, you can select it by clicking the Browse button in the **SELECT USER DICTIONARY** section.

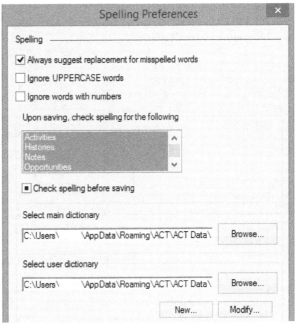

**Figure 2-35** Spelling Preferences dialog box

## User Dictionaries

These dictionaries are used to save words that are not in the main dictionary. This is helpful because once you save a word in this dictionary, it will not be considered a misspelled word in ACT!. If you use Microsoft Office and have created a custom dictionary, you can use it in ACT!.

You can create several user dictionaries. For example, if you are in the legal field you could create a legal dictionary and store the legal words that you need in it. If you need to add or delete words that are in the **USER** dictionary, click the **MODIFY** button shown above in Figure 2-35.

The options on the dialog box shown in Figure 2-36 are used to add and delete the words in the user dictionary.

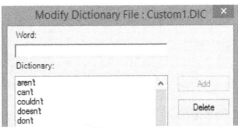

**Figure 2-36** Modify Dictionary File dialog box

2. On the Spelling Preferences dialog box, click on the **ACTIVITIES** option in the list, then press and hold down the Shift key ⇒ Scroll to the end of the list and click on the last option. All of the options should be highlighted, as shown earlier in Figure 2-35.

3. Clear the **CHECK SPELLING BEFORE SAVING** option if you do not want to have the spell checker run automatically each time you create an entry on one of the tabs that you just highlighted. You can run the spell checker manually, as needed.

4. Click OK ⇒ Click the Apply button on the Communication tab.

### Startup Tab Preferences

The options shown in Figure 2-37 determine what will happen each time ACT! is opened and what happens when records are added to the database.

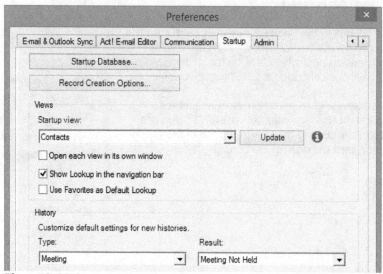

If you primarily use the same ACT! database, you can click the **STARTUP DATABASE** button and select the database that you want to have open automatically when ACT! is opened.

For example, you could select the My_ACTDemo database that you will be using throughout this book. Then, when you are finished using this book, you can select a different database.

The **RECORD CREATION OPTIONS** are covered in Chapter 9.

**Figure 2-37** Startup tab preferences

If you do not want the database to open with the Welcome view, select the view that you want from the **STARTUP VIEW** drop-down list. You can also select the Dashboard option.

Click the **UPDATE** button to apply the Views options, to all authorized login accounts for the database.

If checked, the **SHOW LOOKUP IN THE NAVIGATION BAR** option shown above in Figure 2-37, will display the lookup search options in the Navigation bar, as shown earlier at the top of Figure 2-19. Check the option, then click the Apply button.

### Admin Tab Preferences

The options shown in Figure 2-38 are used to set default options for features that you will probably use on a regular basis.

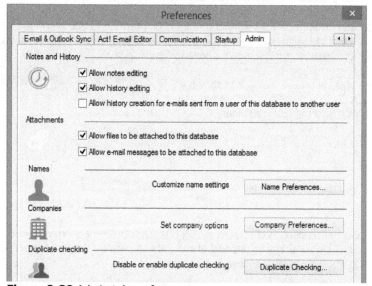

The **NAME PREFERENCES** options are covered in Chapter 14.

The **COMPANY PREFERENCES** options are covered in Chapter 5.

The **DUPLICATE CHECKING** options are used to select how ACT! handles duplicate contact, company and group records in the database.

**Figure 2-38** Admin tab preferences

 Administrator or manager rights are needed to change the **ALLOW HISTORY EDITING** and **DUPLICATE CHECKING** options.

### Exercise 2.2: Select A Database And View To Automatically Open With ACT!

Earlier you learned that a database could be selected to open automatically when ACT! is opened. You will select the copy of the database that you just created to open automatically when you open ACT!. This will be the database that you use to complete the exercises in the rest of this book.

1. Tools ⇒ Preferences ⇒ Startup tab.

2. Click the **STARTUP DATABASE** button.

3. Select the **NAMED DATABASE** option ⇒ Click the button at the end of the drop-down list field.

4. Double-click on the My_ACTDemo2018.pad file in your folder.

   You should have the options selected that are shown in Figure 2-39. Click OK.

**Figure 2-39** Startup Database dialog box options

5. On the Startup tab, open the Startup view drop-down list and select **CONTACTS**.

6. Click Apply. The next time that you open ACT!, the database and startup view that you selected in this exercise will automatically open.

## Using The Duplicate Checking Options

1. Click the **DUPLICATE CHECKING** button on the Admin tab ⇒ Open the **RECORD TYPE** drop-down list and select Company.

2. Change the first **THEN ON** field to <None>, as shown in Figure 2-40.

   The options shown, will prompt anyone using the database when they create a company record that has the exact company name, as a record already in the database.

**Figure 2-40** Duplicate checking options for company records

3. Click OK, then click the Apply button ⇒ Click OK to close the Preferences dialog box.

4. File ⇒ Exit, to close ACT!, then reopen ACT!. The database may need to be verified. This is only done the first time that a database is opened. Look at the top of the workspace. You should see the name of the database in the Title bar.

## Exercise 2.3: Viewing Layouts

ACT! comes with the two basic layout styles that are shown in Figure 2-41 for the Contact, Group, Company and Opportunity detail views. These two layouts come with new databases that you create. The demo database has an additional layout, named ACT Demo.

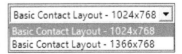

**Figure 2-41** Basic layouts

 Saving the ACT Demo database with a new name (like you did in Exercise 1.4) does not bring over the ACT Demo layout.

Layouts are the background, fields and tabs in the workspace. These options can be modified to better meet your needs or you can create your own layout. Fields and tabs can be added, re-arranged or hidden as needed.

The options in this drop-down list contain layouts for the type of view (contact, company, group or opportunity) that is currently displayed. Each layout for each view can contain different fields. For example, the Basic Contact Layout 1366x768 displays more fields than the Basic Contact Layout 1024x768.

 The Basic Contact Layout - 800x600 was removed in ACT! Pro v17.

1. Open the **LAYOUT** drop-down list on the Detail View toolbar and select **BASIC CONTACT LAYOUT - 1024x768**, if it is not already selected.

2. File ⇒ Save, to save the changes.

It is possible that a database will require more than one layout. Different people or groups of people that are using the database may need to see different fields or may need to have the fields appear in a different order. Images and text can also be added to a layout. You can switch layouts at any time.

### The Views In ACT!

There are several views in ACT! including Contacts, Groups and Companies that you can view records and reports in.

In addition to being able to select a view on the Navigation pane, a view can also be selected on the **VIEW** menu, as shown in Figure 2-42.

 The items on a menu like the one shown in Figure 2-42 that have an icon in the left column means that the option is on at least one toolbar in the software.

**Figure 2-42** View menu options

# CREATING AND EDITING CONTACT RECORDS

In this chapter, you will learn about contact records, including the following:

☑ Adding and deleting contact records
☑ Enter information on the Notes, Documents and Personal Info tabs
☑ Editing contact information
☑ Using the Date field calendar
☑ Attaching files on the Documents tab
☑ Creating relationships
☑ Duplicating contact information

CHAPTER 3

## What Is A Contact?

A contact in ACT! is any person or group of people that you need to have up to date information on. When many people hear the word **CONTACT**, they immediately think of a business contact. It is true that many people use ACT! strictly for managing business contacts, but you can have friends, family members, prospects and vendors, as well as, business contacts in the same ACT! database. As you will see, ACT! handles much more than names and addresses.

If you are brand new to ACT!, this chapter and the next one are probably the most important ones for you to fully understand, because creating, editing and looking up contacts are the tasks that you will spend most of your time doing. The key thing to remember when entering data is to be consistent. This will make finding contacts in the database easier and the reports will be more accurate.

### Contact Detail View Toolbar

Figure 3-1 shows the Contact detail view toolbar. Table 3-1 explains the buttons on the toolbar. The buttons provide quick access to some of the most used options for contacts. Each view (contact, company, group etc) has its own toolbar. For example, the Contact list and Contact detail views have a similar toolbar. You will see that not all buttons are enabled for both views.

**Figure 3-1** Contact detail view toolbar

| Button | Description |
|--------|-------------|
| 1 | Displays the Contact detail view. |
| 2 | Displays the Contact list view. |
| 3 | Displays the first record. (1) |
| 4 | Displays the previous record. (1) |
| 5 | The **RECORD COUNTER** displays the record number (By default, contacts are displayed in alphabetical order) of the contact that is currently displayed and how many contact records are in the database. **42 OF 201** means that you are currently viewing record 42 and that there are 201 records in the database. (1) |
| 6 | Displays the next record. (1) |
| 7 | Displays the last record. (1) |
| 8 | Saves the record. (2) |
| 9 | Opens the Quick Print Options dialog box, which has options for printing the current view. |
| 10 | Duplicates the current contact record. |
| 11 | Opens the word processor. |
| 12 | Call the contact on the phone through the Dialer application. (2) |
| 13 | Is used to attach a file to the contact record. |
| 14 | Opens Internet Explorer to the Google Maps web site and displays a map based on the address of the contact record that is currently displayed. |
| 15 | Is used to select a layout for the view. (2) |

**Table 3-1** Contact detail view toolbar buttons explained

(1) This option is either for the entire database or current lookup, which is a subset of records in the database.
(2) This option is only available from the Contact detail view.

### Contact List View Toolbar

In addition to the buttons shown above in Figure 3-1, the buttons shown in Figure 3-2 are available. They are at the end of the toolbar. Table 3-2 explains the buttons on the toolbar.

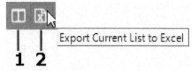

**Figure 3-2** Contact list view toolbar buttons

| Button | Description |
|--------|-------------|
| 1 | Is used to customize the columns in the view. |
| 2 | Exports the data to an Excel spreadsheet. |

**Table 3-2** Contact list view toolbar buttons explained

If you cannot remember the name of a button on the toolbar, hold the mouse pointer over the button. You will see the name of the button, as illustrated above in Figure 3-2. This is known as a **TOOL TIP**.

 **List View Buttons**
The buttons shown above in Figure 3-2 are also available on the Company, Group, Task List and Opportunity list views.

## Difference Between The Enter And Tab Keys

You can use both of these keys to move from field to field when adding or editing data. The **TAB** key is used to move from field to field on the layout. The Tab key stops at every field by default.

The **ENTER** key is used to move from field to field also. The difference is that the Enter key does not stop at every field. It stops at the most used fields. The order that these keys move in can be changed.

## Exercise 3.1: Creating A New Contact Record

You do not have to enter information in all of the fields, but you should enter enough information to make the contact record meaningful. You will learn how to enter data on several of the tabs on the Contact detail view in this exercise.

1.  Click the **NEW** button on the Global toolbar. You will see a blank record. Notice that the record counter, on the toolbar, has been incremented by one. There should now be 202 records in the database.

 You can also press the **INSERT** key to add a new contact or select Contacts ⇒ New Contact.

2.  Type `Sarah Baker` in the Contact field, then press the Tab key.

Notice that the contacts first name has automatically been filled in the Salutation field. That is because you selected the option on the Preferences dialog box, to automatically fill in the salutation field with the contacts first name.

The button at the end of the Contact field, on the Contact detail view, opens the dialog box shown in Figure 3-3.

This button is called an **ELLIPSIS BUTTON** in ACT!. In other software, this is called the Browse button, which provides the same functionality.

By default, ACT! automatically splits a contact name into three fields. Initially, the options on this dialog box display what ACT! thinks the first, middle and last name are, based on the preferences selected on the Contact Name dialog box.

**Figure 3-3** Contact Name dialog box

If a name has not been separated correctly, open the drop-down list for the name that is not correct and select the correct name. This may happen when someone's first or last name is two names like Johnnie Mae Westbrook. In this example, the contacts first name is Johnnie Mae. By default, ACT! will interpret it as shown in Figure 3-4. These separation options are what enables contacts to be sorted or used in a lookup by first or last name, even though the first and last name are stored in the same field.

By default, ACT! has been set up to not use Mr., Mrs., Ms., Esq., MD, PhD and Dr. as part of the first, middle or last name. I entered my name with "Dr" in front of it, then opened the Contact Name dialog box and saw that ACT! separated my name correctly, as shown in Figure 3-5. You can change these options as needed.

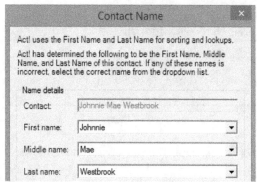

**Figure 3-4** Contact with two first names　　**Figure 3-5** Contact name separated correctly

3. In the Company field type `Capri Book Company`.

4. Open the Title field drop-down list and select the Sales Manager title, illustrated in Figure 3-6.

   The **EDIT LIST VALUES** option is used to add, edit or delete the values in the drop-down list.

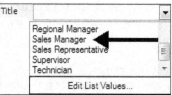

**Figure 3-6** Title field drop-down list values

5. Type `pur` in the Department field, then press the Tab key. Notice that the Purchasing department has been filled in automatically.

6. In the Phone field type `765 555 5330`. (Do not put spaces between the numbers. I typed it that way to make it easier for you to read.) Notice that the phone number was automatically formatted.

## Phone Number Formatting

Like the salutation field, the phone number fields also have default formatting. The ellipsis button at the end of the Phone and Mobile fields will open the dialog box shown in Figure 3-7. The options shown are used to change how the phone number will be formatted. The default phone number format is for the US. If you enter a phone number for a different country and do not know the correct format for the country, open the Country field drop-down list shown in Figure 3-7 and select the country. After you click OK on the Enter Phone Number dialog box, the phone number will be formatted for the country that you selected.

The **EDIT FORMATS** button, on the Enter Phone Number dialog box, opens the dialog box shown in Figure 3-8. You can create your own phone number format or select one of the other formats shown in Figure 3-8 to be the new default format.

**Figure 3-7** Enter Phone Number dialog box

**Figure 3-8** Edit Phone Formats dialog box

**Using Country Codes**
The **COUNTRY CODE** is the prefix that you have to enter before you dial the area code. The Country Code for the United States is 1, as shown above in Figure 3-7 in brackets. Being able to look up the country code in the Country field drop-down list is helpful if you have contacts in other countries and do not know the country code.

7. Enter the information in Table 3-3, in the appropriate fields on the Contact detail view.

The top portion of the contact record should look like the one shown in Figure 3-9.

This is the contact record that you will use to enter data on various tabs in the remainder of this exercise.

| Field | Type This |
|-------|-----------|
| Address 1 | 123 Main St |
| City | Los Angeles |
| State | CA |
| Zip | 90277 |
| Country | USA |
| ID/Status | Supplier |

**Table 3-3** Contact information

**Figure 3-9** Information for a new contact

As shown above in Figure 3-9, there are two address fields. ACT! actually has three address fields. The Basic Layout 1024x768 view only displays two of them. All three fields are for one address, not three different addresses. Often, the physical street address goes in the Address 1 field and the other two address fields are used to enter the floor, suite or room number, for example.

Some company addresses also include a building name. These are examples of the type of address information that could be entered in the second and third address fields. If a contact has more than one company address, like a street address and a PO Box, you could use fields on the User Fields tab, as long as the layout for that tab is modified to reflect what the fields are being used for.

### The Notes Tab

The data on this tab is a history of each note that you or another user of the database creates for the contact, company, group or opportunity. The entries on this tab are created automatically each time a note is created. An unlimited number of notes can be created.

### Insert Note Dialog Box Toolbar

Table 3-4 explains the buttons on the Insert Note dialog box toolbar shown in Figure 3-10.

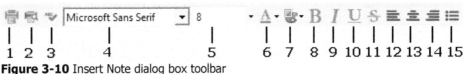

**Figure 3-10** Insert Note dialog box toolbar

| Button | Description |
|--------|-------------|
| 1 | Prints the note. |
| 2 | Displays the note to show how it will look when it is printed. |
| 3 | Spell checks the note. |
| 4 | Change the font for in the note. |
| 5 | Change the font size for the note. |
| 6 | Change the font color of the note. |
| 7 | Change the background color of the note. |
| 8 | Makes the selected text in the note bold. |
| 9 | Makes the selected text in the note italic. |
| 10 | Underlines the selected in the note text. |

**Table 3-4** Insert Note dialog box toolbar buttons explained

| Button | Description |
|--------|-------------|
| 11 | Draws a line through the selected text. This is usually done to indicate text that you want to delete. |
| 12 | Left aligns the text in the body of the note. This is the default alignment for text. |
| 13 | Centers the text in the body of the note. |
| 14 | Right aligns the text in the body of the note. |
| 15 | Creates a bulleted list in the body of the note. |

**Table 3-4** Insert Note dialog box toolbar buttons explained (Continued)

1. On the **NOTES** tab, click the **INSERT NEW NOTE** button illustrated in Figure 3-11. Notice that the Date and Time fields are filled in automatically on the Insert Note dialog box.

If you had created a My Record in this database, your name would be in the **RECORD MANAGER** field.

**Figure 3-11** Insert New Note button illustrated on the Notes tab

2. In the field at the bottom of the dialog box, type `This is my first note. It has an attachment and is associated to contacts at Liberty.`

The **CONTACT** button on the Insert Note dialog box, opens the dialog box shown in Figure 3-12.

If you need to attach the same note to other contacts, select the other contacts on this dialog box.

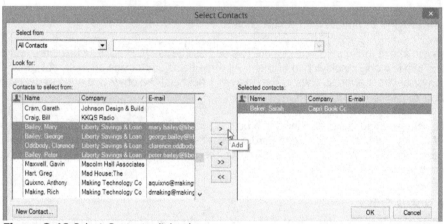

**Figure 3-12** Select Contacts dialog box

 **Sorting Contact Records On The Select Contacts Dialog Box**
If you click on a column heading in the **CONTACTS TO SELECT FROM** list or the **SELECTED CONTACTS** list, you can sort the contacts in ascending or descending order.

## New Contact Dialog Box

Clicking the **NEW CONTACT** button shown above in Figure 3-12, opens the dialog box shown in Figure 3-13.

This dialog box is used to create a new contact record.

**Figure 3-13** New Contact dialog box

## Add/Remove Dialog Box

The ellipsis button at the end of the **SHARE WITH** field, on the Insert Note dialog box, opens the dialog box shown in Figure 3-14.

The options on this dialog box are used to share the note with everyone in a group, company or opportunity. By default when you click the button at the end of the Share with field, you will see a message about sharing public notes. Click OK to close the message window.

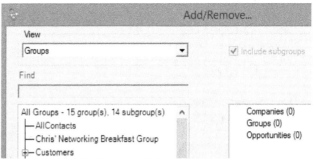

**Figure 3-14** Add/Remove dialog box

3.   Click the Contact button on the Insert Note dialog box.

4.   Sort the contacts by the Company column ⇒ Select the four contacts at Liberty Savings & Loan, as shown earlier in Figure 3-12, by clicking on the first contact at the company, then press and hold down the Shift key and click on the last contact at Liberty.

5.   Click the **ADD** button shown earlier in Figure 3-12.

There should be five names in the **SELECTED CONTACTS** list, on the Select Contacts dialog box, as shown in Figure 3-15.

**Figure 3-15** Contacts that will have the note attached

6.   Click OK to close the Select Contacts dialog box.

## How To Attach A File To A Contact Record

The **ATTACH BUTTON** on the Insert Note dialog box provides two options to attach a file to a note, as shown in Figure 3-16. The options are explained below.

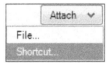

**Figure 3-16** Attach button options

①   Selecting the **FILE** option stores a copy of the file with the note. Select this option if you know for sure that you will not need to see any changes that may be made to the original document, when the document is opened from inside of ACT!. This option also increases the size of the database.

②   The **SHORTCUT** option creates a link to a file. The link is not dynamic, which means that if the file is moved to another folder, renamed or deleted, the shortcut will no longer work.

If the attached file needs to be opened by other users of the database and the shortcut attachment option is selected, the file needs to be in a location (a folder) that other users have access to, like a server. I don't know how the computers in your office are networked, but I doubt that the person down the hall from you, that needs to open an attachment, has access to the hard drive on your computer. If you find out that they do, you need to call your IT department immediately and have them change the status of your hard drive to not be shared. <smile>

1.   Click the **ATTACH** button on the Insert Note dialog box ⇒ Select the File option.

2. Double-click on the **C3 ATTACH** file in your folder.

   The Insert Note dialog box should look like the one shown in Figure 3-17. You will have a different date and time.

   Checking the **PRIVATE OPTION** will prevent other people that use the database from viewing the note. You would be the only person that could see this note.

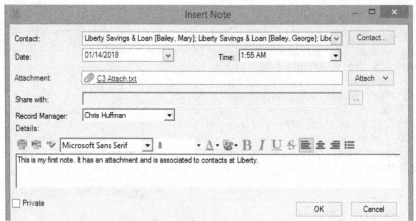

**Figure 3-17** Insert Note dialog box

3. Click OK to close the Insert Note dialog box.

4. Click OK on the **SPELL CHECK STATUS** dialog box if you enabled the automatic spell checker option on the Preferences dialog box. If you wanted to spell check the note manually, click the **CHECK SPELLING** button on the Insert Note dialog box toolbar. The entry on the Notes tab should look like the one shown in Figure 3-18.

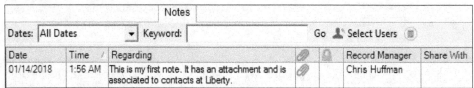

**Figure 3-18** Information added to the Notes tab

**Attached Documents**
When you attach a file in ACT!, a copy of the file is placed in the Attachments folder of the database. The original copy of the file is still where is was before you attached it. If you make changes to the original file (the one outside of ACT!), you will not see the changes when you open the attachment in ACT!. The opposite is also true. Changes made to the attached copy of the file will not be seen in the original file. You can edit the attached documents, as well as, view, email and print them. You have the three options explained below to manage attachments:

① You can reattach the original file to the note, if the original file was changed and you need the changes attached to the note.
② You can copy the original file that you changed, to the Attachments folder in ACT!, as long as the original file still has the same file name. This will overwrite the file in the Attachments folder.
③ You can make the changes to the copy of the file that is in the Attachments folder.

**Tips For Viewing And Deleting Attachments On The Notes Tab**
① By default, notes are displayed with the most recent one at the top of the list.
② To view an attachment, double-click on the paper clip icon, on the note that has the attachment that you want to view.
③ To delete an attachment from a note, double-click on the note. Click the Attach button, then select **FILE**. You will see the message shown in Figure 3-19. Click Yes and the attachment will be deleted.

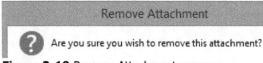

**Figure 3-19** Remove Attachment message

## Attaching Files On The Documents Tab

Earlier you attached a document to a note. Notice that the C3 Attach file is not displayed on this tab. That is because it is attached to a note. The Documents tab displays the documents that are associated with the current contact. The documents on this tab cannot be linked to another contact from this tab. There is an option on the Documents tab that is used to attach a document to the current contact.

1.  On the **DOCUMENTS** tab, click the **ADD DOCUMENT** button ⇒ Select the File option. You can also right-click in the white space on the Documents tab and select Add.

2.  Double-click on the **C3 DOCUMENTS TAB** file in your folder.

    You will see a reference to the document, as shown in Figure 3-20.

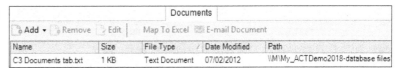

**Figure 3-20** File added to the Documents tab

> **Tips For Viewing And Deleting Attachments On The Documents Tab**
> ① To view an attachment on the Documents tab, double-click on the attachment.
> ② To delete an attachment on the Documents tab, right-click on it and select **REMOVE**.

## Relationships Tab

This tab is used to create and display contact relationships. The Relate Contact dialog box looks similar to the Insert Note dialog box.

If you want to relate the contact to one other contact, open the first drop-down list and select the contact. You can also relate the contact to more than one contact at the same time, like some or all contacts in a company or group, by selecting the group or company, on the Select Contacts dialog box.

1.  On the **RELATIONSHIPS** tab, click the **RELATE CONTACT** button. At the top of the dialog box, you should see the name Sarah Baker.

2.  On the Relate Contact dialog box ⇒ Contacts button ⇒ Select Contacts. You will see the Select Contacts dialog box.

3.  Open the Select from drop-down list and select Companies ⇒ Open the drop-down list to the right and select Verge Records.

4.  Add all of the contacts from the company to the Selected contacts list, then click OK.

5.  Open the **DEFINE RELATIONSHIP** drop-down list for Sarah Baker and select Business Partner.

6.  Open the next drop-down list and select Vendor.

7.  In the Details field at the bottom of the dialog box, type This relationship is for the record company to write a jingle for a commercial.

    Your dialog box should have the options shown in Figure 3-21. Click OK. You will see a separate entry for each contact at Verge Records on the Relationships tab, as shown in Figure 3-22.

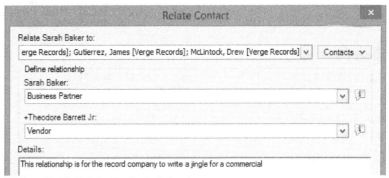

**Figure 3-21** Relate Contact dialog box

| Relationships | | | | | |
|---|---|---|---|---|---|
| **Relate Contact** Edit Relationship | | | | | |
| Relationship From | Contact | Company | E-mail | Title | ID/Status |
| Vendor | Theodore Barrett Jr | Verge Records | Theo@vergereco... | Chief Engineer | Influencer;Prospect |
| Vendor | Theodore Barrett Sr | Verge Records | | CEO | Prospect |
| Vendor | James Gutierrez | Verge Records | JamesGutierrez... | Administrative... | Gate Keeper |
| Vendor | Paul Henderson | Verge Records | PaulH@vergerec... | Assistant Engineer | Prospect |
| Vendor | Drew McLintock | Verge Records | DMclintock.verger... | Assistant Engineer | Gate Keeper |

**Figure 3-22** Contacts added to the Relationships tab

 The formatting toolbar on the Relate Contact dialog box was removed in ACT! 2011.

## Entering Information On The Personal Info Tab

In addition to the fields for the contacts home address, the following fields are also available on this tab:

① The **PERSONAL E-MAIL** field should not be used for the business e-mail address, especially if you plan to use the Mail Merge wizard to create an email mail merge. The wizard does not use this field.
② The **MESSENGER ID** field is used to store the contacts Instant Messenger ID or screen name.

 **Editing The Personal Email Field**
This field among others, can be edited differently then most of the contact fields. You can delete the contents of the field and re-type it or you can right-click in the field and select **EDIT PERSONAL E-MAIL**, as shown in Figure 3-23. If selected, this option selects the information in the field so that you do not have to delete it before you start typing in the field.

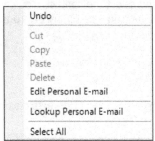

Undo

Cut
Copy
Paste
Delete
Edit Personal E-mail

Lookup Personal E-mail

Select All

**Figure 3-23** Personal Email field shortcut menu

1. On the **PERSONAL INFO** tab, in the Address 1 field, type `1899 Peyton Place Village Drive`.

2. Add the information in Table 3-5 to the record.

| Field | Type This |
|---|---|
| City | Sacramento |
| State | CA |
| Zip | 99990 |
| Home Phone | 7815551308 |

**Table 3-5** Home Address information

## Using The Date Field Calendar

Date fields, like the Birthday field, will have a calendar like the one shown in Figure 3-24. You can use the calendar to select the date or you can type the date in the field. Find the month and year in the calendar, then click on the day that you need, by using the options that are explained below.

The **TODAY** button will add the current date to the field.

Clicking the **LEFT ARROW** button at the top of the calendar will display previous months.

Clicking the **RIGHT ARROW** button will display future months.

**Figure 3-24** Date field calendar

What I like about date fields is that you do not have to type a four digit year or type a zero as the first digit of a month or day. You can type 6/2/09 and ACT! will convert it to the date shown in Figure 3-25.

**Figure 3-25** Date field converted

The **BIRTHDAY** field does not require you to enter the year the contact was born. Entering the day and month is sufficient. The current year will be filled in automatically if you do not enter it. Chapter 4 covers this and other **ANNUAL EVENT** fields and how to use them as a lookup field.

3. Click on the arrow at the end of the Birthday field, then select your next birthday on the calendar. The information on the Personal Info tab should look similar to the information shown in Figure 3-26.

Notice that the phone number was not automatically formatted.

That is because the Home Phone field is a Free Form format field. [See Phone Number Formatting, earlier in this chapter]

**Figure 3-26** Personal Info tab fields

## Contact Access Tab

The majority of fields shown in Figure 3-27 are filled in and updated automatically. The values cannot be changed.

**Figure 3-27** Contact Access tab fields

The **RECORD MANAGER** field lists the current owner of the contact record. The owner can be manually changed to another user by the current record owner.

The **CREATE DATE** and **RECORD CREATOR** fields store the date that the record was created and the name of the user that created the contact record. I do not know why the Create Date field has a drop-down list because this field is filled in automatically when the record is created and it can't be changed.

The **EDIT DATE** and **EDITED BY** fields store the date that the record was last edited and the user that edited the record. These fields cannot be changed.

The **ACCESS LEVEL** options are used to make the contact record **PUBLIC** (anyone with rights to the database can view it) or **PRIVATE** (only the Record Manager can view it).

 The **LATEST ACTIVITIES TAB** was removed in ACT! v17. The fields are in the Latest Activities section, on the top half of the contact detail view.

## User Fields Tab

The fields shown in Figure 3-28 are free form. They are used to enter data that does not fit into any of the fields that currently exist in the database. The labels for these fields can be changed to something meaningful for the data that you enter in the field.

While the fields on the User Fields tab seem like a good idea to use, they can be dangerous if more than one person is using the database. That is because by default, any user that has rights to modify the layout, add, edit or delete information, can do just that.

**Figure 3-28** User Fields tab fields

For example, one user may decide to use the User 2 field to store an alternate email address for the contact. Another user may use the User 2 field to store the date that they mailed the contact a sample product. If this happens, one of these types of data will have to be moved to a different field. This may have to be done manually, record by record, which is probably not something that you want to do.

## Saving Data

If any of the fields on the view that you are using have the **GENERATE HISTORY OPTION** enabled, a history record will be created and will appear on the History tab when the record is saved. There are two ways to save the data that you enter, as explained below.

   ①  Move to another record.
   ②  Click the Save Changes button on the toolbar.

## Exercise 3.2: Duplicating Contact Information

In Exercise 3.1, you created a contact record with a company that was not already in the database. In this exercise, you will create a contact record based on information from an existing contact record. This is known as duplicating a contact. This will save you time because you do not have to retype the company information. Duplicating a contact record that has the company information that you need, duplicates data in some of the fields in the top half of the Contact detail view. There are two ways that you can duplicate records, as explained below:

   ①  You can duplicate the primary fields, which are the company, phone, fax, address, city, state, zip code, country and web site fields. These are the primary fields that ACT! sets up as the default. You can make other fields primary fields as needed.
   ②  All of the fields can be duplicated. If this option is selected, the only fields not duplicated are the contact name and e-mail address fields.

 | Opportunity fields cannot be used as primary contact fields. |

## Creating A New Contact Based On The Primary Fields

1. Display the contact Jonathan Jenkins. (**Hint**: If you have the Lookup Search options displayed in the Navigation bar, you can type the name in the **CONTAINS** field, then click the Go button.)

2. Click the **DUPLICATE CONTACT** button on the Contacts toolbar. You should see the dialog box shown in Figure 3-29.

   Select the **DUPLICATE DATA FROM PRIMARY FIELDS** option, if it is not already selected, then click OK. You should see a new record with the primary fields filled in.

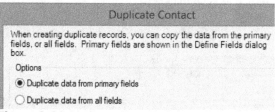

**Figure 3-29** Duplicate Contact dialog box

3. Click Yes, when prompted that the changes affect the lookup/sort criteria.

4. Add the information in Table 3-6 to the new contact record. The top half of the contact record should look like the one shown in Figure 3-30.

| Field | Type This |
|-------|-----------|
| Contact | Dan Day |
| Title | Analyst |
| Department | Engineering |

**Table 3-6** Duplicate contact information

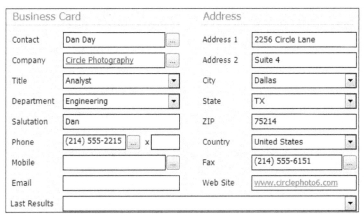

**Figure 3-30** Contact information

 **Other Ways To Open The Duplicate Contact Dialog Box**
Display the contact record that you want to duplicate, then select one of the options listed below.

① Right-click on a blank space in the top half of the Contact detail view and select **DUPLICATE CONTACT**.
② Contacts ⇒ Duplicate Contact.
───────────────────────────────────────────────

## Contact Detail View Related Tasks

The options shown in Figure 3-31 are primarily found on the detail view. Some of the options are also on list view. The options are explained below.

**VIEW ALL CONTACTS** Is the same as selecting Lookup ⇒ All Contacts. This option is helpful when you have already created a lookup and now want to display all of the records. It is quicker to use this link, then opening the Lookup menu and selecting the option. It may just be my laptop, but the View All Contacts link takes longer to display all of the records then the option on the Lookup menu does.

**WRITE LETTER** Opens the ACT! Word Processor, shown in Figure 3-32, if the word processor is selected as the default, and displays a letter template.

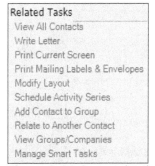

**Figure 3-31** Contact detail view related tasks

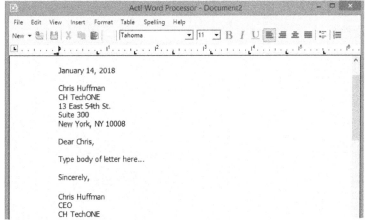

**Figure 3-32** Letter template

**PRINT CURRENT SCREEN** Opens the Quick Print Options dialog box, so that you can select options for how the screen will be printed.

**PRINT MAILING LABELS & ENVELOPES** Opens the Print dialog box, which has options for printing labels and envelopes.

**MODIFY LAYOUT** Opens the currently displayed layout in the Layout Designer, so that the layout can be changed.

**SCHEDULE ACTIVITY SERIES** Opens the Schedule Activity Series dialog box. Activity series remind me of a project plan or mini to-do list that has all of the tasks that you need to do, to complete a project. An activity series is used to schedule pre-defined activities with contacts. An activity series saves you time because you do not have to remember all of the tasks or create a series of activities manually for each contact.

**ADD CONTACT TO GROUP** Opens the Add/Remove dialog box to select groups and companies to add the contact to.

**RELATE TO ANOTHER CONTACT** Opens the Relate Contact dialog box. [See Relationships Tab, earlier in this chapter]

**VIEW GROUPS/COMPANIES** Opens the dialog box shown in Figure 3-33.

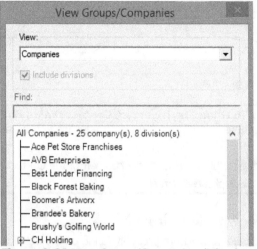

**Figure 3-33** View Groups/Companies dialog box

**MANAGE SMART TASKS** Smart Tasks are similar to an activity series because they are a series of related tasks. The difference is that Smart Tasks are automatic and cause an action like scheduling an activity as a follow up or automatically sending an email to contacts based on a condition, to be run without your intervention. Smart Tasks can be created for contact or opportunity records.

### Contact List View Related Tasks

The options shown in Figure 3-34 are for the Contact list view. The options that are only on the list view are explained below. The others were explained in the previous section.

**EXPORT TO EXCEL** Exports the contacts that are displayed on the list view to Excel.

**Figure 3-34** Contact list view related tasks

**IMPORT CONTACTS** Opens the Import Wizard, which is used to import data from a variety of file types, as shown in Figure 3-35.

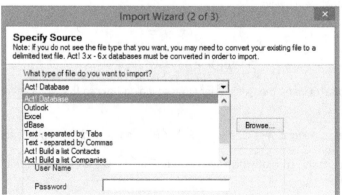

**Figure 3-35** Import Wizard

**CHANGE COLUMNS** Opens the Customize Columns dialog box, which is used to add, remove and change the order that the columns are displayed in, on the Contact list view.

**WRITE E-MAIL USING TEMPLATE** Opens the Template folder (for the database) so that you can select a template to use for the email that you want to create. Once you select the template, a new email window will open and the template that you selected, will be displayed. If you selected multiple contacts on the Contacts tab, a mail merge document will be created for each contact record.

**MAIL MERGE CONTACTS** Opens the Mail Merge Wizard.

**SORT LIST** Opens the Sort dialog box, to sort the contacts displayed in the view.

**CREATE GROUP OF CONTACTS** Displays the Group detail view. All of the contacts displayed in the view will be added to the group that you create.

# FINDING CONTACTS IN A DATABASE

Overview

In this chapter you will learn how to use the following search techniques:

- ☑ Lookup options on the Navigation Pane
- ☑ Lookup command
- ☑ Keyword Search lookups
- ☑ Multiple field lookups
- ☑ Narrow lookup option
- ☑ Add to lookup option
- ☑ Universal search feature
- ☑ Annual Events lookup

You will also learn the following:

- ☑ How to modify more than one record at the same time
- ☑ How to sort records
- ☑ How to delete records

**CHAPTER 4**

## Finding Records

Having a database with hundreds or thousands of contacts is great. Being able to find the contacts that you need to access quickly, is a core reason of putting information into a database. ACT! comes with several lookup options to find contacts. Depending on the contacts that you need to find, one lookup option is probably a better solution then the other lookup options. Many of the lookup options are covered in this chapter. Some are specifically for contacts and others can be used to look up other types of records.

## Lookup Options On The Navigation Pane

At the top of the Navigation Pane you will see the lookup section shown in Figure 4-1, if the lookup option is enabled on the Preferences dialog box.

This section of the Navigation Pane is used to find records. The drop-down list field (the Contact Field in Figure 4-1) contains all of the fields that can be searched.

**Figure 4-1** Contacts Navigation Pane lookup options

Each of the other views on the Navigation Pane also has a lookup section. The options in the drop-down list change, depending on the view that is displayed. The options in this section provide quick access to some of the lookup options in ACT!.

The drop-down list is used to select the field that you want to search on. Fields on the tabs of the detail views are also included in this list.

The **MORE OPTIONS** link opens the Lookup dialog box.

The steps below demonstrate how to use the lookup options.

1.  Open the drop-down list and select the field that you want to search on.

2.  In the **CONTAINS FIELD**, type the value that the field that you selected must have, then click the Go button.

## Exercise 4.1: Using The Lookup Options On The Navigation Pane

1.  In the Related Tasks section of the Navigation Pane, click the View All Contacts link.

2.  In the Lookup section, open the Contact Field drop-down list ⇒ Select Company.

3.  Type `Circle` in the **CONTAINS** field ⇒ Click the Go button. You will see all of the contact records in the Contact list view that have the word Circle in the Company field.

## The Lookup Command

The Lookup command is used to find records based on the criteria that you select. Other software packages use the term **QUERY** when discussing finding specific records. Both terms provide the same functionality. You can find all contacts in one state or all contacts that have the same title. You can use the Lookup command to find contacts by Company, First Name, Last Name, Phone Number, City, State, Zip Code or ID/Status. Later you will learn how to find contacts using other fields. The biggest limitation to lookups is that the criteria cannot be saved. After you complete the lookup exercises, hopefully, you will better understand why it is so important to enter data correctly and to enter as much data as possible for each record that you create.

## Lookup Contacts Dialog Box Options

This dialog box provides several options to help you find the records that you need. The options are explained below.

The **OPERATOR** options shown in Figure 4-2 are used to select the criteria to find the records. These options are used to include or exclude records.

The **SEARCH FOR** options shown in Figure 4-3 are used to select the type of records to search, to find the contacts that you are looking for.

The **CURRENT LOOKUP** options shown in Figure 4-4 are used to select the type of lookup that you want to create. The options are explained in Table 4-1.

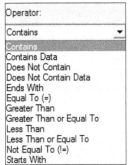

**Figure 4-2** Operator criteria options

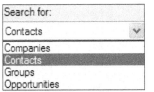

**Figure 4-3** Record type search options

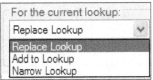

**Figure 4-4** Lookup options

| Option | Description |
|---|---|
| Replace Lookup | This is the default option. It creates a new lookup. |
| Add to Lookup | Adds the contacts from the lookup that you are creating now, to the previous lookup that you created. |
| Narrow Lookup | Searches the records from the previous lookup to exclude (remove) records from it, based on the criteria that you select in the lookup that you are creating now. |

**Table 4-1** Current lookup drop-down list field options explained

### Exercise 4.2: Using The Lookup Command

1. Lookup menu ⇒ State.

2. Open the **VALUE** drop-down list to the far right and select NY or type NY in the field.

3. If you see the **SHOW MORE OPTIONS** option on the dialog box, click the button before it. You should have the options shown in Figure 4-5.

   Click OK.

   You should see record 1 of 26 displayed on the Contact list view.

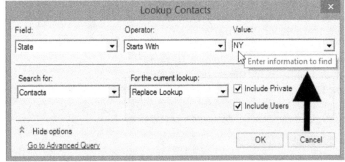

**Figure 4-5** Lookup Contacts dialog box

On Figure 4-5 above, the **INCLUDE PRIVATE OPTION** is used to search your private records. The **INCLUDE USERS OPTION** will retrieve other database users "My Records", if they meet the search criteria.

The result of a lookup will only display records that match the criteria that you select. Notice that the view changed to the Contact list view. If you click the Detail View button on the toolbar, you will be able to see more information for each of the contacts that were retrieved by the lookup.

Notice that the information on the Status bar in the lower left corner of the workspace, displays **LOOKUP: STATE**. This lets you know that the records displayed are based on a lookup for the State field.

4. Lookup ⇒ All Contacts, or click the View All Contacts link in the Related Tasks section of the Navigation Pane. All of the contacts will be displayed.

5. Click the Detail View button on the Contacts toolbar.

| **Contact Detail View Lookup Shortcut** |
|---|
| Using the lookup options on the menu or clicking the **MORE OPTIONS** link in the Lookup section of the Navigation Pane is probably how most people create a lookup, but there is another way. Right-click in the field on the Contact detail view that you want to use as the lookup field and select **LOOKUP [FIELD NAME]**, as illustrated in Figure 4-6. The Lookup Contacts dialog box will open. This also works on fields on tabs that you can enter data, like the fields on the Personal Info tab. |

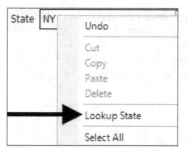

**Figure 4-6** State field shortcut menu

## Exercise 4.3: Using Keyword Search Lookups

Keyword search lookups are used to find records based on information in any field. You can perform a keyword search for a word or phrase in any field, including fields on the tabs. This is different from the lookup that you created in the previous exercise. The lookup that you created in the previous exercise searched for records that **START WITH** the value that you typed in or selected. Keyword searches are different. They retrieve records that have the value any place in a field.

As you will see, the **OPERATOR** field on the Lookup dialog box has other options to search for data. The Keyword Search feature is very helpful when you remember a word or phrase, but do not remember what field it is in. The difference between these two options is that the Lookup only searches in one field in one table, while the Keyword Search, searches all fields in all of the tables that you select. Depending on how many tables you select to search in, the keyword search could take a while, because all of the fields are searched, including fields on the System tabs, which each have their own table in the database.

1.  Lookup ⇒ Advanced ⇒ Search on Keywords. You should see the Search on Keywords dialog box.

2.  Type `Sales` in the **SEARCH FOR** field.

3.  Open the **TYPE** drop-down list and select **CONTACTS**, then clear the **OPPORTUNITIES** option in the Look in section. You should have the options selected that are shown in Figure 4-7.

These options will search for the word "Sales" in all contact, activity, history, notes and relationships fields.

The **FIELDS** option in the Look in section includes all fields for the record type that is selected.

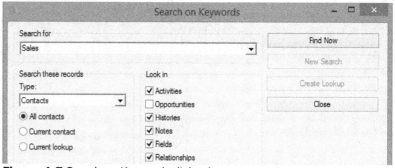

**Figure 4-7** Search on Keywords dialog box

4.  Click the **FIND NOW** button. The records shown at the bottom of the dialog box match the criteria that you selected.

You should see that the keyword search criteria "Sales" was found over 100 times. This is not necessarily the number of records that have the search criteria. It is the number of fields that have the word "Sales" in it. This often means that several records have the word "Sales" in more than one field.

## Viewing The Keyword Search Results

When you view records retrieved from the search, the Search on Keywords dialog box stays open. This allows you to go back to it to select other records to view in detail. You can also change the search options and perform another search, without starting over. There are several options that you can select from to view the results in the Contact detail view, as explained below.

①  You can scroll through the list of records at the bottom of the Search on Keywords dialog box. You may recognize the records that you are looking for.

② If you right-click on a single record at the bottom of the dialog box and select **GO TO RECORD**, as illustrated in Figure 4-8, the detail record will be displayed.

③ You can select more than one record to view, by clicking on one record, then pressing and holding down the **CTRL** key and clicking on the other records that you want to view, as shown in Figure 4-9. Once the records are selected, right-click and select **LOOKUP SELECTED RECORDS**, as shown in Figure 4-8.

④ Click the **CREATE LOOKUP** button at the top of the Search on Keywords dialog box. This option will create a lookup to display every record (on the Contact List view) with the record type that you select on the dialog box.

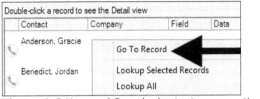

**Figure 4-8** Keyword Search shortcut menu options

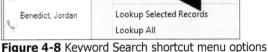

**Figure 4-9** Multiple records selected to view

5. Select the first 10 records on the Search on Keywords dialog box, then right-click on any of the highlighted records and select **LOOKUP SELECTED RECORDS**.

Notice that the dialog box is minimized in the lower left corner of the workspace. The reason that there are only eight contact records displayed, is because some of these contact records have more than one field that has the word "Sales" in it.

6. Close the Search on Keywords dialog box. (Click the X on the dialog box, without restoring it first) ⇒ Lookup ⇒ All Contacts.

> **Keyword Search Viewing Tips**
> ① Selecting the **LOOKUP ALL** option, on the shortcut menu shown earlier in Figure 4-8, is the same as clicking the Create Lookup button, on the dialog box.
> ② Double-clicking on a record in the bottom half of the Search on Keywords dialog box is the same as right-clicking on a record and selecting Go To Record.
> ③ To select several adjacent records, click on the first one, then press and hold down the **SHIFT** key and click on the last record that you want to view.

### Exercise 4.4: How To Create A Lookup Using Multiple Fields

Exercise 4.2 covered how to perform a lookup using one field. In this exercise you will learn how to look up records using more than one field. If you wanted to email managers that are in Boise, you would have to search two fields. You would have to search the City field for "Boise" and you would have to search the Title field for "Manager".

If you open the Lookup menu you will see the City field. You will not see the Title field. It appears that you cannot search the Title field. The **OTHER FIELDS** option on the Lookup menu contains the fields that are not listed on the Lookup menu. You can also right-click in the Title field on the view and select the lookup option from the shortcut menu.

1. Lookup ⇒ City.

2. Type `Boise` in the Value field, then press Enter. There are three contacts in Boise. Notice that two contacts have the Manager title.

### Using The Narrow Lookup Option

Until now, when you performed a lookup, the Replace Lookup option was used. The Replace Lookup option tells ACT! to remove the records from the previous lookup and start over.

The **NARROW LOOKUP** option is used to reduce the number of contacts that are from the result of the previous lookup. In this exercise, the previous lookup selected all contacts in Boise. Now you want to find the managers in Boise. If you selected the Replace lookup option you would get all managers, no matter what city they are in. This is not what you want in this exercise. The Narrow Lookup option will only search the records that were retrieved from the previous lookup.

1.  Lookup ⇒ Other Fields ⇒ Open the Field drop-down list and select Title.

 The **OTHER FIELDS** option does not provide any additional fields to search on, that are not already in the Field drop-down list. If the field that you want to search on, is not on the Lookup menu, you can select any field to open the Lookup Contacts dialog box and select the field that you need from the **FIELD** drop-down list.

2.  Open the Value drop-down list and select Manager.

3.  Select the **NARROW LOOKUP** option.

    The Lookup Contacts dialog box should have the options shown in Figure 4-10.

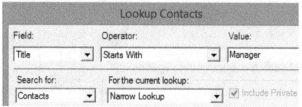

**Figure 4-10** Options to search for a specific job title

4.  Click OK. You should now have two records in the lookup. This means that one of the three original contact records retrieved does not have "Manager" in the Title field.

This may seem like a lot of work to remove one record. If the database retrieved thousands of records that met your initial lookup criteria, being able to perform another lookup to remove 1,000 records from the search automatically, makes this a good feature to use.

### Exercise 4.5: Using The Add To Lookup Option

If you wanted to find contacts with a Texas address or are sales reps, using the Replace Lookup and Narrow Lookup options together would not give you the results that you are looking for. The **ADD TO LOOKUP** option is used to combine the results from different lookups. The records from the various lookups do not have to be related. This is the type of lookup that you will learn how to create in this exercise.

1.  Lookup ⇒ State. Type TX in the Value field.

2.  Make sure that the **REPLACE LOOKUP** option is selected. Click OK. 14 records should have been retrieved.

3.  Lookup ⇒ Other Fields ⇒ Select Title from the Field drop-down list ⇒ Select Sales Representative from the Value drop-down list.

When performing lookups, you should select an item from the Value drop-down list as much as possible, even though the Value field will allow you to type in an entry. If you type in an entry and what you type in is not used on any record, you will not retrieve the records that you expect.

4.  Select the **ADD TO LOOKUP** option. Click OK. There should be 20 records displayed. All of the records in the lookup either have "TX" in the State field or "Sales Representative" in the Title field. If someone typed "Texas" in the State field on contact records, those records would not be retrieved in this search.

### Universal Search

At the right side of the Global toolbar is the Search tool. It can be used to search for any information regardless of the view that is currently displayed. For example, you could search for opportunities from a Group view.

Operators like "AND" and "OR" can also be used to combine terms that you want to search for. The question mark (used to replace one character) and asterisk (used to replace two or more characters) wildcard characters can also be used in the Universal search field. The steps bellow show you how to use this search feature.

1.  From any view that has the Search field at the end of the Global toolbar, type in the phrase, words or terms that you want to search for. For example, type in Sales or presentation.

2.  Click the Go button. You will see the screen shown in Figure 4-11.

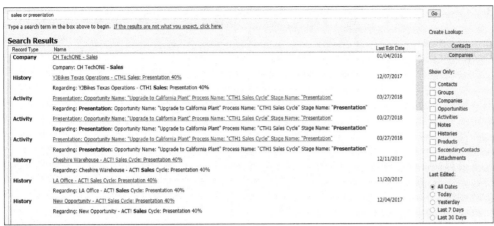

**Figure 4-11** Screen results window

The options explained below are on the right side of the window. Using them is are optional. To view a record, click on a link in the **NAME COLUMN**.

The **SHOW ONLY** options are used to select (filter) the search results by record type.

The **LAST EDITED** options are used to select a date range.

### Finding Contact Records That Are Missing Information

The goal of Exercise 4.4 was to find contacts that meet specific criteria to send an email to. In order to send the contacts an email, they need to have an email address. You can use the Lookup command to find contacts that do or do not have an email address. Searching for records that do not have data in certain fields is a good way to keep contacts from having data missing.

### Exercise 4.6: Find Contacts Without An Email Address

In this exercise you will find all contacts that do not have an email address.

1.  Lookup ⇒ E-mail Address ⇒ Select the **DOES NOT CONTAIN DATA** operator, illustrated in Figure 4-12.

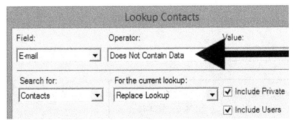

**Figure 4-12** Options to find all contacts without an email address

2.  Click OK. To verify that the records do not have an email address, click the Detail View button. View a few records and look at the Email field. You will see that the field is empty.

The reason that I had you view the records on the Contact detail view is because the Email field is not displayed by default, on the Contact list view. You will learn how to modify a layout to display the fields that you need.

### Exercise 4.7: Find Contacts That You Added To The Database

One way to help keep data accurate and consistent is to review it. Everyone that uses the database should do this periodically. The frequency that data is checked and verified depends on how many records are added and how often data is modified.

In this exercise you will create a lookup that finds all contacts that you added to the database in the last month. The fields that you need for this search are the Record Creator and Create Date fields on the Contact Access tab.

1. Lookup ⇒ Other Fields.

   Select the options shown in Figure 4-13.
   You have to type in the Record Creators
   name, which for the exercises in this book,
   is Chris Huffman.

   Click OK.

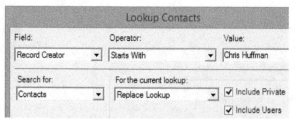

**Figure 4-13** Record Creator field lookup criteria

2. Lookup ⇒ Other Fields ⇒
   Select the options shown in Figure 4-14, then click OK.

   You should see the two records shown in Figure 4-15.
   These records should look familiar because you created
   them earlier, in this book. If it has been more than 30
   days since you completed Exercise 3.1 and 3.2, you will
   not retrieve these records.

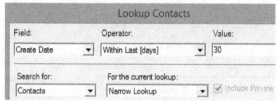

**Figure 4-14** Create Date field lookup criteria

| | | Company | Title | Contact | Phone |
|---|---|---|---|---|---|
| | | Capri Book Comany | Sales Manager | Sarah Baker | (765) 555-5330 |
| | | Circle Photography | Analyst | Dan Day | (214) 555-2215 |

**Figure 4-15** Contacts that you added to the database in the last 30 days

## Annual Events Lookup

Annual events is another type of lookup. Examples of annual events are anniversaries, birthdays and yearly salary
reviews. By default, annual events do not appear on calendars, but they can be added to a calendar. Creating a lookup
is one way to be able to view annual events.

 Annual event fields only search the month and day portion of the date field, because they are tracked from
year to year.

## Exercise 4.8: Lookup Annual Events

In this exercise you will create a lookup to find all contacts with a birthday between January 1, 2018 and
March 31, 2018.

1. Lookup ⇒ Annual Events.

   The options in the **SEARCH FOR** drop-down list shown in
   Figure 4-16, display all of the types of annual events
   that are currently being used in the database.

**Figure 4-16** Annual event types

2. Accept the Birth Date search option ⇒ Select the **DATE RANGE** option.

 **Tips For Selecting A Different Date**
   ① An easy way to select a different year is to change the year of the date displayed at the top of the
   drop-down list.
   ② Type the date you want in the Date field, instead of selecting it on the calendar.

3. Open the first date drop-down list field and select January 1, 2018, as shown in Figure 4-17 ⇒ Open the second
   date drop-down list field and select March 31, 2018. You should have the options selected that are shown in
   Figure 4-18.

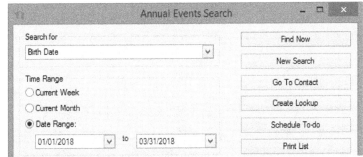

**Figure 4-17** Date field calendar

**Figure 4-18** Birth Date annual event search options

If you click the **SCHEDULE TO-DO** button on the Annual Events Search dialog box, you can create an activity for the contact that is selected at the bottom of the Annual Events Search dialog box. The contacts name will appear on the Schedule Activities dialog box. This option will not recognize more than one selected contact.

4. Click the **FIND NOW** button. You will see the contacts (at the bottom of the dialog box) that have a birthday in the date range that you selected.

5. Close the Annual Events Search dialog box, then display all of the contacts.

> **Annual Events Search Viewing Tips**
> The records shown at the bottom of the Annual Events Search dialog box match the criteria. The options explained below are how you can view the results.
>
> ① You can search for more than one annual event at the same time. As shown earlier in Figure 4-16, you can check more than one annual event type or you can select the **ALL** option to lookup all of the annual event types that are in the database.
> ② If you right-click on a single record at the bottom of the Annual Events Search dialog box and select **GO TO CONTACT**, the record will be displayed.
> ③ Double-clicking on a record is the same as right-clicking and selecting **GO TO CONTACT**.
> ④ Click the **CREATE LOOKUP** button on the Annual Events Search dialog box. This will create a lookup that displays every record that is at the bottom of the dialog box, in the Contact detail view.

### ACT! Annual Events Report

The **PRINT LIST** button on the Annual Events Search dialog box will create and print the report shown in Figure 4-19, if the Birth Date option is selected in the drop-down list, shown earlier in Figure 4-16.

The report shown in Figure 4-20 is created if the First Purchase option is selected. If both options, shown earlier in Figure 4-16, are selected, both fields will be displayed on the report.

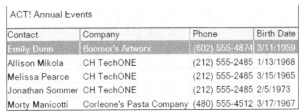

**Figure 4-19** ACT! Annual Events Birth Date report

**Figure 4-20** ACT! Annual Events First Purchase report

### Contact Activity Lookup

This type of lookup is used to find contacts whose records were or were not updated since a certain date. The lookup searches on any or all of the following tabs: Notes, History, Activities, Opportunities and Contact Access. This lookup is useful if you have a lot of contacts that you need to keep up with on a regular basis. It is also a good way to make sure that the data is accurate and that none of your contacts are being neglected or have fallen off of your radar, as they say.

## Exercise 4.9: Find Contacts That Have Not Been Updated

In this exercise you will search for contacts that have not had the notes, opportunities or activities updated since February 1, 2017.

1. Lookup ⇒ Contact Activity.

2. Check the **NOT CHANGED** option ⇒ Change the **SINCE DATE** to 2/1/2017.

 I am not sure why, but the value in the **SINCE DATE** field is saved in ACT!. This means that the next time that you open the Contact Activity dialog box, the date that you selected the last time that you used the dialog box, will automatically be in this field.

3. If selected, clear the following options: Contact fields and Histories ⇒ Check the Notes, Opportunities and Activities options. You should have the options selected that are shown in Figure 4-21.

 The Histories and Activities options allow specific categories to be searched for, as shown in Figure 4-22.

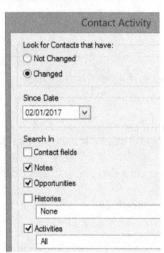

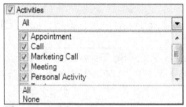

**Figure 4-22** Activity options

**Figure 4-21** Contact Activity dialog box options

4. Click OK. The records on the Contact list view is the list that you would work from, because the contact records have not been updated in a long time.

 **Contact Activity Lookup Tips**
① Lookups are not case sensitive. Typing "Marketing" or "marketing" will return the same results.
② **LOOKUP ⇒ PREVIOUS** displays up to the last nine searches that you ran, as shown in Figure 4-23. You can select the search that you want to run again. When you reopen ACT!, the previous searches will not be available because they are not saved.
③ Right-click in a field in the top half of the Contact detail view and select Lookup (Field Name) to open the Lookup dialog box.
④ When only one record meets the lookup criteria, it is displayed in the Contact detail view. You do not have to display all contacts before creating a lookup.

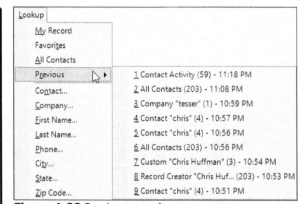

**Figure 4-23** Previous searches

## Modifying Several Records At The Same Time

You may have the need to change the data in the same field on several records. You could make the changes one record at a time or you could create a lookup to retrieve all of the records that you need to change and change all of them at the same time.

 | If you do not create a lookup first, the changes will be made to every record in the database. |

If you have several company contacts at the same address and the company moves, you could look up the company address that you need to change and change all of the records at the same time, if the address fields are not linked. You can also change data on the User Fields, Personal Info and Secondary Contacts tabs this way.

The **REPLACE FIELD** command is used to change the data in a field for multiple records at the same time.

### Exercise 4.10: How To Modify Several Records At The Same Time

In this exercise you will change the value in the Last Results field and add a note to a user defined field for all contacts in NY. The tasks that you will learn in this exercise are helpful for updating several records at the same time, as well as, keeping the data consistent and accurate.

 | Depending on the change that you are making, it is a good idea to make a back up copy of the database before modifying several records at the same time. This is known as a **GLOBAL** change. This type of change cannot be undone with a mouse click. You do not have to create a back up copy now, because this is a practice database. |

### Change The Value In The Last Results Field

1. Create a lookup to find all contacts in NY. The lookup should retrieve 26 records.

2. Edit ⇒ Replace Field. You will see the Replace Data dialog box.

3. Open the Replace contents of drop-down list and select the **LAST RESULTS** field.

4. Open the Value drop-down list and select **DISCUSSED OPPORTUNITIES**, as shown in Figure 4-24.

**Figure 4-24** Replace data options for the Last Results field

5. Click OK. The Replace/Swap/Copy message lets you know that all records in the current lookup will be modified ⇒ Click Yes to modify the records.

### Change The Value In A User Defined Field

In this part of the exercise you will use the Replace Field command to change the value in a user defined field. User defined fields are free form fields that are used to enter data, that there is no existing field for.

1. Edit ⇒ Replace Field.

2. Select the User 10 field from the first drop-down list ⇒ Type Should this record be private? in the **VALUE** field, as shown in Figure 4-25.

**Figure 4-25** Replace data options for the User 10 field

3. Click OK, then click Yes to modify the records.

Observe the following information about the 26 records in the lookup, by clicking the Detail View button.

① The **LAST RESULTS** field (in the top section of the view) has been set to Discussed opportunities.

② On the Contact Access tab, the **EDIT DATE** field has today's date.

③ On the User Fields tab, the **USER 10** field has the text that you typed in the Value field, shown above in Figure 4-25.

### Exercise 4.11: How To Delete Data From Several Records At The Same Time

Just like you can add or change data in a field for multiple records, you can also delete data from a field for multiple records at the same time. You will learn how in this exercise.

1. With the 26 NY records still in the lookup, Edit ⇒ Replace Field.

2. Select the User 10 field from the first drop-down list and leave the Value field empty. Leaving the Value field empty will overwrite the data in the field with blanks, which produces the same effect as deleting data in the field.

3. Click OK, then click Yes. You can view the information on the User Fields tab. You will see that the User 10 field for the 26 records is now blank.

### Using The Contact List View

Until now, you have been using the Contact detail view to look at records. The Detail view only displays one record at a time. The Contact list view resembles a spreadsheet and displays all of the contacts that you have the right to see. Options not covered on the Contact list view in this chapter are covered in Chapter 9. [See Chapter 9, Tagging Contacts]

The first two columns on the Contact list view shown in Figure 4-26, are used to visually bring records to your attention.

The first column will have an icon in it if the contact record is a user of the database.

The second column will display a lock icon if the record was marked private by the current user (you).

| | | Company | Title |
| --- | --- | --- | --- |
| | 🔒 | A1 Services-US Oper | VP of Sales |
| | | A1 Services-US Oper | President US Operations |
| | | AVB Enterprises | CEO |
| | 🔒 | CH Gourmet Coffee | Public Relations Manager |
| 👤 | | CH TechONE | Vice President of US Operations |
| 👤 | | CH TechONE | Sales Representative |

**Figure 4-26** Contact list view

### Sort Records Using Column Headings In The Contact List View

You can sort the records in the Contact list view by clicking on the column heading that you want to sort on. The default sort order is based on the Company field.

1. Lookup ⇒ All Contacts. On the Contact list view, click on the Contact column heading.

Notice that the records are now sorted by the contacts last name, even though the first and last names are in the same column. The Last name field is the field that the Contact column actually sorts on.

You should see a triangle in the Contact column heading. If the triangle points up like this ▲, the records are sorted in ascending (A to Z or 1 to 10) order. If the triangle points down like this ▼, the records are sorted in descending (Z to A or 10 to 1) order.

 If your database has hundreds or thousands of records, you may not want to scroll down the list even though the records are currently sorted to find the contact that you need. If that is the case, the steps below show you how to find to a specific record in the list without scrolling.

2. At the far right of the window, open the Options drop-down list shown in Figure 4-27 and select Show Look For.

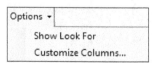

**Figure 4-27** Options drop-down list

3. Click on the column heading, not the arrow on the column heading, of the field that has the value that you want to look for, to sort the list. In this exercise, click on the Contact column.

4. Start typing the first few letters of what you are looking for. You do not have to click in a field, just type. In this example, type `York`, because that is a contacts last name.

You will see that the first contact in the list that matches what you typed in, is highlighted. Also notice that the letters that you typed in are in the **LOOK FOR** field even though you did not click in this field, before you typed in the information.

The more letters that you type, the closer ACT! will be able to find the record that you are looking for. This works for all columns, as long as the list is sorted on that column before you start typing in the search criteria.

### View Detail Information From The Contact List View

If you want to view all of the data for a contact from the Contact list view, double-click on the contact that you want to view. If you click on a field that is hyperlinked (blue), like the company or web site fields, you will open the Company detail record or the web site.

### How To Select And View Specific Records

If you have a database with thousands of records, you will probably not want to see all of the records in the Contact list view. You can select (highlight) any of the records and only view the records that you select.

1. Click the List View button ⇒ Click on the Company column heading. The records should be in ascending, alphabetical order, by company. If not, click on the Company column heading again.

2. Click on the first record with the company name A1 Services ⇒ Press and hold down the Shift key, then click on the last record with the same company name.

3. Press and hold down the Ctrl key, then select all of the Beautiful Friendship company records.

   The Contact list view should look like the one shown in Figure 4-28.

**Figure 4-28** Contact list view with records selected

4. Right-click in the Contact list view on a highlighted record and select **LOOKUP SELECTED CONTACTS**, as illustrated in Figure 4-29.

   In the Contact list view you should now only see the eight records that you selected.

**Figure 4-29** Contact list view shortcut menu

### Exercise 4.12: Sorting Records

Earlier, you learned how to sort records in the Contact list view by clicking on a column heading. That is how to sort on a single column. If you want to sort on more than one column or sort on a column that is not displayed on the Contact list view, you have to use the Sort dialog box. Follow the steps below to learn how to sort records in the Contact list view, using the Sort dialog box.

1. Lookup ⇒ All Contacts.

2. Edit ⇒ Sort. You should see the Sort dialog box.

3. Open the **SORT BY** drop-down list. You will see all of the fields on the current layout ⇒ Select the State field ⇒ Select the **ASCENDING** sort order option.

4. Open the **AND THEN BY** drop-down list and select the Referred By field (which is not displayed on the Contact list view) ⇒ Select the Descending sort order option.

5.  You should have the options selected, that are shown in Figure 4-30.

    Click OK. The records are now sorted by the State and Referred By fields.

**Figure 4-30** Sort dialog box options

## Deleting Contact Data

If you no longer need to keep information on a particular contact or secondary contact, you can delete the record. Once you delete a record, it is gone forever unless you restore it from a back up copy of the database. The contact record is deleted from all companies that it is associated or linked to. The contact record is also deleted from any group that it is a member of. When deleting a contact you have the following options:

①  Delete the current contact.
②  Delete all of the contacts in the current lookup.
③  Select the contacts on the list view, then right-click and select Delete Contact.

When you delete a contact, the Notes and History records for the contact are also deleted. The programmer in me knows that just deleting records from a database is usually not the best solution. A better solution would be to export the records that you do not need to another database. You can name this database anything that you like. This second database is sometimes referred to as a **HISTORY** or **ARCHIVE DATABASE**, meaning that it does not contain any current or active records. Once you export the records from the live database to the second database, you can delete them from the live database.

In other databases, I created a field called Inactive. When this field is checked, the code behind it disabled all of the fields, so that they could not be changed by users. The record could only be enabled again, by an administrator of the database, which is usually a department manager.

## Exercise 4.13: How To Delete Contact Records

In this exercise, you will learn how to delete a single contact record and how to delete more than one record at the same time.

### How To Delete One Record

1.  Right-click on the record for William Cadbury that does not have a company name and select **DELETE CONTACT**.

2.  Click the Delete Contact button shown in Figure 4-31, then click Yes to confirm that you want to delete the record.

**Figure 4-31** Delete contact confirmation dialog box

### How To Delete Multiple Records At The Same Time

If you need to delete several records, when possible, create a lookup to find the records that you want to delete.

1.  Lookup ⇒ Company ⇒ Type A1 in the Value field.

2.  Press Enter or click OK. Five records should be displayed.

3.  Contacts ⇒ Delete Contact.

4.  Click the **DELETE LOOKUP** button, shown above in Figure 4-31 ⇒ Click Yes to confirm that you want to delete the five records in the lookup. In a few seconds, you will see a message that tells you that no more records match the lookup criteria ⇒ Click OK.

## View The My Record

Now that you have edited and deleted records, you can check the History tab to see the entries for the changes that you made to the database.

1.  Lookup ⇒ My Record.

2.  On the History tab, the first seven entries should be for the records that you deleted or changed, as shown in Figure 4-32.

    The **REGARDING & DETAILS** column is used to let you know what the change to the record is.

| Date | Time | Result | Regarding & Details |
|------|------|--------|---------------------|
| 01/15/2018 | 3:16 AM | Contact Deleted | Contact Andy Harrison has been deleted. |
| 01/15/2018 | 3:16 AM | Contact Deleted | Contact Amanda Form has been deleted. |
| 01/15/2018 | 3:16 AM | Contact Deleted | Contact Angela Ives has been deleted. |
| 01/15/2018 | 3:16 AM | Contact Deleted | Contact Ann Goodall has been deleted. |
| 01/15/2018 | 3:16 AM | Contact Deleted | Contact Pat Gourmet has been deleted. |
| 01/15/2018 | 3:14 AM | Contact Deleted | Contact William Cadbury has been deleted. |
| 01/15/2018 | 1:42 AM | Field Changed | Field changed<br>Field Last Results changed from "" to "Discussed opportunities" |

**Figure 4-32** History log of deleted and changed records

3.  Lookup ⇒ All Contacts. There should be 197 records in the database.

# CREATING COMPANY AND DIVISION RECORDS

Overview

In this chapter you will learn about the following company and division record options:

- ☑ Using the Companies tree
- ☑ Creating company and division records
- ☑ Associating and linking contacts to companies
- ☑ Duplicating company and division records
- ☑ Using the Company Lookup command

CHAPTER 5

## Company And Division Records

The Company record type allows contacts associated with a company to be managed easier. By "managed", I mean that the company view is used to view all of the activities, history, notes and opportunities for all of the contacts associated with the selected company. If a company has a lot of contacts, it may be easier to manage the contacts if divisions were created for the company, similar to companies that have divisions and departments. Companies in ACT! can have them also. It is also possible that you may not need any divisions for the companies, in the database that you create. Figure 5-1 shows the Company detail view.

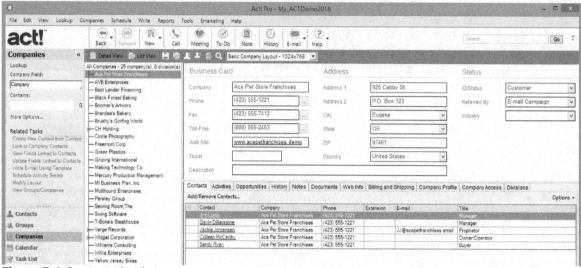

**Figure 5-1** Company detail view

In a way, a company record is similar to a group. This may be why the groups and companies are on the same tab on the Contact detail view. You can see all of the companies and groups except dynamic groups that a contact is a member of. It would be nice if there was a way to know if the entries on this tab are a company or group. Contacts can be associated with more than one company.

An example of when you would associate a contact to more than one company would be if one consultant (a contact) did work for multiple companies that are in your database. You can create activities, notes and opportunities, as well as, attach documents to a company record. In ACT!, any of the following are acceptable ways to categorize contacts in a company. These categories would be divisions that you create. I am sure that you can come up with several others.

    ① By department    ② By title    ③ By contacts home state

Keep in mind that company records in ACT! do not have the same limitations as brick and mortar companies. Company records in ACT! function more like folders, meaning that the contact records associated to a company, do not have to have anything related. While the company records displayed in the Companies tree have the name of a company, you can create a company record with any name that you want. You could create a company record that has your first name as the company name.

In addition to being able to create 15 levels of divisions per company record, you can also create **SUBDIVISIONS**. Subdivisions are used to further divide the contacts into categories per company, which makes it easier to manage hundreds or thousands of contacts associated with the company record.

An example of when it would be appropriate to create subdivisions would be for a company that has 1,000 sales reps. I would create a division called "Sales Reps". I would then create subdivisions for each of the product lines the company has like telephones, digital cameras, camcorders and televisions. Then add the sales reps to the appropriate subdivisions based on the product lines that the sales rep sells. As you can see, divisions and subdivisions can be used to organize contacts in the way that works best for you. A contact that is in a division does not have to also be part of the company. This means that you can add a contact to a division without being required to associate it to the company. Divisions are independent of the company that they are created under.

## Company vs Group Records

In this chapter you will learn how to create company records. In the next chapter you will learn how to create group records. On the surface, company and group records may appear to be the same and have the same functionality, but there are some differences.

Company records have more functionality than group records. For example, company records have more fields that can be used to automatically fill in fields on a contact record. The opposite is also true. Fields on a contact record can be used to fill in fields on a company record.

Creating a group is like saving a lookup because the records do not have to have the same data in a specific field. When you view contacts from the Company detail view you can see the notes, activities and opportunities for all of the contacts in the company on the same tab. The same is true if contact records are viewed from the Group detail view.

## Company Detail View Toolbar

Many of the buttons on the Company detail view toolbar are the same as the contact and group view toolbars. Figure 5-2 shows the Company detail view toolbar. Table 5-1 explains the buttons on the toolbar.

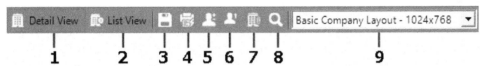

**Figure 5-2** Company detail view toolbar

| Button | Description |
|--------|-------------|
| 1 | Displays the Company detail view. |
| 2 | Displays the Company list view. |
| 3 | Saves the record. (1) (2) |
| 4 | Opens the Quick Print Options dialog box. |
| 5 | Adds or removes a contact from a company. (2) |
| 6 | Updates the linked contacts for the selected company. |
| 7 | Attach a file. (2) |
| 8 | Creates a lookup of the selected company. |
| 9 | Is used to select a different layout. (1) |

**Table 5-1** Company detail view toolbar buttons explained

(1) This option is only available from the Company detail view.
(2) This option applies to companies and divisions.

## Companies Tree

The Companies tree is on the left side of the Company detail view. At the top of the Companies tree, the number of companies and divisions are displayed. The tree displays all of the companies, divisions and subdivisions in the database, as illustrated in Figure 5-3.

A plus sign in front of an entry in the tree means that there is at least one division below it.

If you click on an entry in the tree, you will see the detail information for it on the right side of the window. The companies and divisions at this level are recognized as divisions.

**Figure 5-3** Companies tree

Company records in the Companies tree may or may not contain the same companies that you see in the Contacts view. For example, in the Contact list view you will see the following companies, Cadbury, County Tennis Supplies and Liberty. If you look in the Companies tree, you will not see an entry for these companies. It is not a requirement that every company have a company record.

You can use the tree to complete several tasks including moving, creating and deleting a company.

Any task that you can do for a company, you can also do for a division or subdivision. Like other features in ACT!, the Companies tree has a shortcut menu, as shown in Figure 5-4.

**Figure 5-4** Companies tree shortcut menu

### Exercise 5.1: Create Contact Records

To complete some of the company exercises, you need to add more contact records to the database.

1.  Create contact records for the following names. You only have to enter the name in each record. John Doe, Jennifer Doe, Charles Smith, Mary Wood and Bill Grant.

2.  Create contact records for the following names: Laura Smith and Tom Wood. Type `Lookup` in the Company field for these two records. They will be used later in this chapter to lookup contacts and link them to a company.

### Exercise 5.2: Create A Company Record

1.  Click the **COMPANIES** button on the Navigation Pane.

2.  Click the **NEW** button on the Global toolbar ⇒ Create records for the two companies in Table 5-2. The first record should look like the one shown in Figure 5-5. You will see both companies in the Companies tree.

| Field | Company #1 | Company #2 |
|---|---|---|
| Company | My Company | My Other Company |
| Address 1 | 123 Main St | 456 South St |
| City | Hitsville | Hollywood |
| State | CA | CA |

**Table 5-2** New companies record data

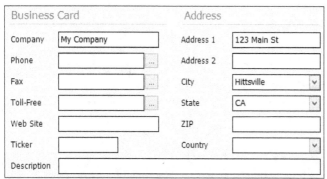

**Figure 5-5** New company record

 ACT! will try to prevent you from creating duplicate records.

If you enter a company name that already exists in the database, you will see the warning message shown in Figure 5-6, when you try to go to another company record.

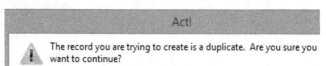

**Figure 5-6** Duplicate company warning message

If you recall, in Chapter 2, you changed how ACT! checks for duplicate companies.

If you click Yes, the company record that you just created will be added to the database.
If you click No, you will have to change the company name to save the record.

### Exercise 5.3: Create Divisions For A Company

Creating a division uses the same screen, as the one for creating a company record.

1.  Display the company (or division) record that you want to create a division for. For this exercise click on the company, My Company in the Companies tree.

2.  Right-click on the Company Name in the tree, and select **NEW DIVISION** ⇒ Type `Finance` in the Company field.

3.  If you click on the company in the tree, you will see the division. You will also see the **HIERARCHY** of the company and its divisions on the Divisions tab, as illustrated at the bottom of Figure 5-7.

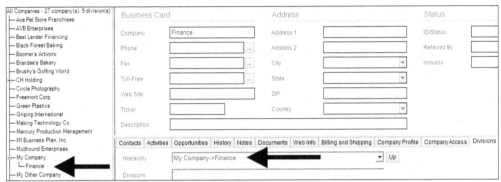

**Figure 5-7** Division associated to a company

4.  Create the divisions in Table 5-3 under the company listed.

| Company | Division |
|---|---|
| My Company | Technology Division |
| My Other Company | Marketing |
| My Other Company | Sales Division |

**Table 5-3** Divisions to create

### Associating Contacts To Companies And Divisions

Contacts can exist in an ACT! database without being linked or associated to a company. Companies can be in the database without having contacts linked to them. There is no requirement that contacts and companies be linked or associated, so do not be alarmed if you have contact records that are not linked to company records or vice versa. Although, I am not sure why someone would create a company and not associate any contacts to it, it is acceptable in ACT!. There are two ways to associate contacts to companies as explained below.

①  **MANUALLY** This method entails creating the link between a contact and a company. ACT! refers to this type of link as a **STATIC LINK**. That is because the link will remain intact until you manually change it.
②  **AUTOMATICALLY** This method entails creating a query that selects the contact records that will be linked to a company. ACT! refers to this type of a link as a **DYNAMIC LINK** because the contacts associated to a company will change automatically, depending on whether or not the data in the contact record meets the criteria in the query. A contact record can meet the criteria in the query this week and not meet the criteria next week, if the data in any of the contact record fields that the query uses, changes.

### Exercise 5.4: Associate A Contact To A Company Record

There are several ways to associate contacts to a company record. In this exercise you will learn different ways to accomplish this task. Contact records can be associated to companies from the contact record. The opposite is also true. Contact records can be associated to companies from the company record.

1.  Display the My Other Company record in the Company detail view ⇒ On the Divisions tab, you should see the two divisions that you created for the company.

2.  Click the Add/Remove Contacts to Company button on the Company toolbar.

3. Click the **CONTACTS** button on the Add/Remove Contacts dialog box ⇒ Type Doe in the Look for field.

4. Select the contact record for John Doe, then click the Add button.

5. Click OK. The contact should be in the **STATIC MEMBERS** section of the dialog box, as shown in Figure 5-8.

   Click OK. You will see the contact John Doe on the Contacts tab, on the Company detail record.

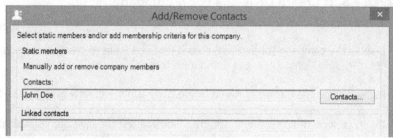

**Figure 5-8** Add/Remove Contacts dialog box

> **More Ways To Open The Add/Remove Contacts Dialog Box From A Company View**
> ① Companies ⇒ Add/Remove Contacts.
> ② Right-click on the company name in the Companies tree or Company column (in the Company list view) and select Company Membership ⇒ Add/Remove Contacts.
> ③ Contacts tab ⇒ Click the Add/Remove Contacts button.
> ④ Companies detail view ⇒ Contacts tab ⇒ On a blank space in the Contact List section, right-click and select Company Membership ⇒ Add/Remove Contacts, on the shortcut menu.

> **How To Open The Add/Remove Dialog Box From A Contact View**
> Below are several ways to open the Add/Remove dialog box shown in Figure 5-9.
> ① Contacts ⇒ Add Selected to Company.
> ② Contact list view ⇒ Right-click in the grid and select Add Contacts to Company from the shortcut menu.
> ③ Contacts detail view ⇒ Groups/Companies tab ⇒ Select Companies and Divisions in the **SHOW FOR** drop-down list ⇒ Click the Add/Remove Companies button, illustrated in Figure 5-10.

The entries in the list on the right are companies, divisions, subdivisions and groups that the contact is a member of.

I find this dialog box helpful because you can add and remove companies, divisions and groups for the contact at the same time.

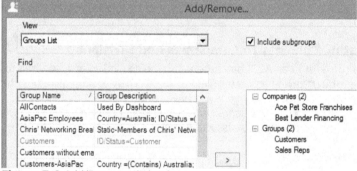

**Figure 5-9** Add/Remove dialog box

**Figure 5-10** Company options on the Groups/Companies tab on the Contact detail view

### Exercise 5.5: Create A Company Record From A Contact Record

Earlier, you created a company record from scratch. Creating a company record from a contact record that has the address information for the company will keep you from having to type the same information in again. You can create a company record from a contact record by following the steps below.

1. Select a contact that has the company information that you want to use. In this exercise select the contact Jane Bellamy of Boomers Artworx.

2. Contacts ⇒ Create Company from Contact.

The Company detail view will open and the company name and address fields will automatically be filled in. If you needed to make any changes to the information for the new company record, you could. Notice in the Companies tree that the company name is similar to another company. The difference is the apostrophe in the other company name.

### Exercise 5.6: Create A Contact Record From A Company Record

Creating a contact record from a company record that has the address information will keep you from having to type in the same information again. You can create a contact record from a company record by following the steps below.

1. Select the company in the Companies tree that has the information for the contact record that you want to create. In this exercise, click on the company Circle Photography, in the Companies tree.

2. Companies ⇒ Create Contact from Company. The Contact detail view will open and the company name and address fields will automatically be filled in.

3. Type `Test Record` in the Contact field, then display another record.

### Refreshing Linked Data In Contact Records

It is possible that you may not be viewing the most current data in the database. This happens when there are several people adding and editing records in the database. To make sure that you are viewing the most current data, refresh the data of the contact record that is displayed in the Contact detail view.

Contacts ⇒ Update Linked Contact, will refresh the data. If this option is not enabled on the menu, it means that the contact is not linked to a company record.

### Company Preferences

Tools ⇒ Preferences ⇒ Admin tab ⇒ Company Preferences button, will open the Company Preferences dialog box shown in Figure 5-11.

The **COMPANY CREATION** option is used to set up the automatic creation of companies when X number of contacts have the same company name.

**X** equals the number of contacts that you select. If enabled, these companies are created behind the scenes.

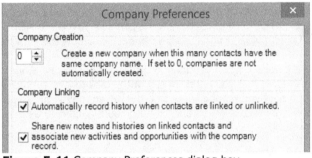

**Figure 5-11** Company Preferences dialog box

**Company Creation Option**

① Keep in mind that if enabled, blank company records will be created, when at least X number of contact records do not have data in the Company field.

② You may want to enable this feature on a test copy of a database to see what changes will take place. I set the creation option to two on the My_ACTDemo database and ACT! wanted to create 23 new companies, as shown in Figure 5-12.

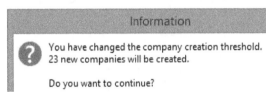

**Figure 5-12** Company creation message

If checked, the **AUTOMATICALLY RECORD HISTORY . . .** option will create a history record each time a contact record is linked or unlinked.

If checked, the **SHARE NEW NOTES . . .** option will keep a contacts notes and history records with the original company, even if a contacts company changes.

### Linking Company And Contact Records

If you scroll through the contact records, you will see that some company names are blue and underlined and others are not. The company names that are blue and underlined are hyperlinked. You can click on this link to open the company, division or subdivision record.

Fields on the contact record that are linked will automatically be updated when the corresponding field in the company record is updated. This means that if the company name field on the company record changes from DEF Company to HIJ Company, any contact records that are linked to the DEF company on the company name field will automatically be updated. Contact records that have the same name, but are not linked, will not be updated to the new company name.

The ellipsis button at the end of the Company field on a contact record that is not already linked, opens the dialog box shown in Figure 5-13.

If the contacts company name already exists in the database, you can link the contact to the company by selecting the company name on the dialog box.

If the contact record is linked to a company, the **UNLINK FROM COMPANY DIALOG BOX** shown later in Figure 5-28, opens.

**Figure 5-13** Link To Company dialog box

### Associate vs Linking

On the surface, these terms sound like they have the same functionality. Understanding the difference is important if you have the need to make some contacts private. In ACT!, associating and linking have different functionality as explained below. I find it somewhat deceiving how the "Private" option works.

In "My world", when you mark a contact as private, whether or not the contact is "linked" to a company, any information that you enter on any of the tabs for the contact is also marked as private by default. The exception would be if you manually override the private option for a specific piece of information. If a history record is created, the history record would also be automatically marked as private. Well, I started this paragraph off by saying in "My world".

The scenario that I just described is **NOT** how the private option works in ACT! if the contact record is marked as private and "linked" to a company record. When a note or history record is created for a contact that is linked to a company record, the note or history record is visible (available for other users to see) from the company record by default. If this is not what you want to happen, you have to also mark the note as private, on the Insert Note dialog box.

Depending on a users rights, they may not be able to see all of the contact information that is displayed under the company record. Users that have rights to the contact record will be able to view the activity and opportunity records that are displayed under the company record.

**Linking Issues**

Overall, linking contacts to companies is a good feature to have and use. Depending on how sensitive some of the contact data is, you may not want it to be shared. Some contact data is automatically shared. I think that it is important that you understand how linking works in ACT!.

By default, contact notes, history, activity and opportunity records are displayed under the company record that they are linked to. I thought that if the link between a contact and company was removed, that the contacts history, activity and opportunity records would also be removed from the company record, but that is **NOT** the case.

I can understand why they are not automatically removed because the primary purpose of company records is to build a profile of the company, which includes the interactions with all of the contacts associated or linked with the company. I just wanted to let you know that the contacts linked data is not automatically removed from the company record when the contact record is unlinked.

**Solutions**

If the contact is linked to a different company, these records are moved to the new company. Fortunately, there are ways to prevent notes and history records that you want to remain private, from being displayed under the company record.

① As you already learned, when you create a note you can mark it as **PRIVATE**.

② If you know that you do not want any contact note and history records to be displayed under company records, clear the **SHARE NEW NOTES . . .** option, shown earlier in Figure 5-11. With this option cleared (not checked), you can share a specific note if you have the need to do so.

Contacts can be associated to multiple companies and divisions, but can only be linked to one company.

## Associating Companies And Groups

You can associate companies and groups to the following types of records: Activity, history, notes and opportunity with relative ease, as you will learn throughout this book. Each of the dialog boxes listed below have an **ASSOCIATE WITH** or **SHARE WITH** field. Click the ellipsis button at the end of these fields, then select the companies and groups that you want to associate to the record.

① Schedule Activities [See Chapter 7, Figure 7-1]
② New History [See Chapter 9, Figure 9-14]
③ Edit History [See Chapter 9, Figure 9-18]
④ Insert Note [See Chapter 3, Figure 3-17]

## Exercise 5.7: Creating Manual Links Between Contacts And Companies

In this exercise you will learn several ways to link contact and company records.

## Manually Link A New Contact With A Company

In this part of the exercise you will create the contact record and then link it to a company.

1. Open a new contact record and enter the name Jane Doe.

2. Click the ellipsis button next to the Company field ⇒ Select the company, My Company and click OK. You will see that the company name is a link on the Contact detail view.

3. Click the Save Changes button. If you click on the company link, you will see the company record on the Company detail view.

## Manually Link An Existing Contact With A Company

In this part of the exercise you will learn how to link an existing contact to a company.

1. Right-click in the Contact field in the Contact detail view and select **LOOKUP CONTACT**.

2.  Type `Charles Smith` in the Value field, then press Enter.

3.  Click the ellipsis button next to the Company field ⇒ Select the company, My Company, then click OK.

> **Link Or Associate Contacts To Divisions Or Subdivisions**
> You can link or associate a contact to a division or subdivision, the same way that you link a contact to a company. In both parts of Exercise 5.7 above, instead of selecting a company, select a division or subdivision.

### Exercise 5.8: Link Multiple Contact Records To A Company Record

This type of linking is another example of the static link option that you read about earlier. This is one way that you can change the company that several contacts are linked to, at one time.

1.  Create a lookup that retrieves records that have **LOOKUP** in the Company field.

2.  Select (highlight) both records in the Contact list view ⇒ Contacts ⇒ Link to Company.

3.  Select the company, My Other Company, then click OK.

4.  Click OK when prompted that no more records match the search criteria.

If you look at the My Other Company record on the Company detail view, you will see that both contacts (Laura Smith and Tom Wood) have the new company name. Their records old company name was "Lookup".

### Exercise 5.9: Understanding The Power Of Linking

In the previous exercise, you linked two contact records to a company record. Figure 5-14 shows the company and contacts associated with it.

Notice that the Company field for John Doe is blank. This is how you can visually tell which contacts are linked to a company and which ones are associated to a company. In this exercise you will rename the company.

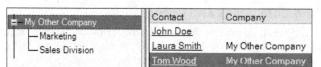

**Figure 5-14** Contacts linked and associated to the same company

1.  Open the My Other Company record in the Company detail view.

2.  Change the Company name to `My New Company`.

3.  View ⇒ Refresh. This will update the company name throughout the database ⇒ When prompted to update contacts linked to this company, Click Yes.

### Linking And Unlinking Contact And Company Fields

You have learned that you can link the company name field on the contact record to the company name field in the company record. This is also true for other fields on the contact record.

An important concept to remember about linking fields is that the fields that you want to link should be the same data type or a compatible data type. Otherwise, you will have trouble linking the fields. For example, you should not try to link a date field to an email field.

> If you created a linked company record field, it is applied to all company records, not just a particular record. The same is true if you unlink a company record field.

## Viewing Linked Fields

Companies ⇒ View Linked Fields, will display how company fields are linked to contact fields, as shown in Figure 5-15.

The **DEFINE FIELDS** button opens a dialog box that is used to create, edit or delete fields. You will learn more about this functionality in the next exercise.

**Figure 5-15** View Linked Fields dialog box

## Exercise 5.10: Create A Linked Billing Address Field

In this exercise you will modify the Billing Address 1 field in the company record so that it is linked to the contact User 5 field. This is not a link that you would create in a live database, because it really does not make a lot of sense. The fields that are normally linked between contact and company records are already linked in this database, as shown above in Figure 5-15. Therefore, I had to select fields that are not already linked, to demonstrate how to use the linking feature.

1. Tools ⇒ Define Fields.
   Notice that the database is locked, as illustrated in Figure 5-16.

   **Figure 5-16** Locked database notification illustrated

2. Open the **VIEW FIELDS FOR** drop-down list on the Define Fields dialog box and select Companies, if it is not already selected.

3. Click on the Billing Address 1 field.

   Click the **EDIT FIELD** link, illustrated in Figure 5-17, then click Next.

   **Figure 5-17** Edit Field link illustrated

4. On the Customize field behavior screen, check the **LINK TO CONTACT FIELD** option ⇒ Open the drop-down list. Notice that some fields are not enabled in the drop-down list. You cannot select these fields to link to, because they have already been linked to a field.

5. Scroll down the list and select the User 5 field ⇒ Click Finish.

   In Figure 5-18, you will see that the Billing Address 1 field is linked to the User 5 contact field.

   Click Close.

   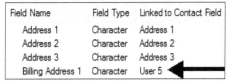

   **Figure 5-18** Billing Address 1 field linked to the User 5 contact field

### Billing And Shipping Tab

The fields shown in Figure 5-19 are used to store the billing and shipping address of the company, division or subdivision.

**Figure 5-19** Billing and Shipping tab fields

### Updating Contact Address Fields From The Linked Company Record

If a company moves, you would update the address fields on the company record. The next step is to update the contact records that are linked to the company record so that they display the updated address information. Before changing the company record, it is a good idea to view the linked contacts to make sure that they have the address that you are about to change.

Companies can have several locations which means that there would be different addresses for the same company. You could create divisions under the company or create a different company record for each location. The steps below show you how to change the address on the company record and update the linked contact records. For now you can read the steps. In the next exercise you will be able to practice this technique.

1. Open the company record and change the information in the linked field, then save the changes.

2. Click the **UPDATES LINKED CONTACTS FOR THE CURRENT COMPANY** button on the Companies toolbar.

3. Click **YES** when you see the message shown in Figure 5-20.

**Figure 5-20** Update linked contacts message

### Exercise 5.11: Use The Linked Field Created In Exercise 5.10

To use the linked field that you created in Exercise 5.10, you will enter data in the Company Billing Address 1 field and observe how the linked contact records are updated.

1. Select the company My New Company ⇒ Click on the Billing and Shipping tab.

2. Type Test field link in the Billing Address 1 field.

3. Click the **UPDATES LINKED CONTACTS FOR THE CURRENT COMPANY** button on the Companies toolbar ⇒ Click Yes, when you see the message shown above in Figure 5-20. The contact records will now be updated.

4. On the Contacts tab on the Company detail view, double-click on one of the records that has the company name, My New Company.

5.  On the User Fields tab of the contact record, you should see the text that you entered in the Billing Address 1 field in the User 5 field, as shown in Figure 5-21.

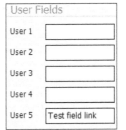

**Figure 5-21** User 5 field updated

 **User Fields Tab**
In the exercise that you just completed, you added data to a user field. If this were a live database you would rename the user field and update the layout. If you do not do this, other people that use the database will not know what type of data should be entered in the field.

## Company Profile Tab

The fields shown in Figure 5-22 track the region, revenue, SIC Code and more for each company, division and subdivision.

**Figure 5-22** Company Profile tab fields

## Company Access Tab

The fields shown in Figure 5-23, except for the Access Level options are updated by ACT! automatically.

These fields store when the company record was created, by who and when it was last changed.

**Figure 5-23** Company Access tab fields

RECORD MANAGER, EDITED ON and EDITED BY fields [ See Chapter 3, Contact Access Tab]

## Unlink A Company Record Field

If you have a company record field that is linked, but no longer need it to be linked, follow the steps below. You do not have to complete these steps now.

1.  Tools ⇒ Define Fields.

2.  Select the field that you want to unlink, then click the EDIT FIELD link.

3.  Click Next ⇒ Clear the LINK TO CONTACT FIELD option, shown in Figure 5-24.

    Click Finish, then click Close.

    Previously linked contact record fields that have data will keep the data even though the field is no longer linked to a company record field.

**Customize field behavior**
Specify formats or rules for entering data in the field.

Default value (optional):

Field format (optional):

☐ Link to contact field:

Note: Fields can only be linked to other fields of a compatible data type.

**Figure 5-24** Customize field behavior options

## Adding Contacts To Divisions

There are several ways to add contacts to divisions, as explained below. It would be easier if we could use drop and drag to add or move a contact record from one company or division to another one.

① Right-click on the division in the Companies tree and select **COMPANY MEMBERSHIP** ⇒ **ADD/REMOVE CONTACTS**. (3)

② Right-click on the contact on the Company detail view and select **COMPANY MEMBERSHIP** ⇒ **ADD/REMOVE CONTACTS**. (3)

③ Right-click on the contact on the Company detail view and select **COMPANY MEMBERSHIP** ⇒ **ADD SELECTED TO COMPANY**. You will see the Add/Remove dialog box.

(3) You will see the Add/Remove Contacts dialog box.

## Exercise 5.12: Duplicating Company And Division Records

You can duplicate a company that has divisions, but the divisions are not duplicated. This is known as **DUPLICATING** a company. The process is similar to duplicating contacts.

1. In the Company detail view, right-click on the company, My Company and select Duplicate.

2. On the dialog box shown in Figure 5-25, select the option **DUPLICATE DATA FROM ALL FIELDS**, then click OK.

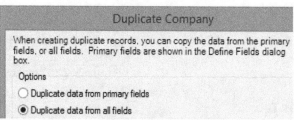

**Figure 5-25** Duplicate Company dialog box

3. Click the Save Changes button ⇒ Click Yes when prompted to continue.

4. You will see a company record that looks like the one that you duplicated. Type `My Duplicate Company` in the Company field.

5. View ⇒ Refresh. Click on the new company in the tree.

## Looking Up Companies

Looking up companies is similar to looking up contacts. Lookup ⇒ Name, will display the Lookup Companies dialog box, which is similar to the dialog box that you use to look up contacts. The differences are explained below.

① The Title bar on the dialog box has "Lookup Companies" instead of "Lookup Contacts".

② The fields in the first drop-down list are company related fields.

## Exercise 5.13: Finding Companies

It is really important to make sure that the company data is as accurate as possible. Often, when adding a new company, you may not know or have all of the information that you want to enter for the company. From time to time, it is a good idea to either look up records that do not have data in certain fields or create reports that show records that are missing data. If your company does a variety of promotional campaigns, it may be important to track how each contact was obtained. You could use the Referred By field to store this information. In this exercise you will find companies where the Referred By field is empty.

1. Lookup ⇒ Other Fields.

2. Open the Field drop-down list and select Referred By.

3. Open the Operator drop-down list and select the option **DOES NOT CONTAIN DATA** ⇒ Click OK.

The companies and divisions that you see in the Company list view, do not have data in the Referred By field. (The Referred By field is not displayed on this view. It is on the Company detail view.) Someone should try to fill in this information.

## Create A Company Note And Attachment

Creating a note for a company is the same process as creating a note for a contact. Creating a note for a company uses the same Insert Note dialog box that is used for creating notes for contacts. Creating a note with an attachment is also the same process as attaching a file to a contact record. Right-click on the company in the Companies tree that you want to create a note for and select **INSERT COMPANY NOTE**. The company name will automatically be filled in the Share with field on the Insert Note dialog box.

## Viewing Company Notes

Over time, the number of notes for companies can grow. If contacts are associated with a company, the Notes tab on the Company detail view will have even more notes for you to sift through.

As shown in Figure 5-26, the Notes tab on the Company detail view has the **SHOW FOR** drop-down list. This field is used to filter the records that are displayed on the view. The options are explained below.

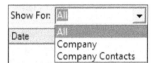

**Figure 5-26** Notes tab on the Company detail view

**ALL** displays both company and company contact notes.
**COMPANY** only displays notes that are created from a company record.
**COMPANY CONTACTS** only displays notes that were created for a contact associated with the company.
The difference between the Company and Company Contacts options are the level that the notes are created at.

## Moving Companies And Divisions

Earlier in this chapter you read that in the Companies tree you can drag companies and divisions to new locations. If you do not like to drag them, you can use the **MOVE** option on the shortcut menu. You can complete this task from either company view. The steps below explain the process.

1.  Right-click on the company or division that you want to move and select **MOVE**.

2.  Select one of the options explained below.

    ① On the dialog box shown in Figure 5-27, select the **PROMOTE DIVISION TO COMPANY** option to make the division that you selected a company.
    ② Select the **CHANGE TO BE DIVISION OF** option if you want the company or division that you selected to be a division of another company.

If you select a company before opening this dialog box and select the Promote option, nothing will change.

**Figure 5-27** Move dialog box

3.  Select the company that you want to move it to on the Move dialog box, then click OK.

> **Deleting A Company Record**
> If you need to delete a company record, any division records under it will be promoted to a company record, unless you delete the division records first. You will not receive a warning that the company record that you are deleting has division records.

### Removing Links Between Contact And Company Records

If a contact record is linked on the Company (name) field, it cannot be changed until you remove the link. You already learned that contact notes and history records that appear under the company record are not automatically removed. Removing the link between the contact and company is how the contact notes and history records remain under the company record. When you have the need to remove links, you can follow the steps below.

1.  Open the contact record (in the Contact detail view) that you want to remove the company link from.

2.  Click the ellipsis button at the end of the Company field. You will see the dialog box shown in Figure 5-28.

    The **UNLINK FROM COMPANY** option will remove the link between the contact and company records.

**Figure 5-28** Unlink from Company dialog box

The **LINK TO A DIFFERENT COMPANY** option shown above in Figure 5-28, is used to link the contact to a different company. This would be helpful if the contact needs to be moved to a different company.

Selecting this option, then clicking OK, opens the dialog box shown in Figure 5-29. It is used to select the company that you want to move the contact to.

The company or division that you want to move the contact to, must already have a record in the database.

**Figure 5-29** Link To Company dialog box

3.  Click OK on the Unlink from Company dialog box. The link will be removed from the Company field.

### Company Detail View Related Tasks

The options shown in Figure 5-30 are primarily on the detail view. Some options are also on the list view. The options are explained below.

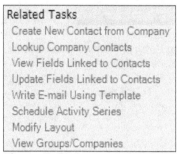

**Figure 5-30** Company detail view related tasks

**CREATE NEW CONTACT FROM COMPANY** Opens a new contact record with the company fields filled in, that are filled in on the company record that was displayed before clicking on the link.

**LOOKUP COMPANY CONTACTS** Displays the contacts that are on the Company Contacts tab on the Contact list view.

**VIEW FIELDS LINKED TO CONTACTS** Opens the View Linked Fields dialog box.

**UPDATE FIELDS LINKED TO CONTACTS** Displays the message shown earlier in Figure 5-20, which is used to update the linked field data for contacts linked to the company that is selected.

**WRITE E-MAIL USING TEMPLATE** [See Chapter 3, below Figure 3-35]

**SCHEDULE ACTIVITY SERIES** [See Chapter 3, below Figure 3-32]

MODIFY LAYOUT [See Chapter 3, below Figure 3-32]

VIEW GROUPS/COMPANIES Opens the View Groups/Companies dialog box, which displays a list of the companies, divisions and groups in the database.

## Using The Company List View

While the Company detail view is probably the company view that you will use most often, the Company list view provides the same functionality. The Company list view shown in Figure 5-31, has the same shortcut menu options as the Companies tree. Actually, the shortcut menu in the Company list view has more options. Like the Contact list view, you can sort on the column headings in the Company list view. If there are a lot of companies in the list you may have a need to filter them.

**Figure 5-31** Company list view

The EDIT MODE option is used to modify records in the Contact list view.

The INCLUDE DIVISIONS option displays all of the divisions and subdivisions in the database. The problem is that the default options on the Company list view do not provide a visual way to know which record is a company, division or subdivision or which company a division or subdivision record belongs to.

If you customize the view and add the HAS DIVISIONS, DIVISION and HIERARCHY LEVEL fields to the view, you will be able to tell a division from a company, but not which division a company belongs to, as shown in Figure 5-32.

Hierarchy Level 0 is a company record.

Hierarchy Level 1 is a company or division record.

Hierarchy Level 2 is a division record.

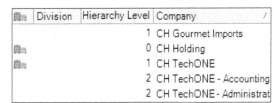

**Figure 5-32** Company list view with division fields

## Create A New Division

To create a new division from the Company list view, right-click on the company that you want to create the division for and select NEW DIVISION.

## Company List View Related Tasks

The options shown in Figure 5-33 are for the Company list view. The options that are only on the list view are explained below.

PRINT CURRENT SCREEN Opens the Quick Print Options dialog box, so that you can select options for how the screen will be printed.

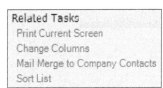

**Figure 5-33** Company list view related tasks

CHANGE COLUMNS Opens the Customize Columns dialog box, which is used to add, remove and change the order that the columns are displayed on the company list view.

**MAIL MERGE TO COMPANY CONTACTS** Opens the Mail Merge Wizard, shown in Figure 5-34.

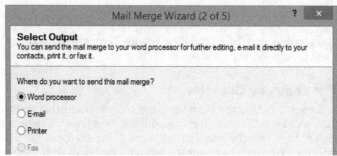

**Figure 5-34** Mail Merge Wizard

**SORT LIST** Opens the Sort dialog box to sort the companies displayed in the view.

# GROUPING CONTACTS

Overview

In this chapter you will learn about the following group and subgroup record options:

- ☑ Using the Groups tree
- ☑ Creating groups
- ☑ Adding contacts to a group or subgroup
- ☑ Managing group notes and attachments
- ☑ Saving the result of a lookup as a group or company
- ☑ Creating subgroups
- ☑ Converting a group to a company
- ☑ The Convert Groups to Companies Wizard

CHAPTER 6

## Groups Overview

Grouping records is another way for you to be able to categorize and find contacts. You have learned how to use the lookup command to find contacts. The limitation to using the lookup command is that all of the contact records that you want to find have to have the same information in the same field. You could think of the group option as a free form way to classify or categorize contacts, because the contacts that you add to a group do not have to have any data in common. Like company records, group records can have 15 levels. You can create as many groups as you need.

If you wanted to group certain contacts together because they are all involved in the same project, you could create a group. You can add a contact to as many groups as needed. Grouping helps you find and organize contacts quickly. The main benefit to creating groups over creating lookups, is that the group information is saved. Figure 6-1 shows the Group detail view.

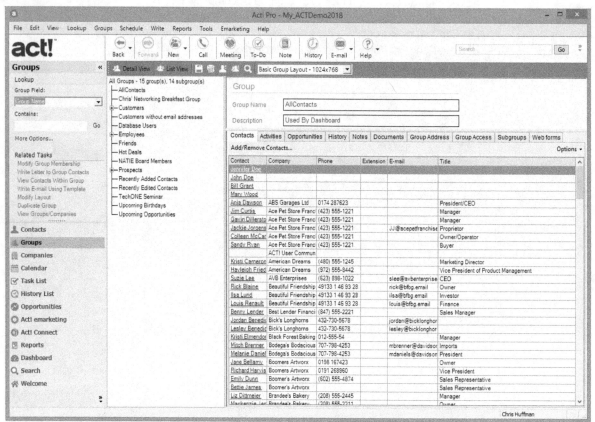

**Figure 6-1** Group detail view

The top right section of the Group detail view displays the group name and description of the group that is selected in the tree. The bottom right section displays the tabs available for groups. For example, the Group Access tab shows information about when the group was created, whether or not the group is private and who created it. The names on the Contacts tab are the contacts or companies that are in the group.

## Group Detail View Toolbar

Figure 6-2 shows the Group detail view toolbar. Table 6-1 explains the buttons on the toolbar.

**Figure 6-2** Group detail view toolbar

| Button | Description |
|--------|-------------|
| 1 | Displays the Group detail view. |
| 2 | Displays the Group list view. |
| 3 | Saves the record. (1) |
| 4 | Opens the Quick Print Options dialog box. |
| 5 | Adds or removes a contact from a group. (2) |
| 6 | Attach a file. (2) |
| 7 | Creates a lookup of the group that is selected. |
| 8 | Is used to select a layout. (1) |

**Table 6-1** Group detail view toolbar buttons explained

(1) This option is only available on the Group detail view.
(2) This option applies to groups and subgroups.

## Good Groups And Not So Good Groups

These are the types of groups that you can create. An example of a not so good group would be a static group that contains contacts in the same state. This is not a good use of a group for two reasons: 1) You can create a lookup by state to accomplish this. 2) Creating a dynamic group displays all contacts in the state, even those that were added to the database after the group was created.

An example of a good group would be a group that contains contacts that attended an insurance seminar that you were a guest speaker at. This is a good group because there is no existing field that you could create a lookup on to find these contacts. It is also a good group because the contacts are a specific number of contacts. More contacts would not be added or removed from this group, four months from now. You could create an activity for the contacts in the group. It would appear on the Activities tab for the group.

## Groups Tree

The Groups tree is on the left side of the Group detail view. At the top of the Groups tree, the number of groups and subgroups are displayed, as shown earlier in Figure 6-1. If you click on a group in the tree, you will see the subgroups on the Subgroups tab. A plus sign in front of a group means that there is at least one subgroup below it.

The Employees group has two subgroups; International Employees and USA Employees. The International Employees group has two subgroups, as shown in Figure 6-3, AsiaPac Employees and European Employees.

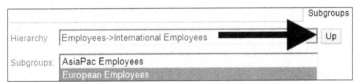

**Figure 6-3** Groups and Subgroups on the Subgroups tab

 The **UP** button, illustrated above in Figure 6-3, is enabled if the group or subgroup that is selected is part of a larger group. Clicking this button will move up the hierarchy, one level at a time. This button is also on the Company detail view. If you double-click on any subgroup shown, the detail record for the subgroup will be displayed.

## Exercise 6.1: How To Create A Group

1. Click the **GROUPS** button in the Navigation Pane.

2. Click the **NEW** button on the Global toolbar. You should see a new group record at the top, on the right of the window.

 You can also right-click on a blank space in the Groups tree section and select **NEW GROUP**.

3. In the Group Name field, type `Potential Customer`

4. Press the Tab key ⇒ In the Description field, type `This group contains contacts that are interested in the next version of the book.`

The Description field can have up to 128 characters.

5. Click the Save Changes button ⇒ Click on the Subgroups tab.

   The group record should look like the one shown in Figure 6-4.

   Notice that the **HIERARCHY** field was filled in automatically and that the group appears on the left side of the window.

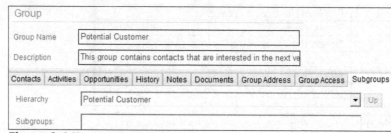

**Figure 6-4** New group record created

## Adding Contacts To A Group

The ways that you can add contacts to a group (or subgroup) are explained below.

① You can scroll through the entire list of contacts in the Contact list view and select the contacts that you want, one by one and add them to a group. This is known as a **STATIC GROUP**. The contacts stay in the group, until you remove them.

② If possible, you can use the lookup command to find at least some of the contact records that you want to add to a group.

③ Select an existing group and add contacts from the existing group to the new group.

④ Contacts can automatically be added to a group if they meet the criteria of the query. This is known as a **DYNAMIC GROUP** because contacts are added and removed based on whether or not they meet the criteria. There is no intervention on your part after creating the query. This type of group is updated each time the Groups/Companies tab on the Contact detail or Group detail view is displayed.

An example is a group for contacts that have the Sales Rep title. Contacts added to the database that have this title would automatically be added to the group. Any contact in the group whose title changes from Sales Rep would automatically be removed from the group. Chapter 13 covers creating this type of group.

The benefit of using the last three options explained above to add contacts to a group is that you do not have to scroll through all of the records in the database to select contacts to add to a group.

 When you add a contact that has a note to a group, the contacts notes are displayed on the Groups Notes tab, unless the note is marked private. The owner of the private note will see the note on the Groups Notes tab, but other database users will not.

## Exercise 6.2: How To Add Contacts One At A Time To A Group

The contacts that you will add to the group in this exercise, are static.

1. Select (or create) the group that you want to add contacts to ⇒ In this exercise, select the Potential Customer group.

2. Click the **ADD/REMOVE CONTACTS TO GROUP** button on the toolbar or click the **ADD/REMOVE CONTACTS** button on the Contacts tab. You will see the Add/Remove Contacts dialog box.

3. Click the Contacts button.

4. Click on the contact Ashley Allan, then press and hold down the **CTRL** key and click on the following names: Bruce Baker, Sarah Baker and Kirby York.

5. Click the **ADD** button.

   The four contacts that you selected should be displayed in the **SELECTED CONTACTS** list, as shown in Figure 6-5.

**Figure 6-5** Contacts selected to be added to the group

The options in the **SELECT FROM** drop-down list and the (Group names) drop-down list to the right of it, are used to narrow or widen the number of names that appear in the **CONTACTS TO SELECT FROM** list. If you select the **GROUPS** option from the first drop-down list and the Customers group from the second drop-down list you will see the contacts shown on the left of Figure 6-6.

If the database has a lot of names and you do not want to scroll through the list, you can type the name that you want to add to the group in the **LOOK FOR** field.

**Figure 6-6** Contacts from an existing group

 If you scroll through the list of names on the left, you will see that the names that you have already selected for the group are grayed out. This lets you know that the contact is already a member of the current group or has been selected to be a member of the current group.

6. Click OK. You should see the contacts in the **STATIC MEMBERS** section of the Add/Remove Contacts dialog box ⇒ Click OK. The contacts will now be added to the Potential Customer group. You will see the contacts on the Contacts tab, as shown in Figure 6-7.

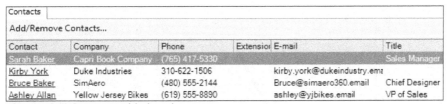

**Figure 6-7** Contacts added to the group

 To add a contact to a group, you can right-click on a contact record on either contact view and select **ADD CONTACT TO GROUP**.

### Looking Up Groups

Looking up groups is similar to looking up companies. Lookup ⇒ Field name from a group view or Lookup ⇒ Groups ⇒ Select an option from a different view, will display the same dialog box that is used to look up contacts. The differences on the Lookup dialog box for groups are the same as the differences between contacts and companies.

### Exercise 6.3: Finding Group Records

You have already learned how to find (look up) all of the contacts that were associated with a company. Looking up contacts that are in the same group is basically the same process. In this exercise you will create a lookup for groups that do not have data in the Address 1 field.

1. Lookup ⇒ Other Fields.

2. Open the Field drop-down list and select the Address 1 field.

3. Open the Operator drop-down list and select the **DOES NOT CONTAIN DATA** option, then click OK.

You will see the groups that do not have any information in the Address 1 field. If you double-click on any group in the Group list view and then click on the Group Address tab, you will see that the Address 1 field is empty.

### Exercise 6.4: How To Rename A Group

The steps below show you how to rename a group. If you need to rename a subgroup, select the subgroup in step 1 instead of a group.

1. Click on the group that you want to rename in the Groups tree. In this exercise click on the Potential Customer group.

2. Type in the name for the new group. Type the word Book after the word **POTENTIAL** in the Group Name field on the right ⇒ Click the Save Changes button. The group will be renamed and the new name is displayed on the Groups tree.

 The reason that I click the Save Changes button is because it refreshes the view. If you clicked on another group or subgroup in the tree and then come back to the group that you changed, you would see that the group was renamed.

### Exercise 6.5: Add Contacts To An Existing Group

In this exercise you will find contacts in Arizona and add them to the Potential Book Customer group. To add contacts to a subgroup, select the subgroup in step 3 below instead of a group.

### Create The Lookup And Add The Contacts To The Group

1. Create a lookup to find all contacts in AZ. There should be 19 records in the Contact list view.

2. Select (highlight) all of the records, then right-click on the highlighted records and select **ADD CONTACTS TO GROUP**, as illustrated in Figure 6-8.

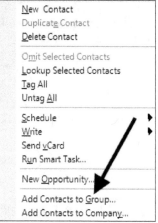

**Figure 6-8** Option to add the contacts to a group illustrated

 If you do not want to right-click on the records, you can use Contacts ⇒ Add Selected to Group.

3. Click on the Potential Book Customer group shown in Figure 6-9, then click OK.

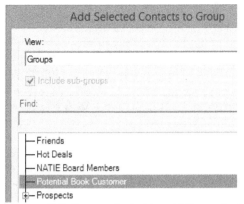

**Figure 6-9** Group selected to add the contacts to

### View The Contacts In The Group

1. Click the Groups button on the Navigation Pane ⇒ Click on the Potential Book Customer group in the Groups tree.

2. On the Contacts tab, you should see the contacts that you just added, plus the contacts that you added in a prior exercise.

### Exercise 6.6: Use The Lookup Command To Add Contacts To A Group

You can use this option when you have several records that have something in common that you want to add to the same group or subgroup. In this exercise you will create a lookup to find all contacts that have the Sales Representative title. After that, you will create a group and add the contacts to a group.

1. Create a lookup that finds all contacts that have Sales Representative as the title. Five records should have been retrieved. (**Hint**: Lookup ⇒ Contacts ⇒ Other Fields)

2. Click the arrow on the New button on the Global toolbar and select Group, as shown in Figure 6-10.

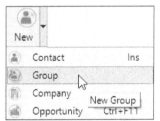

**Figure 6-10** New button options

3. Type `Sales Reps` in the Group Name field ⇒ Type `This group contains all of the sales reps` in the Description field.

4. Click the Add/Remove Contacts button on the Contacts tab ⇒ Click the Contacts button.

5. Select the **CURRENT LOOKUP** option from the Select from drop-down list.

   You should only see the contacts from the lookup that you created, in the list of names on the left side of the dialog box, as shown in Figure 6-11.

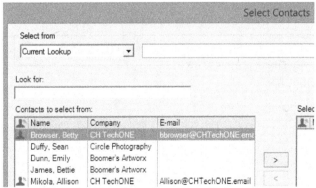

**Figure 6-11** Contacts from the current look up

6. Click the **ADD ALL>>** button. All of the contacts should be in the **SELECTED CONTACTS** list on the right side of the dialog box ⇒ Click OK twice to close both dialog boxes.

7. In the Group detail view, click on the Sales Reps group in the Groups tree, if it is not already selected. On the Contacts tab you will see the five contacts that are in the group.

### How To View The Groups That A Contact Is A Member Of

1. Click on the link for Emily Dunn.

2. On the Groups/Companies tab in the Contact detail view, open the **SHOW FOR** drop-down list and select Groups and Subgroups, if it is not already selected. You will see that this contact is a member of the Sales Rep group that you just created and the Potential Book Customer group that you created earlier in this chapter.

 If you do not see the groups, save the database. Open and close a different database, then reopen your demo database.

### Exercise 6.7: How To Manage Group Notes And Attachments

The Notes tab on the Group detail view is used to view notes for the group, just like you can view notes for a contact. If you create a note for the group, you only have to type it in once and it will be associated with all contacts in the group. You can also assign a contacts note to a group. There are several ways to create a note for a group.

 All of the group management of notes and attachments discussed in this exercise also apply to creating, editing and maintaining company notes and attachments.

### How To Create A Group Note And Attach A File To The Group Note

In addition to adding a note to a group, you can attach files like charts, spreadsheets or sales literature to a group. Doing this allows you to keep all of the attachments for the group in one place.

1. Click the Groups button ⇒ Click on the Potential Book Customer group.

2. On the Notes tab, click the **INSERT NEW NOTE** button. You should see the Potential Book Customer group name in the Share with field, on the Insert Note dialog box.

3. Type `These contacts have requested a book catalog` in the field at the bottom of the dialog box.

4. Select the text that you just typed and change the font to Comic Sans MS, then change the font size to 12.

5. Change the color to red. The color option is to the right of the Font size drop-down list ⇒ Leave the dialog box open to complete the next part of the exercise.

### How To Attach A File To A Group

Attaching a file to a group record is the same process as attaching a file to a contact record.

1. Click the **ATTACH** button, then select File.

2. Double-click on the C3 Attach file in your folder.

    The note should look like the one shown in Figure 6-12.

    Click OK.

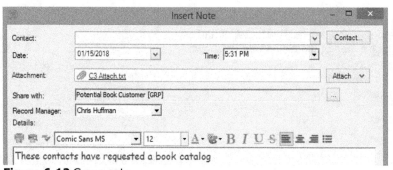

**Figure 6-12** Group note

### View The Group Notes And Attachments

1. On the Notes tab, open the **SHOW FOR** drop-down list and select Group. The entry should be the one for the note shown above in Figure 6-12.

2. Click on the Attachment (paper clip) icon for the note. The attached file will open. Close the attached file.

### Exercise 6.8: Assign A Contact Note To A Group And Individual Contacts

In this exercise you will complete the following tasks:

① Create two notes for a contact that is in a group.
② Associate one of the notes to contacts in the group, that the contact in the task above is a member of.
③ Associate one of the notes to one contact that is not in the group.
④ Associate the second note to a group that the contact in the first task above, is not a member of.

### Add The Contact To Another Group

1. Click on the Potential Book Customer group on the Group detail view.

2. On the Contacts tab, right-click on the contact Sarah Baker ⇒ Select Group Membership ⇒ Add Selected to Group.

3. Scroll down the list of groups on the left of the dialog box and select the Prospects - Hot Opportunities group, then click the Add button.

   The contact should be a member of the two groups shown on the right of Figure 6-13.

   Click OK.

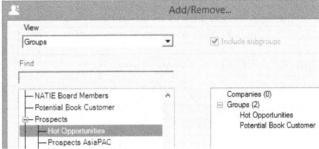
**Figure 6-13** Add/Remove dialog box

### Create The Notes

In this part of the exercise you will create the notes for Sarah Baker.

1. Open the Contact detail view for the contact Sarah Baker. (**Hint**: If you are in the Group detail view, click on the contacts name on the Contacts tab).

2. Click on the Notes tab, then create the notes in Table 6-2.

| Note | Details Field | Formatting |
|------|--------------|-----------|
| 1 | This is the first contact note for S Baker. It will be applied to individual contacts in 2 groups and 1 contact that is not in a group. | Change the font size to 10 ⇒ Change the text color to green and bold. |
| 2 | This is the second contact note for S Baker. It will be applied to the group via the Insert Note dialog box. | Change the color of the text to purple, bold and italic. Complete steps 3 and 4 below, before closing this note. |

**Table 6-2** Notes to create for Sarah Baker

3. Click the button at the end of the **SHARE WITH** field on the Insert Note dialog box ⇒ Click OK to share the note, as indicated in Figure 6-14.

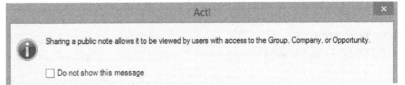
**Figure 6-14** Sharing a public note message

4. Select the Potential Book Customer group and add it to the list, then click OK.

   You should have the options shown in Figure 6-15 ⇒ Click OK to close the Insert Note dialog box.

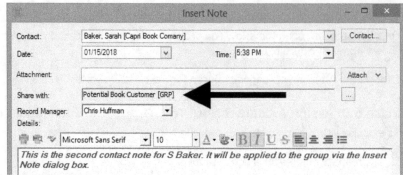

**Figure 6-15** Note associated to a group

## Associate The Notes

In this part of the exercise you will associate the two notes that you just created to other contacts.

1. Locate the first note (in green) that you created in Table 6-2, for Sarah Baker in either the Contact detail or Group detail view, then double-click on the note.

2. Click the **CONTACT** button on the Edit Note dialog box ⇒ Add the contact George Bailey to the Selected contacts list.

3. Open the **SELECT FROM** drop-down list on the Select Contacts dialog box and select Groups ⇒ Select the Sales Reps group from the next drop-down list. You will see the contacts in the group on the left side of the dialog box.

4. Add Bettie James to the selected contact list.

5. Select the Prospects group from the second drop-down list at the top of the dialog box ⇒ Add the contacts Mary Bailey and Kirby York.

   You should have the contacts selected that are shown in Figure 6-16.

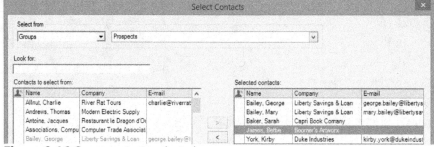

**Figure 6-16** Group contacts selected

6. Click OK twice to close both dialog boxes ⇒ When you see the dialog box shown in Figure 6-17, select the first option, then click OK.

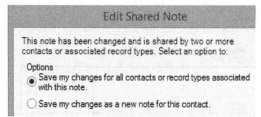

**Figure 6-17** Edit shared note options

 **Editing A Shared Note**
After creating a note, you may need to update the information in the note. When you modify a note that is shared with groups or contacts, you will see the dialog box shown above in Figure 6-17. Select the option for how you want the changes that you make to the note to be applied.

## View The Notes

1. Create a contact lookup by last name. Search for Bailey. You will see three contacts.

2. Switch to the Contact detail view. George and Mary Bailey will have the first note in Table 6-2 (in green). Peter Bailey does not. This is correct.

3. Switch to the Group detail view. The note with green text should also be available in the Prospects group. If you do not see the note, select **GROUP CONTACTS** in the Show for drop-down list.

4. View the Potential Book Customer group notes. You will see the second note (in purple) that you created in Table 6-2. You will also see the note (in green), because it was created by Chris Huffman (aka you), who is a member of the Potential Book Customer group.

### Show For Drop-Down List Options

The options in the **SHOW FOR** drop-down list, shown in Figure 6-18, are available on the Activities, Opportunities, History and Notes tabs in the Group detail view. The options are used to filter the records that are displayed on the tab.

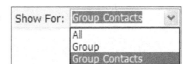

**Figure 6-18** Show For drop-down list options

 By default, group level notes cannot be viewed on the Notes tab in the Contact detail view. To know if there is a group note for the contact, click on the Groups/Companies tab on the Contact detail view. Double-click on the group, then click on the Notes tab in the Group detail view.

### Preview Area

If the note is long, you will not see all of it on the Notes tab. If you look to the far right of the workspace, you should see a shaded area. This is the Preview area.

If you click on a note, you will see the entire note in the Preview area (on the right side of Figure 6-19). You can resize the Preview area by placing the mouse pointer in the position illustrated in Figure 6-19, then drag the mouse pointer in the direction that you want to resize the section to.

If you do not want to have the Preview area visible, you can hide it by clicking on the **OPTIONS BUTTON** shown in Figure 6-19 and clearing the **SHOW PREVIEW** option, shown on the right of the figure. You can do this on any Notes tab.

**Figure 6-19** Mouse pointer in position to resize a section of the tab

### Exercise 6.9: How To Save The Result Of A Lookup As A Group Or Company

If you create a lookup that you will need to use over and over, you can save it as a Group or Company by following the steps below. The number of records in this type of group or company can change. If the value in the field that the lookup is using changes and now meets the criteria, the contact record will automatically be added to the group or company. If the value in a contact record field changes and no longer meets the lookup criteria, the record will automatically be removed from the group or company.

In this exercise you will save the results of the lookup as a group and a company. On your own, you do not have to save the same lookup results both ways. Select the option that works best for you.

1. Create an Email Address lookup for contacts that do not have an email address. 99 records should be retrieved.

2. Lookup ⇒ Groups ⇒ Save Lookup as Group.

3. Type `My Group Lookup No Email Address` as the group name ⇒ View ⇒ Refresh, or press the F5 key.

4. Lookup ⇒ Companies ⇒ Save Lookup as Company.

5. Type `My Company Lookup No Email Address` as the company name ⇒ View ⇒ Refresh, or press the F5 key.

If you view the records under the company and group that you just created, you will see that both have the same records. Normally, you would not save the same records to a group and company. It is done here for illustration purposes so that you can learn both methods of saving the result of a lookup.

## Subgroups

A subgroup is usually a subset of the contacts in the group. In the previous exercise you created a group that contains contacts that do not have an email address. If you wanted to further categorize the contacts in the group by company, title, state, status or just about anything that you can think of, you can create a subgroup. Subgroups can be 15 levels deep, meaning subgroups can have subgroups. Subgroups are similar to the divisions that companies have.

## Exercise 6.10: Creating Subgroups

In this exercise you will create two subgroups for the My Group Lookup No Email Address group: One for sales reps without an email address and one for contacts without a title.

1. In the Group detail view, right-click on the My Group Lookup No Email Address group in the Groups tree and select **NEW SUBGROUP**.

2. Type `Sales Reps with no email` in the Group Name field.

3. In the Description field, type `This subgroup contains sales reps that do not have an email address.`

4. Click on the My Group Lookup No Email Address group in the Groups tree. You should see the subgroup in the Groups tree.

5. Create another subgroup under the My Group Lookup No Email Address group. Use `No Title` as the subgroup name.

6. In the Description field, type `These contacts do not have a title.`

   You should have the subgroups shown in Figure 6-20.

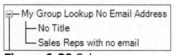

**Figure 6-20** Subgroups

## Exercise 6.11: Moving Contact Records Between Groups And Subgroups

After the subgroups are created, it is a good idea to move the appropriate records from the group to a subgroup, if applicable. In this exercise you will move contacts that have the Sales Rep title to the corresponding subgroup and contacts that do not have a title to a different subgroup. There are two ways to move contact records between groups and subgroups, as explained below:

① Move the contacts manually using the Add/Remove dialog box.
② Use a query.

## Moving Records Manually

Currently, moving contacts from one group to another and removing them from the original group is a two step process, as explained below.

① Add the contacts from the first group to the second group.
② Remove the contacts (that are linked to a company) from the original group unless you need the contact in the group and related subgroup. There is no way currently to complete this step from the Group detail view.

> **Moving Contact Records**
> Keep in mind that when the term "move" is used, you are actually copying records in one group to another group. This means that the records are in two groups. Currently, the only automated work around for this is to create dynamic groups. I think that it would be very useful to be able to move records by dropping and dragging them between groups.

## Step 1: Add The Contacts To The New Group

In this part of the exercise you will add records to each of the subgroups that you created.

1.  Click on the My Group Lookup No Email Address group ⇒ Click on the Contacts tab.

2.  Sort the contacts by the Title field. The contacts that do not have a title should be at the top of the list.

3.  Select all of the contacts without a title, then right-click on the selected contacts ⇒
    Select Group Membership ⇒
    Add Selected to Group ⇒
    Scroll down the list and select the **NO TITLE** subgroup, illustrated in Figure 6-21, then click OK.

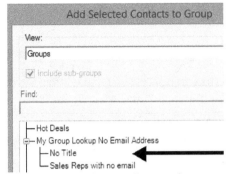

**Figure 6-21** Subgroup illustrated

4.  In the My Group Lookup No Email Address group, select the three contacts with Sales Representative in the Title field. Right-click on the selected records. Group Membership ⇒ Add Selected to Group.

5.  Scroll down the list and select the **SALES REPS WITH NO EMAIL** subgroup.

6.  If you click on the Sales Reps with no email subgroup, you will see the contacts that you added, as shown in Figure 6-22.

**Figure 6-22** Contacts in a subgroup

## Step 2: Remove The Contacts From The Original Group

As stated earlier, there is no way to remove linked contacts from a group from the Group detail view. They have to be removed from the Contacts Groups/Companies tab. In this part of the exercise you will remove the three contacts that you added to the Sales Reps with no email subgroup from the My Group Lookup No Email Address group.

1.  Click on the Sales Reps with no email subgroup ⇒ Click on the Contacts tab.

2.  Click on the first contacts name. The Contact detail view will open.

3.  Groups/Companies tab ⇒ Add/Remove Groups button.

4. On the right side of the Add/Remove dialog box, you will see the groups that the contact is a member of, as shown in Figure 6-23.

   Click on the second group shown, then click the Remove button.

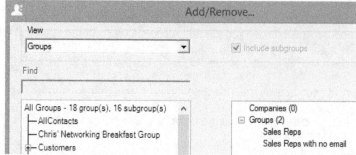

**Figure 6-23** Add/Remove dialog box

5. Click OK. The group should be removed from the contact. On your own, you would repeat these steps for each contact that you want to remove from the group.

### Deleting Groups Or Subgroups

You may have a need to delete a group or a subgroup. When you delete a group or subgroup, the contacts in the group or subgroup, their notes and attachments are not deleted. The groups notes, history records and attachments are deleted.

Subgroups of the group that will be deleted are not deleted. The subgroup is automatically promoted to a group. If you need to delete a group or subgroup, you can follow the steps below. For now, you can read the steps because you do not need to delete a group or subgroup.

1. Right-click on the group or subgroup in the Group detail or Group list view and select Delete.

2. Click Yes, when prompted to delete the current group or subgroup.

### Removing Contacts That Are Not Linked From Companies Or Groups

Exercise 6.1 covered how to remove contacts that were linked to a company from a group. There may be times when you need to remove contacts that are not linked from a company, division, group or subgroup. Examples would be if the contact leaves the company or you copied a contact in a group to a subgroup. If this is the case, you can follow the steps below to remove contacts that are not linked to a company, division or group record. For now, you can read this section because you do not need to remove a contact from a company or group.

1. Right-click on the company, division, group or subgroup that has contacts that you want to remove in the tree, then select the appropriate option below.

   ① Company Membership ⇒ Add/Remove Contacts.
   ② Group Membership ⇒ Add/Remove Contacts.

2. Click the Contacts button on the Add/Remove Contacts dialog box.

3. Select the names that you want to remove in the **SELECTED CONTACTS** list, then click the Remove button.

4. Once you have removed the contact records, click OK twice to close both dialog boxes.

### Converting A Group To A Company

Groups and subgroups can be converted to a company by using the **CONVERT GROUPS TO COMPANIES WIZARD**. If the group or subgroup that you convert has subgroups, the subgroups are not converted by default. They move up the hierarchy and quite possibly become a group. Contacts that are in the group or subgroup that is being converted, automatically become members of the company or what the group is converted to.

One reason that you may want to convert a group to a company is because you need to use a feature (for the contact records that are currently in a group) that only a company record has. In the next exercise you will convert the My Group Lookup No Email group to a company.

Once you convert a group to a company, it cannot be converted back to a group.

## Move Group Option

This option is used to promote a subgroup to a group or make a group a subgroup of another group. The steps below demonstrate how to move a group or subgroup. For now, just read this section.

1. In either group view, click on the group or subgroup that you want to move (promote).

2. Groups ⇒ Move Group. On the dialog box shown in Figure 6-24, select one of the options explained below.

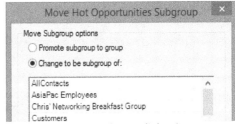

① **PROMOTE SUBGROUP TO GROUP** This option is only available for subgroups. When selected, the subgroup is promoted to a group and the contacts are retained in the group.

② **CHANGE TO BE SUBGROUP OF** Select this option to make the group (or subgroup) a subgroup of a different group.

**Figure 6-24** Move Group dialog box

 The **MOVE** option is also available for companies.

## Group Address Tab

The fields shown in Figure 6-25 are used to enter an address for the group if applicable.

**Figure 6-25** Group Address tab fields

## Group Access Tab

The fields shown in Figure 6-26 are filled in and updated by ACT! automatically.

The fields were explained in Chapter 3. [See Chapter 3, Contact Access Tab]

**Figure 6-26** Group Access tab fields

## Group Detail View Related Tasks

The options shown in Figure 6-27 are primarily on the detail view. Some options are also on the list view. The options are explained below.

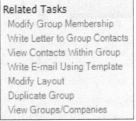

**Figure 6-27** Group detail view related tasks

**MODIFY GROUP MEMBERSHIP** Opens the Add/Remove Contacts dialog box.

**WRITE LETTER TO GROUP CONTACTS** A mail merge of contacts in the group is created and displayed in the word processor. [See Chapter 3, below Figure 3-35]

**VIEW CONTACTS WITHIN GROUP** Displays the contacts in the selected group in the Contact list view. If there is only one contact in the group, it will be displayed in the Contact detail view.

**WRITE E-MAIL USING TEMPLATE** [See Chapter 3, below Figure 3-35]

**MODIFY LAYOUT** [See Chapter 3, below Figure 3-32]

**DUPLICATE GROUP** Opens the dialog box shown in Figure 6-28. The options are used to select which group fields will be duplicated on the new group record.

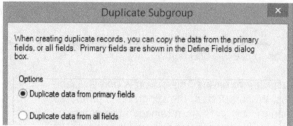

Figure 6-28 Duplicate Group dialog box

**VIEW GROUPS/COMPANIES** [See Chapter 5, below Figure 5-30]

## Group List View

This view provides an easy way to see groups and subgroups, as shown in Figure 6-29.

The icon in the first column indicates that the group has subgroups, which is a benefit over the Company list view.

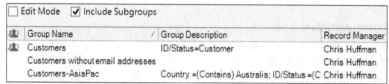

Figure 6-29 Group list view

If you do not want to see the subgroups, clear the **INCLUDE SUBGROUPS** option.

## Group List View Related Tasks

The options shown in Figure 6-30 are for the Group list view. The options that are only on the list view are explained below.

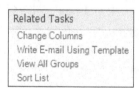

Figure 6-30 Group list view related tasks

**CHANGE COLUMNS** Opens the Customize Columns dialog box, which is used to add, remove and change the order that the columns are displayed on the group list view.

**VIEW ALL GROUPS** Displays all of the groups in the database. It is the same as selecting Lookup ⇒ All groups.

**SORT LIST** Opens the Sort dialog box to sort the groups displayed in the view.

# SCHEDULING ACTIVITIES

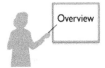

In this chapter you will learn about the following scheduling activity features:

- ☑ Timeless activities
- ☑ Scheduling a To-Do
- ☑ Scheduling the same activity for multiple contacts
- ☑ Sending email to contacts
- ☑ Scheduling activities for other users
- ☑ Using the alarm
- ☑ Rescheduling an activity
- ☑ Handling activity conflicts
- ☑ Group activities
- ☑ Creating and deleting recurring activities
- ☑ Scheduling random activities
- ☑ Filter and sort activities

## Activities Overview

Activities are more formal than notes. I think of activities as a really large, well thought out and detailed to-do list for your contacts. Activities let you keep up with your contacts. While it is tempting to only enter a little information for each activity, you may not remember everything that you know now, when the time comes to complete the task that an activity is for.

There are different types of activities that you can schedule. Some activities that you will schedule with contacts are business related and others are personal. The default activity types that you can schedule with contacts are meetings, telephone calls and to-do's. Each of these activities are basically created the same way. Activities are reminders of tasks that you need to complete. You can also create your own activity types.

It is a good idea to display the contact that you want to schedule the activity with before you open the Schedule Activity dialog box. This is not a requirement because there is an option on the dialog box to select the contact.

If you want to schedule the same activity for more than one contact, select the group or create a lookup that will display the contacts that you want to schedule the activity for.

You can also create the same activity for people that are not part of the same group or lookup, at the same time.

In addition to being able to view activities on the Activities tab on detail views, you can also view activities on the calendar and Task List.

Figure 7-1 shows the Schedule Activity dialog box. Table 7-1 explains the options on the Schedule Activity dialog box.

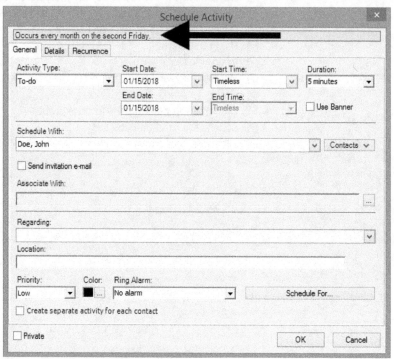

**Figure 7-1** To-Do activity options

| Option | Description |
|---|---|
| Activity Type | Select or change the type of activity that you are creating or editing. This field will initially be filled in based on the option that you select to open this dialog box. For example, if you click the Schedule Meeting button, "Meeting" will be the value displayed in this field when the dialog box is first opened, but you can change it. |
| Start Date | The date that the activity should start. The default value is today's date. |
| Start Time | The time that the activity should start. The default value is **TIMELESS**. |
| End Date & Time | These fields will change automatically, when the duration is selected. |
| Duration | Select the length of time needed to complete the activity. |
| Use Banner | Displays a banner on the daily calendar if the duration of the activity meets the requirement of the **SHOW FULL DAY** banner calendar preferences option. |
| Schedule With | By default, this field contains the contact that was displayed before the dialog box was opened. Other contacts can be added. |
| Contacts Button | The options on this button are used to select contacts for the activity. (1) |
| Send invitation e-mail | If checked, this option will display a message in the banner at the top of the Schedule Activity dialog box stating that contacts will receive an email notification of the activity and users will receive a calendar email invitation. Once the activity is set up, the appropriate emails and invitations will be sent automatically. |
| Associate With | Select the groups, subgroups, companies and divisions that need to be included on the activity. |
| Regarding | Is used to provide a description of the activity. The options that will be displayed in the drop-down list depend on the activity type that is selected. (2) |

**Table 7-1** Schedule Activity dialog box options explained

| Option | Description |
|--------|-------------|
| Location | A free form field that is used to enter where the activity will take place. |
| Priority | Select how important the activity is. Setting a priority is optional. |
| Color | Select the color for the priority. (3) |
| Ring Alarm | If a time is selected from this drop-down list, your computer will beep the number of minutes selected, before the activity is scheduled to start. |
| Schedule For Button | Select a user in the database to assign the activity to. Activities can be scheduled for more than one user. (4) |
| Create separate activity for each contact | This option will create an activity for each contact listed in the Schedule With field. |
| Private | If this option is selected on any tab on the Schedule Activity dialog box, other users of the database will not be able to view the activity. |

**Table 7-1** Schedule Activity dialog box options explained (Continued)

(1)  This button opens the menu shown in Figure 7-2. The options are explained below.
The **SELECT CONTACTS** option is used to select the contacts that the activity is for.
The **NEW CONTACT** option is used to create a new contact, which you can add to the activity.
The **MY RECORD** option is used to add yourself to the activity. If you need to use this option, select it first, then add the other contacts. This option will remove contacts that are already in the Schedule With field, including the original contact that was there.

(2)  Figure 7-3 shows the Regarding field drop-down list options for the Meeting activity type.
Figure 7-4 shows the Regarding field drop-down list options for the To-Do activity type.
If none of the options in the drop-down list meet your needs, you can type in a new description, which can be up to 256 characters. If you know that you will do a lot of searches or use this field as criteria for a query or report, you should customize it so that only options from the drop-down list can be selected.

(3)  By default, each priority level is a different color. If you want to change the color, click the button next to the option. You will see the dialog box shown in Figure 7-5. Keep in mind that the color is associated to a priority level and not the specific activity. If you change the color, the color that you select will automatically be applied to all activities with the same priority, going forward.

(4)  Click the **SCHEDULE FOR** button when you need to schedule the activity for another user of the database. In order to schedule an activity for another user, you must have rights to do so. If you have rights to schedule activities for other users and click this button, you will see the dialog box shown in Figure 7-6. Select the person that you want to schedule the activity for. The activity will display on the users calendar and task list. Don't be surprised when the user (probably a co-worker) does not thank you for giving them more work. <smile>

**Figure 7-2**
Contacts button options

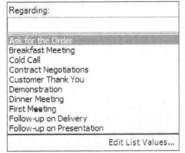

**Figure 7-3** Meeting options

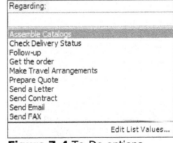

**Figure 7-4** To-Do options

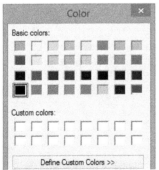

**Figure 7-5** Color dialog box

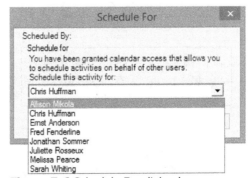

**Figure 7-6** Schedule For dialog box

You will only see users that you have the rights to schedule activities for in the drop-down list on the Schedule For dialog box, shown above in Figure 7-6. Chapter 11 covers how to grant calendar access, which in addition to being able to view entries on another users calendar, is also used to create activities and assign them to other users.

## Activity Types

There are seven types of activities that you can create, as explained in Table 7-2.

| Activity | Is Used To Schedule . . . |
|---|---|
| Appointment | An Outlook appointment. (5) |
| Call | A telephone call. |
| Meeting | A meeting. |
| To-Do | A task that needs to be completed. |
| Marketing Call | A telephone call. You could use this option for cold call telephone sales. (5) |
| Personal Activity | A non business related task. (5) |
| Vacation | Vacation time. (5) |

**Table 7-2** Activity types explained

(5)  There is no button on the Global toolbar for this activity type.

Schedule ⇒ Other, as shown in Figure 7-7, displays the entry point for these activity types.

If you do not want to use the menu options to access these activity types, you can click on any of the schedule activity icons on the Global toolbar to open the Schedule Activity dialog box and then select the activity type from the drop-down list.

**Figure 7-7** Schedule menu options

## Timeless Activities

This type of activity is one that does not have a time associated with it. Many types of To-Do activities, like sending an email or fax can be timeless. When you create a To-Do activity, you will see that the default start time displayed is TIMELESS. You can change the start time to a specific time if you need to. You can select the timeless option as the default for any type of activity on the Preferences dialog box.

 Timeless activities are not displayed on the Daily Calendar.

## Public Or Private Activities

This option is only useful if more than one person uses the database. If the contact record is marked as private, the activities for the contact are marked as private by default. You can make activities private, even if the contact is not private.

The lock symbol illustrated in Figure 7-8, on the Activities tab, denotes that the activity is private.

| | Type | ⟳ | Date | Time | Priority | Scheduled With | Regarding | ❶ | 📎 | 🔒 |
|---|---|---|---|---|---|---|---|---|---|---|
| ☐ | 📞 | | 12/13/2017 | None | Low | Lucy Connor | AS-Follow-up to First Order | | | |
| ☐ | ☑ | | 01/15/2018 | 6:00 AM | High | Lucy Connor | Send Quote | ❶ | | |
| ☐ | ☑ | | 01/16/2018 | None | Low | Lucy Connor | Prepare Quote | | | |
| ☐ | ♥ | | 03/28/2018 | 5:00 PM | Low | Lucy Connor | Presentation | | | 🔒 |

**Figure 7-8** Private activity icon illustrated

Keep the following in mind when deciding whether or not to make an activity private.

① Private activities will partially appear on other users calendars when your name is part of the filter that they use. The actual contents of the activity does not appear, but the word **PRIVATE** appears next to your name.
② When you clear a private activity, it is still marked as private when it is moved to the History tab.
③ Private activities are not displayed in other users Task List.

## Exercise 7.1: How To Schedule A To-Do Activity

In this exercise you will create a To-Do activity. Write down the date that you work on this exercise because you will use the same date in Chapter 11 to view the Daily Calendar.

1.  Look up the contacts that have "Customer" in the **ID/STATUS** field.

2.  Double-click on the record for Jim Curtis.

3.  On the Activities tab of the Contact detail view, click the **TO-DO** button on the Global toolbar. You will see the Schedule Activity dialog box.

4.  Change the Start time to 6 AM.

5.  Open the **REGARDING** drop-down list and select Send Quote.

6.  Change the **PRIORITY** to High. Leave the dialog box open to complete the next part of this exercise.

## Selecting Who To Schedule The Activity With

You cannot schedule an activity without associating it to a contact in the database.

1.  The **SCHEDULE WITH** drop-down list should look like the one shown in Figure 7-9. For now, leave the current contact selected.

    If you click on the Name or Company column heading in the drop-down list, you can change the sort order.

    Clicking the **MY RECORD** button at the bottom of the drop-down list will add the My Record as the person that you want to schedule the activity with.

**Figure 7-9** Schedule With drop-down list

## How To Schedule An Activity For A New Contact

As mentioned earlier, you can schedule the activity for more than one contact. If a contact that you want to schedule the activity with is not in the database, you have to add the contact to the database and then associate it to the activity. This is done by clicking on the Contacts button on the Schedule Activity dialog box and selecting New Contact. Selecting this option will open the New Contact dialog box.

### How To Add A New Contact To An Activity From The Schedule Activity Dialog Box

In this part of the exercise you will create a new contact for the activity.

1. Click the Contacts button on the Schedule Activity dialog box, then select New Contact. You should see the New Contact dialog box.

2. Enter the information in Table 7-3 for the new contact, then click OK.

   The address fields are on the Business Address tab.

| Field | Type This |
|-------|-----------|
| Company | Spice Plus |
| Contact | Jennifer Milton |
| Address | 456 Treasury St |
| City | Astoria |
| State | PA |
| Zip | 10210 |

**Table 7-3** Information for the new contact

### How To Select Multiple Contacts

1. Click the **CONTACTS** button on the Schedule Activity dialog box, then select the Select Contacts option. You will see the Select Contacts dialog box.

 Notice that you can add a new contact from the Select Contacts dialog box also.

You can assign the activity to all contacts, contacts in the current lookup, a group or company. You can also assign the activity on a contact by contact basis, by selecting names from the list.

2. Open the **SELECT FROM** drop-down list and select Current Lookup. You will see the names that are from the ID/Status = Customer lookup that you created earlier in this exercise.

3. Click the **ADD ALL>>** button. You will see all of the contacts from the current lookup in the Selected contacts list.

 If you wanted to assign this activity to other contacts, you could add them now. ACT! will not add names to the Selected contacts list if they have already been selected to be added to the activity.

4. Select the **GROUPS** option from the Select from drop-down list, then open the drop-down list to the right and select the Sales Reps group.

5. Select the first three names (Betty Browser, Sean Duffy and Emily Dunn) from the Sales Reps group by holding down the **CTRL** key and clicking on each name, then click the **ADD>** button. Click OK.

6. Check the **CREATE SEPARATE ACTIVITY FOR EACH CONTACT** option. This will create an entry on the Activities tab of each contact record.

 **Activity Linking Issue**
When an activity is cleared from a contact that is linked to a company record, by default, the history record that is created for the activity can be viewed from the contact record. To prevent this from happening, clear the **ASSOCIATE WITH** field, shown in Figure 7-10.

7. Check the **USE BANNER** option.

   (**Hint**: It is below the Duration field.)

   You should have the options selected that are shown in Figure 7-10.

**Figure 7-10** General tab activity options

## Details Tab Options

The options on this tab are used to add comments, as well as, add an attachment to the activity, if needed. The Details tab is used to enter more text than the Regarding field on the General tab can store.

8. On the Details tab, type `This is a To-Do activity`, as shown in Figure 7-11.

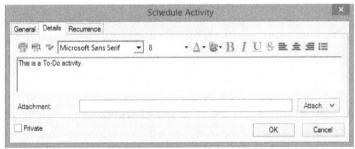

**Figure 7-11** Details tab options

## Recurrence Tab Options

The options on this tab are used to select the frequency of the activity, as well as, the start and end date for a recurring activity.

9. No options need to be selected on this tab. Click OK.

## View The Activity

10. On the Activities tab, scroll through the records.

    You will see the To-Do activity that you created, as illustrated in Figure 7-12.

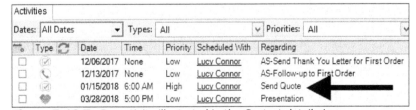

**Figure 7-12** To-Do activity illustrated in the Contact detail view

You may be asking yourself, what if I schedule an activity for a future date? How will I remember it? On the Task List view, you can view all of the activities that are scheduled in the future.

### Send Invitation E-Mail Option

If you select this option on the
Schedule Activity dialog box and
have email software configured to
work with ACT!, once you click OK
on the Schedule Activity dialog box,
the email will be generated.

Your email software will open and
you will see an email similar to the
one shown in Figure 7-13.

I currently do not have email
software configured to work with
ACT!. This figure is from a previous
version of the software.

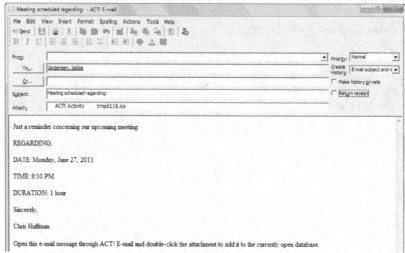

**Figure 7-13** Activity email that will be sent to the contacts

### Viewing An Activity With Multiple Contacts

If the same activity is assigned to more than one contact, you will not see all of the contact names in the SCHEDULED
WITH column on the Activities tab. Instead, you will see a plus sign at the beginning of the list of names, as illustrated
in Figure 7-14. If you click on this link, all of the contacts associated with the activity will be displayed on the Contact
list view.

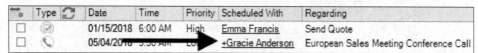

**Figure 7-14** Multiple contacts for an activity illustrated

### Exercise 7.2: Scheduling Activities For Other Users

The SCHEDULE FOR button at the bottom of the General tab on the Schedule Activity dialog box is used to create an
activity for another user of the database. For example, if you wanted a sales manager in your company to send a
thank you note to all of your suppliers, you could schedule the activity for the sales manager. Won't the sales manager
be thrilled! <smile>

### How To Schedule A Call

This activity type is used to create a reminder to call a contact. In this exercise, you will schedule a phone call activity
for another user of the database.

1.  Look up the contact George Agen.

2.  Click the CALL button on the Global toolbar.

3.  Select the Regarding option, Confirm Appointment.

4.  Click the SCHEDULE FOR button. Open the drop-down list and select Allison Mikola, then click OK.

5.  You will see the banner shown in Figure 7-15,
    at the top of the Schedule Activity dialog box.

    Click OK.

**Figure 7-15** Activity banner

**Why I Think It's Best To Schedule Phone Calls Individually**
Looking at the activity illustrated earlier in Figure 7-14, you will not know how many people need to be called, if this was a telephone call activity. You would have to view them on the Contact list view or open the Schedule Activity dialog box to see the contact names, which adds an extra step to the process. If you call and speak to some of the contacts but cannot reach other contacts, it will be difficult to know which contacts you still have to call because there is no way to mark some contacts on the activity as completed and leave others open.

If you do not call all of the contacts, but mark the task as being complete, you may not remember that you still need to call other contacts that are listed on the activity because the activity will no longer appear on the Activities tab or Task List. This is the other reason why I think it is best to schedule phone calls individually. If you want to automatically have activities assigned to multiple contacts scheduled individually, select the option on the Scheduling Preferences dialog box.

## Exercise 7.3: Using The Alarm

This feature is designed to remind you of a scheduled activity. ACT! has to be open in order for the alarm to notify you of an activity. If ACT! is open, the Alarms dialog box will pop up. If ACT! is open, but minimized, the ACT! button on the Windows Taskbar will flash. Your computer will beep if you have the Ring Alarm option enabled. If you only select the Set Alarm option, you will only be notified at the time that activity starts, not before.

The alarm also has a snooze option, which you can use to be reminded of an activity. It works like the snooze button on an alarm clock, by notifying you in advance of the activity. You can reset the alarm to go off again at a later time. You can also clear the alarm option to turn it off completely. Turning off the alarm does not clear the activity.

The snooze option is useful if you need time before the activity to prepare for it. If you want a snooze time that is not in the Ring Alarm field drop-down list, you can type it in. For example, you can enter any of the following times in the field: 46 minutes, 46 hours or 46 days.

1.  Lookup the contact Jim Curtis.

2.  Click the **CALL** button on the Global toolbar.

3.  Open the Start Time drop-down list. Scroll down the list and click in the time slot that is to the nearest, next half hour. (If it is currently 8:20 PM, select 8:30 PM. If it is 4:35 PM, select 5 PM.)

4.  Select the Regarding option Confirm Appointment.

5.  Open the **RING ALARM** drop-down list and select 5 minutes. This means that you will be notified five minutes before this activity starts.

6.  You should have the options selected that are shown in Figure 7-16.

    You will see a different date and time.

    Click OK.

    If there is a conflict alert, select the closest available time in the future.

    You should now see an entry for this activity on the contact record for Jim Curtis.

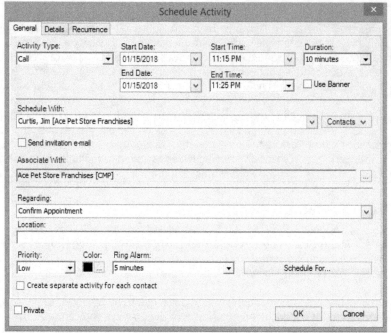

**Figure 7-16** Telephone call activity options

When the Alarms dialog box shown in Figure 7-17 appears, come back to the section below: Alarm Notification Options.

For now, continue going through the book, by going to Exercise 7.4: Handling Activity Conflicts or you can go get a snack. <smile>

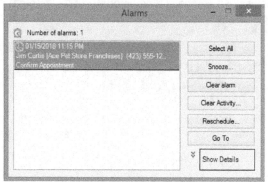

**Figure 7-17** Alarms dialog box

## Alarm Notification Options

You should now see the dialog box shown above in Figure 7-17. The alarm options explained below are available.

**SELECT ALL** Is used to set the same option for all of the activities that are displayed on the Alarms dialog box.

**SNOOZE** Is used to reset the snooze time, on the dialog box shown later in Figure 7-19.

**CLEAR ALARM** Turns the alarm off for the rest of the day. The activity will still stay on your calendar.

**CLEAR ACTIVITY** Opens the Clear Activity dialog box so that you can mark the activity as being complete.

**RESCHEDULE** Opens the Schedule Activity dialog box, which is used to select a different date or time for the activity.

**GO TO** Displays the contact record that the alarm is for.

**SHOW DETAILS** Displays the Activity Details section, shown in Figure 7-18. It is at the bottom of the Alarms dialog box.

When the details are displayed, the Show Details button will change to **HIDE DETAILS**.

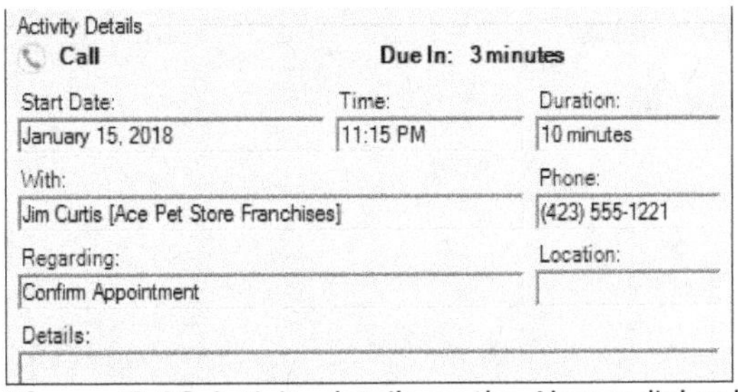

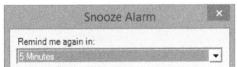

**Figure 7-18** Activity details on the Alarms dialog box

## Setting The Snooze Alarm

The steps below show you how to set the snooze feature. For now, skip this section.

1. Click the Snooze button.

   You should see the dialog box shown in Figure 7-19.

**Figure 7-19** Snooze Alarm dialog box

2. Select the amount of minutes from now that you want to be notified again, of the activity that you have scheduled, then click OK.

3. Click the **CLEAR ALARM** button on the Alarms dialog box, then close the dialog box ⇒ Look up the contact Jim Curtis.

4. Double-click on the Confirm Appointment activity with today's date ⇒ Change the **RING ALARM** option to **NO ALARM**, then click OK.

## Rescheduling An Activity

Rescheduling allows you to change when an activity will take place. The steps below show you how, if the need arises. For now, skip this section.

1. On the Alarms dialog box, shown earlier in Figure 7-17, click on the activity that you want to reschedule.

2. Click the **RESCHEDULE** button. You will see the Schedule Activity dialog box for the activity. If you were doing this for real, you would select a new date or time on the Schedule Activity dialog box.

## Exercise 7.4: Handling Activity Conflicts

ACT! will warn you of activity conflicts and try to keep you from scheduling two activities at the same time. If this occurs, you will be notified when you are creating an activity that conflicts with an existing activity. You will have the option to reschedule the time and/or date of the new activity. In this exercise you will schedule a meeting activity for a time when an activity already exists.

1. Look up the contact Jim Curtis ⇒ Look at the time for the Confirm appointment activity.

2. Click the **MEETING** button on the Global toolbar.

3. Change the Start Date to the same date as the Confirm appointment ⇒ Change the Start Time to one hour before the start time of the Confirm appointment activity. (Yes, I know that this is a date in the past, but stay with me.) You can do this by typing the date in the field or by using the calendar attached to the field.

4. Set the Duration to 2 hours.

   Select the **PRESENTATION** Regarding option.

   You should have the options shown in Figure 7-20.

   Click OK.

   You may see the message shown in Figure 7-21.

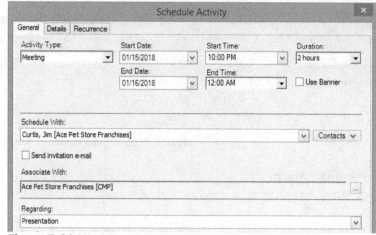

**Figure 7-20** Meeting activity options

Normally, you would not see this dialog box because you would not be trying to schedule an activity for a date in the past, unless you typed in a date in the past by mistake. It is being done here on purpose to demonstrate how to handle activity conflicts.

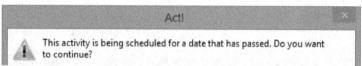

**Figure 7-21** Activity warning message

5. Click Yes to continue. You will see the dialog box shown in Figure 7-22.

   This dialog box is telling you that the activity that you are trying to schedule is conflicting with an existing activity.

   The figure shows that an activity has already been scheduled for the same time frame.

   Therefore, it is probably a good idea to reschedule this activity for another date or time.

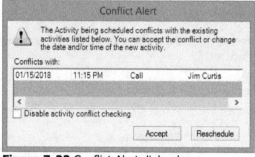

**Figure 7-22** Conflict Alert dialog box

If you still want to schedule this activity, click the **ACCEPT** button. If you want to change the date or time of the activity, click the **RESCHEDULE** button.

## How To Reschedule A Conflicting Activity

1. Click the **RESCHEDULE** button on the Conflict Alert dialog box, shown above in Figure 7-22.

2. Change the Start date to 09/19/2015 ⇒ Change the Start time to 8:00 PM, then click OK. This date and time does not conflict with other activities for the contact.

3. Click Yes when prompted that the activity has been scheduled for a date in the past. I had to pick a date and time that did not already exist for an activity in the database, to demonstrate the reschedule functionality.

## Group Activities

You can schedule an activity for a group. Doing this means that each contact in the group will be associated to the group activity. The group activity will appear on the Activities tab of each contact in the group. The majority of the steps to create a group activity are the same as creating an activity for one contact.

If you want to practice creating a group activity, you can follow the steps below or use the steps when you have the need to create a group activity.

1. Open the Group detail view, then click on the Sales Reps group.

2. Click the Meeting button on the Global toolbar ⇒ Change the Start Date to tomorrow.

Notice that the group name is in the Associate With field on the Schedule Activity dialog box. You can also add individual contacts and other groups to the activity.

3. Click the Contacts button ⇒ Select the Select Contacts option.

4. Open the Select From drop-down list, then select Groups.

5. Open the next drop-down list and select the group, Sales Reps with no email ⇒ Add all of the contacts in the group, to the list, then click OK.

6. Select the **FOLLOW-UP ON PRESENTATION** Regarding option, then click OK. If you click on the Activities tab for the Sales Reps group, you will see the activity that you just created. If you do not see the activity, change the Show For option to Group.

## Recurring Activities

Recurring activities are activities that are repeated on a consistent frequency. The four types of recurring activities that can be created are explained below. The recurring options look somewhat similar, but the fields perform differently. To make sure that you have selected the correct options, read the information in the banner at the top of the dialog box. It briefly explains what the options that you selected represent.

The **EVERY** field determines how many days, weeks, months or years are between each occurrence of the activity.

The **STARTS** field is the date that you want the first occurrence of the recurring activity to begin.

The **ENDS** field is the date that you want the last occurrence of the activity to happen.

There are two ways that recurring activities can be scheduled, as explained below:

① Activities that occur on a regular basis, like monthly staff meetings.
② Activities that occur randomly, like processing payroll every other Friday.

## Recurring Activity Types Explained

① **DAILY** Select this option if the interval for the recurring activity should be in days.

For example, the options shown in Figure 7-23 are for an activity that will happen every five days.

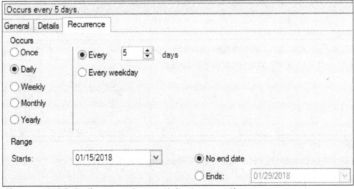

**Figure 7-23** Daily recurring activity type options

② **WEEKLY** Select this option for activities that you want to occur weekly.

The options shown in Figure 7-24 are for a weekly meeting that will take place every Thursday and Friday, indefinitely.

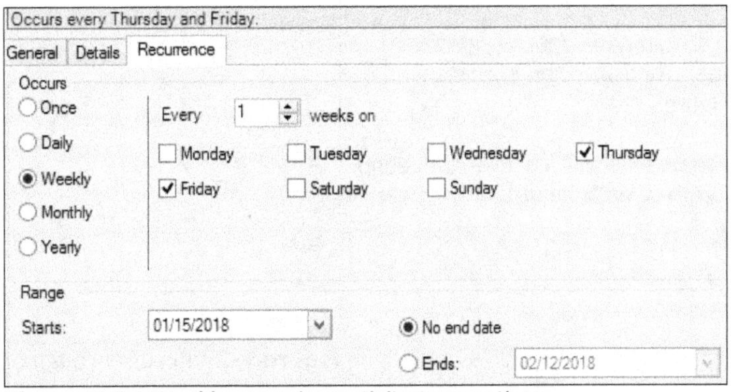

**Figure 7-24** Weekly recurring activity type options

③ **MONTHLY** Select this option for activities that you want to occur monthly.

The options shown in Figure 7-25 will create a monthly activity that takes place on the second Tuesday of every month.

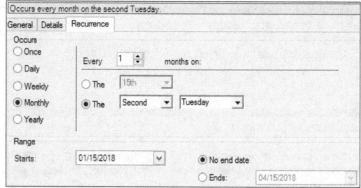

**Figure 7-25** Monthly recurring activity type options

④ **YEARLY** Select this option for activities that you want to occur yearly.

The options shown in Figure 7-26 will create a yearly activity that takes place on the last Tuesday in March.

If you wanted the activity to end, you would enter a date in the **ENDS** field.

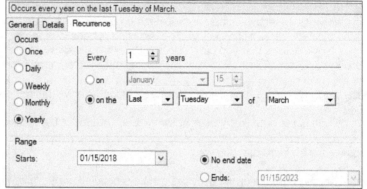

**Figure 7-26** Yearly recurring activity type options

## Exercise 7.5: How To Schedule Recurring Activities

If you know that you will need to have monthly meetings, you can schedule the meeting once and have ACT! automatically schedule the rest of the monthly meetings for the time frame that you specify.

1.   Look up the contact Rick Blaine ⇒ Click the Meeting button.

2.   On the General tab, select the options in Table 7-4 to create the meeting activity.

| Option | Change To |
|---|---|
| Start Date | The 24th of next month |
| Start Time | 3 PM |
| Duration | 2 hours |
| Regarding | Contract Negotiations |

**Table 7-4** Meeting activity options

3.   On the **RECURRENCE** tab, select the Monthly option ⇒ Change the first **THE** option to the 24th.

4.   Select the **ENDS** option and type in the date a year from today.

You should have options selected that are similar to the ones shown in Figure 7-27.

These options will schedule a meeting the 24th of each month for the next year.

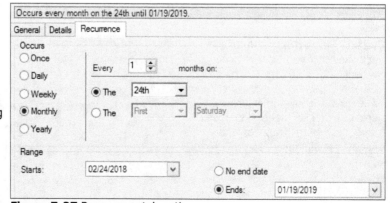

**Figure 7-27** Recurrence tab options

5.  Click OK. If there is a conflict, reschedule the activity and change the Start date on the Schedule Activity dialog box to the 25th. If necessary, change the time also.

On the Activities tab for Rick Blaine, you will see a recurring symbol and meeting that starts on the 24th (or the date that you selected) of next month, as illustrated in Figure 7-28.

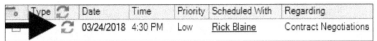

| Type | | Date | Time | Priority | Scheduled With | Regarding |
|---|---|---|---|---|---|---|
| | ⟳ | 03/24/2018 | 4:30 PM | Low | Rick Blaine | Contract Negotiations |

**Figure 7-28** Recurring symbol illustrated

 Only the next occurrence of recurring activities will appear on the Activities tab and Task List. All of the occurrences of a recurring activity will appear on your calendar. This means that you will see each occurrence of a weekly meeting on a calendar, but you will only see the next occurrence of the weekly meeting on the Activities tab. On your own, you may find it helpful to set up an alarm reminder for 1 to 5 days ahead of the meeting.

### Exercise 7.6: How To Schedule Random Activities

Scheduling random activities allows you to schedule a conference call on the last day of the month. In ACT! 2013 and earlier, you could select the 31st and ACT! would schedule the recurring activity on the last day of the month, no matter what the actual last date of the month is. Starting with ACT! v16, that has changed, as you will see in this exercise.

1.  Look up the My Record.

2.  Click the **CALL** button ⇒ On the General tab, select the options in Table 7-5 to create the activity.

| Option | Change To |
|---|---|
| Start Date/Time | Tomorrow, 6 PM |
| Duration | 15 minutes |
| Regarding | Discuss Legal Points |

**Table 7-5** Schedule call activity options

3.  On the Recurrence tab, select the Monthly option.

Open the second drop-down list and select **LAST**.

Open the next drop-down list and select **DAY**.

You should have similar options to those shown in Figure 7-29.

Click OK.

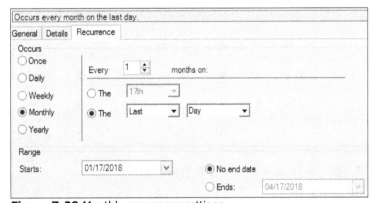

**Figure 7-29** Monthly recurrence settings

On the Activities tab of the My Record (for Chris Huffman), you should see a phone call scheduled for the last day of the current month or the last day of next month, if you are completing this exercise on the last day of the month. The activity will appear on the last day of the month. This may or may not be a workday.

### Scheduling An Activity For The Last Workday Of The Month

In the previous exercise, you created a random recurring activity that would automatically be scheduled for the last calendar day of the month.

If you need to schedule a monthly activity for the last workday of the month, select the monthly options illustrated in Figure 7-30.

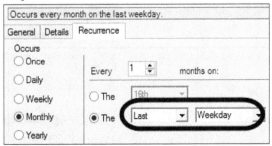

**Figure 7-30** Options for a last workday of the month activity

**Other Ways To Open The Schedule Activity Dialog Box**
The majority of the activities that you created in this chapter used a button on the toolbar to open the Schedule Activity dialog box. There are other ways to open the Schedule Activity dialog box, as explained below.

① Double-click on a time slot on the calendar. This is helpful because it can help prevent you from trying to schedule conflicting activities.
② Open the Schedule menu.
③ On the Activities tab of a Detail view, right-click in the list of activities ⇒ Select Schedule and the type of activity that you want to create, as shown in Figure 7-31.

**Figure 7-31** Activities tab shortcut menu

## Deleting Recurring Activities

If you have scheduled a recurring activity and either no longer need the remaining activities or need to clear (delete) a recurring activity for a specific date, you can.

## How To Clear All Future Recurring Activities

The steps below will show you how to delete all of the remaining occurrences of an activity.

1. Display your My Record.

2. On the Activities tab, right-click on the recurring activity that you want to clear and select the **ERASE ACTIVITY** option.

3. You will see the dialog box shown in Figure 7-32, letting you know that this is a recurring activity.

   Select the **DELETE ALL OCCURRENCES** option, then click OK.

   If your email software opens, close it.

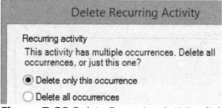

**Figure 7-32** Delete Recurring Activity dialog box

## How To Clear A Single Recurring Activity

The steps below will show you how to clear one occurrence of the remaining occurrences of a recurring activity.

1. On the Activities tab, right-click on the recurring activity that you want to clear and select **CLEAR ACTIVITY**.

2. Select the **ERASE** option on the Clear Activity dialog box, as illustrated in Figure 7-33, then click OK. The activity will be deleted.

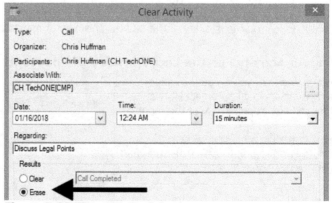

**Figure 7-33** Clear Activity dialog box

## Clearing Activities

It is good practice to clear activities once you complete them. When you clear an activity, a record is automatically created on the History tab of the contact(s) that the activity belongs to. This way, if you need to know whether or not an activity was completed or ever existed, you will be able to easily tell.

## Other Reasons To Clear Activities

① Some reports are based on history records that are created when an activity is cleared. Without history records, the reports will not display the correct records.

② Allows you to schedule follow up activities.

③ You will not be reminded of the activity.

④ Fields on the **LATEST ACTIVITIES SECTION** are updated.

## How To Clear Activities

You have already learned how to clear recurring activities from the Activities tab. Clearing other types of activities is basically the same process. You can right-click on an activity any place except the History tab, then select Clear Activity. The other ways to clear an activity are explained below:

① On the Task List, click in the check box illustrated in Figure 7-34.

② On any calendar view, click in the check box illustrated in Figure 7-35.

③ Select the activity on the Activities tab that you want to clear ⇒ Schedule ⇒ Clear Activity.

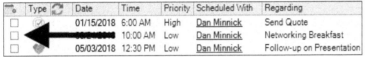

**Figure 7-34** Task List option to clear an activity

**Figure 7-35** Calendar view option to clear an activity

## Exercise 7.7: Clear An Activity For A Contact

When you clear an activity, you can leave the options the way that they are or you can add or change information about the activity, as needed. You should make changes that will help you remember more about the activity in the future.

1. Right-click on the Contract Negotiations activity for Rick Blaine, then select **CLEAR ACTIVITY**.

2. Click the **FOLLOW-UP** button. The follow-up option is used to schedule another activity for the contact. (Amazingly, this is called a follow up activity .<smile>) This is the equivalent of creating a paper trail.

3. Open the **REGARDING** drop-down list and select the Follow-up on Presentation option, then click OK.

4. Select the **MEETING NOT HELD** results option on the Clear Activity dialog box.

5. Check the **ADD ACTIVITY DETAILS TO HISTORY** option, if it is not already checked.

    You should have the options shown in Figure 7-36. Click OK.

    The activity for Contract Negotiations with today's date is no longer on the Activities tab. You should see a new activity with today's date that has "Follow-up on Presentation" in the Regarding field. On the History tab, you will see an entry for the meeting not held activity.

**Figure 7-36** Clear activity options

> **How To Clear More Than One Activity At The Same Time**
> You can clear more than one activity on the Activities tab or the Task List at the same time by selecting the activities that you want to clear, then right-click on them and select CLEAR MULTIPLE ACTIVITIES, as illustrated in Figure 7-37.

**Figure 7-37** Task List multi select shortcut menu

## Clear An Activity For A Group

Clearing a group activity is the same process as clearing an activity for a contact. When you have the need to clear a group activity, you can follow the steps below.

1.  Click the Groups button ⇒ Click on the Activities tab for the group that has the activity that you want to clear.

2.  Right-click on the activity and select CLEAR ACTIVITY.

3.  Select the appropriate options on the Clear Activity dialog box, then click OK.

## Exercise 7.8: How To Filter Activities

You may only want to see certain types of activities or activities in a certain date range. Filtering is used to accomplish both of these tasks. In this exercise you will learn how to filter activities.

1.  Look up the My Record ⇒ On the Activities tab, open the TYPES drop-down list and clear the Vacation option. If there are vacation activities, they will not be displayed now.

2.  Right-click in the Activities tab and select Filter Activities on the shortcut menu. You should see the Filter Activities dialog box.

3.  Open the Dates drop-down list and select TODAY AND FUTURE.

4.  Open the Types drop-down list and clear the Personal Activity option.

    You should have the options selected that are shown in Figure 7-38.

    Click OK.

    There should be less activities displayed now then when you first started this exercise.

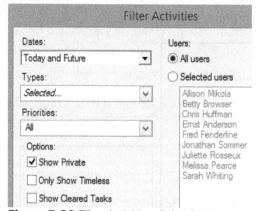

**Figure 7-38** Filter Activities dialog box

> **Sorting Activities**
> You can sort the activities on the Activities tab in ascending or descending order by clicking on the column heading of the field that you want to sort on.

# RUNNING REPORTS

Overview

In this chapter you will learn the following about running reports:

- ☑ Selecting report criteria
- ☑ Custom date ranges
- ☑ Printing calendars, labels and envelopes
- ☑ Using the Quick Print options

**No Shame Book Plug #1**
If you find that your reporting needs have out grown the reporting features in ACT!, you may find my book, No Stress Tech Guide To Using Crystal Reports With ACT! Databases
ISBN 978-1-935208-10-5 helpful, because Crystal Reports can connect to ACT! databases. This means that you will have more functionality available to create the reports that you need.

**CHAPTER 8**

## Reports Overview

ACT! comes with several reports already created that you can use. They are on the Reports menu. In this chapter you will learn how to run some of the reports. The reports that you run can be printed and saved. Reports are probably a key feature in ACT! because we are a report driven society. For many, reports are the only reason they enter contact information in ACT!. Once you have been using ACT! for a while, you will probably see that you are running the same reports on a regular basis. Take some time once you have run reports for about a month and carefully look at the data. Are there columns on the report that do not have any data or very little data? Is the report providing the level of detail that you need? If not, you may need to modify the report and/or enter more data.

The label and envelope options are on the Print dialog box, which is accessed from the File menu. The calendar and address book print options are with the labels and envelopes. Some people think that it is strange that these options are not on the Reports menu, but if you think about it, they are not reports, in the true sense of the word.

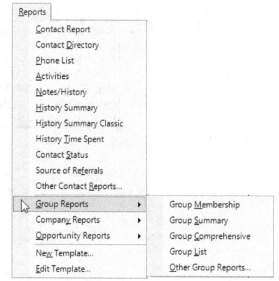

The Reports menu shown in Figure 8-1 is how you access the reports. Notice the **OTHER REPORTS** options. (For example, the Other Contact Reports option and the Other Group Reports option, shown on the sub menu). The wording gives the impression that these options would display more reports.

As a programmer, I was not misled by this wording because these options do not have a triangle like the Group, Company and Opportunity Reports menu options have. A programming standard when a menu option will open a submenu is to put a triangle next to the option.

If you look closely, you will see that the "Other Reports" menu options have three periods (called an **ELLIPSIS**) after them. This is another programming standard. This is used to signify that selecting the option will open a dialog box.

When you select any of the "Other Reports" options, you will see the **SELECT REPORT** dialog box, which has all of the reports that came with ACT!.

**Figure 8-1** Reports menu

If you modify reports or create new ones and other people will use the reports, you could save them in this folder or add them to a menu so that other people can access them. OK, the programming lecturette for today is over! <smile>

## Define Filters Dialog Box

The Define Filters dialog box should reduce any anxiety that you may have about selecting options to run reports, because it is used to select the criteria for each report. Options that are not available for a report are not enabled. You have to create the lookup or run a saved query before selecting a report to run if you do not want to be limited by the options on the Define Filters dialog box. If you know that a certain report needs a query, you should create it and save it. It would be a nice feature to be able to select a saved query or create a lookup from the Define Filters dialog box when selecting other report criteria.

| **Activity, Notes, History And Opportunity Reports** |
| --- |
| The default date range option for these reports is **CURRENT MONTH**. If left unchanged, this may produce unexpected results by not displaying all of the data that you would expect to see. For example, you create a lookup or run a query that retrieves contact records that have a create date from last year.<br><br>If you leave the default date range of the current month selected, the report will not display any activity, note, history or opportunity data from any other time period. Only data for the current month will be displayed on the report. More than likely, you would also be expecting to see data for these types of records from previous years. |

**Tips For Running Reports In This Chapter**
① Unless stated otherwise, make sure that the **SEND THE REPORT OUTPUT TO** option on the General tab on the Define Filters dialog box is set to Preview, unless you want to print the report. The remaining report output options are explained in Table 8-1.
② Make sure that the **EXCLUDE 'MY RECORD'** option is checked on the General tab, on the Define Filters dialog box. Selecting this option will keep the My Record from printing. Not all reports have this option.
③ Save any report that you want to keep in your folder.
④ Close the report when you are finished viewing it.

| File Type | Select This File Type If The Report . . . |
|-----------|-------------------------------------------|
| Rich-Text | Needs to be edited in a word processor. |
| HTML | Will be posted on the Internet. |
| PDF | Will be distributed to someone that does not have ACT!. Either the full version of Adobe Acrobat or the free Adobe Reader is needed to view a PDF file. |
| Text | Needs to be in plain text format. Non text objects like image files are not saved in this format. |
| Printer | Will be printed on paper. |
| Email | Will be sent via email. |

**Table 8-1** Report output file types explained

### Exercise 8.1: Run The Contact Report

This report will print a profile for each contact that is selected. You can filter the report to include or not include the notes, history, opportunities and activity information.

1. Reports ⇒ Contact Report.

2. On the General tab, select the **ALL CONTACTS** option. You should have the options selected that are shown in Figure 8-2.

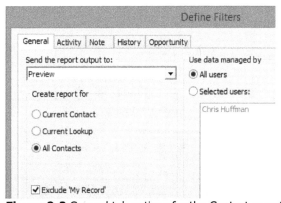

**Figure 8-2** General tab options for the Contact report

If you created a lookup for the records that you want to appear on the report prior to opening the report, select the **CURRENT LOOKUP** option. If you only want the report to use the contact record that you have open, select the **CURRENT CONTACT** option.

3. On the Activity tab, clear the **MEETINGS** option. Clearing this option will keep the meeting activities from printing on the report.

4. Open the **DATE RANGE** drop-down list and select Past.

The **PAST** date range option will only print activities that have a date in the past.
The **CUSTOM** button is used to select a specific date range for the activities that you want to include on the report.

5. Clear the **INCLUDE CLEARED ACTIVITIES** option.

   You should have the options selected that are shown in Figure 8-3.

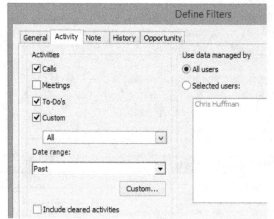

**Figure 8-3** Activity tab options for the Contact report

6. On the Note tab, clear the Notes option.

7. On the History tab, clear the Email and Attachments options ⇒ Select the **ALL** date range option.

8. On the Opportunity tab, clear the Closed-Won, Closed-Lost and Inactive options.

9. Change the Date Range to All, then click OK. The report will open in its own window. In the lower left corner of the Print Preview window, you will see the report pages being created.

## Report Print Preview Toolbar

Like many other windows in ACT!, the Print Preview window has a toolbar, as shown in Figure 8-4. Table 8-2 explains the buttons on the toolbar.

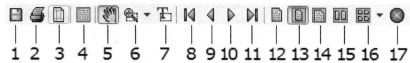

**Figure 8-4** Report print preview toolbar

| Button | Description |
|--------|-------------|
| 1 | Saves the report. |
| 2 | Prints the report. |
| 3 | Is used to change the paper size, margins and orientation of the report. |
| 4 | The Show Navigation Bar button displays the report pages in the thumbnail view, as shown in Figure 8-5. |
| 5 | The Hand Tool button is used to move the report page around in the window. |
| 6 | The Zoom In Tool button is used to change the magnification of the report displayed on the screen. |
| 7 | The Select Text button is used to select text in the report that you want to copy to another document. |
| 8 | Displays the first page of the report. |
| 9 | Displays the previous page of the report. |
| 10 | Displays the next page of the report. |
| 11 | Displays the last page of the report. |
| 12 | The Actual Size button is used to enlarge the report on the screen. |
| 13 | The Full Page button is used to display an entire page of the report, whether or not it is readable. |
| 14 | The Page Width button is used to resize the report so that it is the size of the Print Preview window. |
| 15 | The Two Pages button is used to display two pages of the report, in the window at the same time, as shown in Figure 8-6. |
| 16 | The Four Pages button is used to display four pages of the report in the window at the same time. (1) |
| 17 | Cancels the print preview process from generating the entire report. |

**Table 8-2** Report print preview toolbar buttons explained

## Viewing Other Pages In A Report

Most reports have more than one page. If you want to move around the report quickly, the easiest way to do that is to click the **SHOW NAVIGATION BAR** button on the toolbar.

This will let you view a thumbnail of each page of the report, as shown in Figure 8-5. This option is useful if the report is large. You can scroll down the thumbnails and click on the page that you want to view.

Scrolling down the thumbnails and clicking on page 32 is faster then clicking the Next Page ▶ button 31 times, if the current page is the first page of the report.

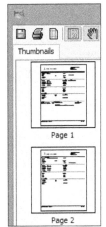

**Figure 8-5** Report preview thumbnail option

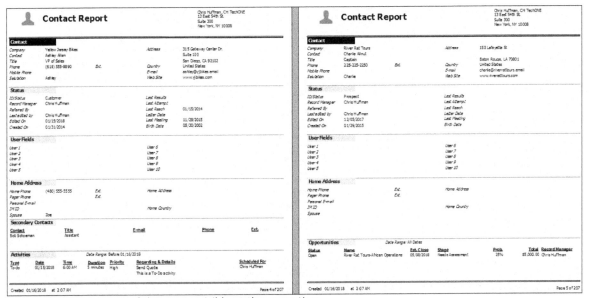

**Figure 8-6** Two pages of the report visible at the same time

(1) Clicking on the arrow at the end of the **FOUR PAGES** button displays the grid shown in Figure 8-7. This is used to select how many pages of the report to display in the window.

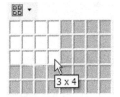

When you want to display a specific number of pages in the report, click in the first square in the upper left corner of the grid, then drag the mouse to the right and then down until you see the number of rows and columns that you need. In the example shown, 12 pages of the report will be displayed on the screen.

**Figure 8-7** Four Pages button options

## Preview And Save The Report

1. Click the **ZOOM IN TOOL** button, then click on the report three times. The report will be displayed much larger. Compare this report to the report shown earlier in Figure 8-6.

2. Click the **FILE SAVE** button on the Print Preview window toolbar. You should see the folder that you created. For now, you can accept the default file name, then click the Save button.

## The Contact Directory Report

This report is similar to the contact report in the previous exercise.

The difference is that the Activities, Notes, History and Opportunities tabs are not on this report.

This report prints the contact address information, as shown in Figure 8-8.

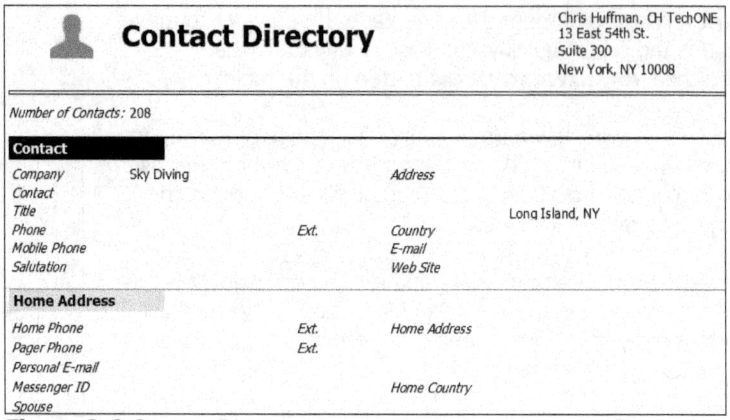

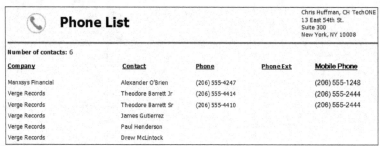

**Figure 8-8** Contact Directory report

## Exercise 8.2: Run The Phone List Report

This report will print the company, contact, phone, mobile phone and extension fields. Earlier in this chapter you learned that if you wanted to only print records based on the result of a lookup or contacts in a specific group, you have to create the lookup or select the group before you run the report. In this exercise you will create a lookup before running the report.

1. Create a lookup to find all contacts in the state of Washington. You should have six records displayed.

2. Reports ⇒ Phone List.

3. Select the Current lookup option, if it is not already selected, then click OK.

   Figure 8-9 shows some of the records on the report.

Phone List

Chris Huffman, CH TechONE
13 East 54th St.
Suite 300
New York, NY 10008

Number of contacts: 6

| Company | Contact | Phone | Phone Ext | Mobile Phone |
|---|---|---|---|---|
| Manxsys Financial | Alexander O'Brien | (206) 555-4247 | | (206) 555-1248 |
| Verge Records | Theodore Barrett Jr | (206) 555-4414 | | (206) 555-2444 |
| Verge Records | Theodore Barrett Sr | (206) 555-4410 | | (206) 555-2444 |
| Verge Records | James Gutierrez | | | |
| Verge Records | Paul Henderson | | | |
| Verge Records | Drew McLintock | | | |

**Figure 8-9** Phone List report

## Exercise 8.3: Run The Activities Report

This report will print the activities that are scheduled and completed with contacts. The default option is to print the report for all users in the database.

1. Reports ⇒ Activities.

2. On the General tab, select the All Contacts option.

3. On the Activity tab, clear the Meetings and Include cleared activities options.

## How To Create A Custom Date Range

Often, you may have the need to print a report to include information for a few weeks or a few months. To do this you need to create a custom date range.

1. On the Activity tab, click the **CUSTOM** button. You will see the Select Date Range dialog box.

2. Click the **<** arrow on the **FROM** calendar until you see January 2018, then click on the 1st.

3. Type 02/28/2018 in the **TO** field, then press the Tab key.

   You should have the options shown in Figure 8-10.

   Click OK.

**Figure 8-10** Date range options selected

4. You should have the options selected on the Activity tab that are shown in Figure 8-11.

   Click OK.

   The report should look similar to the one shown in Figure 8-12.

**Figure 8-11** Activity tab options

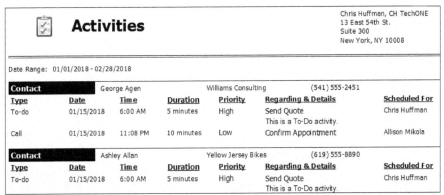

**Figure 8-12** Activities report

## Exercise 8.4: Run The Company Comprehensive Report

This report will display the following data for a company: Contacts, notes, history, activities and opportunities. This report can be used to produce a company profile. You can select options including a date range for each type of data. For example, you can select the All date range for history records and a date range for last year, for notes. The good thing is that the date range that you select for each type of data, prints at the beginning of that section of the report. The Company Summary report, which is similar, does not print contacts or notes.

1. Create a company lookup for Ace Pet Store Franchises.

2. Reports ⇒ Company Reports ⇒ Company Comprehensive.

3. On the General tab, select the Current lookup option.

4. On the Activity tab, create a date range for all of 2018.

5. On the Note tab, select the date range All.

6. On the History tab, select the date range 01/01/2017 to 12/31/2018.

7. On the Opportunity tab, create the date range 01/01/2017 to 12/31/2018, then click OK.

Figure 8-13 shows the first page of the report.

**Figure 8-13** First page of the Company Comprehensive report

## Other Reports

The reports that you have run so far in this chapter are just the beginning. Below are two more reports that you many find useful.

### Notes/History Report

This report prints the notes and history records for the contacts that you select, as shown in Figure 8-14.

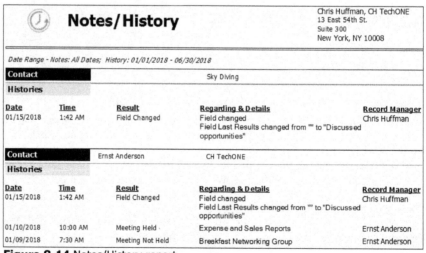

**Figure 8-14** Notes/History report

## Source Of Referrals Report

The report shown in Figure 8-15, is based on the value in the Referred By field.

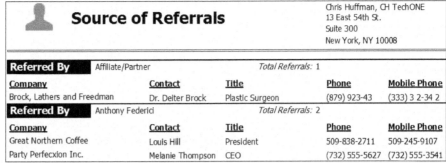

**Figure 8-15** Source of Referrals report

 The first section of the report will list all contact records that do not have data in the Referred By field. If necessary, to get around this, create a lookup to exclude contact records if the Referred By field is blank.

## Reports View

This view displays all of the reports that you have access to. Reports that you run frequently can be added to the Favorites section of the view by, checking the box in the **FAVORITE REPORTS** column shown at the bottom of Figure 8-16.

Table 8-3 explains the buttons on the toolbar.

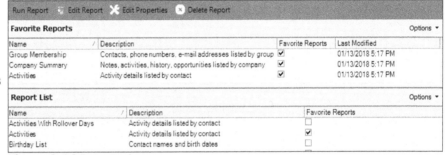

**Figure 8-16** Reports view

The **OPTIONS** button, shown in the upper right corner of Figure 8-16, is used to customize the columns in the Reports view. Each section of the Reports view can be customized individually. Columns can be added, renamed and reordered. At the top of Figure 8-16, the Last Modified column was added to the Favorite Reports section.

| Button | Description |
|---|---|
| Run Report | Displays the Define Filters dialog box to run the selected report. |
| Edit Report | Displays the report in the Report Designer, so that it can be modified. |
| Edit Properties | Opens the dialog box shown in Figure 8-17. The report name displayed in the Reports view can be changed and a description can be added or changed. |
| Delete Report | Is used to delete the report for all users. This option will delete the report from the hard drive. Use this option with caution. |

**Table 8-3** Reports view toolbar buttons explained

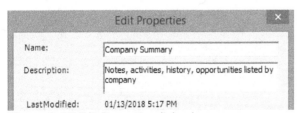

**Figure 8-17** Edit Properties dialog box

## Reports View Related Tasks

The **NEW REPORT TEMPLATE** option shown in Figure 8-18 opens the Report Designer, which you can use to create a new report.

**Figure 8-18** Reports view related tasks

## Printing In ACT!

So far in this chapter, you have learned how to print reports that come with ACT!. Reports are not the only thing that can be printed from ACT!. The remaining exercises in this chapter show you how to print labels, envelopes, an address book and how to use the Quick Print options on the File menu.

### Exercise 8.5: How To Print Labels

There are several label templates that you can select from. There is also a template that you can use to create a custom label.

 If you do not use Avery brand labels, you should be able to find the Avery label size equivalent that you use on your box of labels.

1. File ⇒ Print.

2. Select the **LABELS** Printout type ⇒ Select the Avery 5160 (label size) Paper type ⇒ Click the Print button.

3. Select the appropriate **CREATE REPORT FOR** option on the Define Filters dialog box, then click OK.

   The labels should look similar to the ones shown in Figure 8-19.

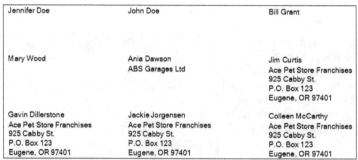

**Figure 8-19** Labels

 **Selecting Where To Start Printing Labels**
Unless you print the same number of names and addresses that the sheet of labels has, you will always have sheets of partially used labels. You can select where the labels should start to print on the sheet.

The options on the **POSITION TAB** (File ⇒ Print ⇒ Select the label size, then click the Print button) on the Define Filters dialog box, shown in Figure 8-20, are used to select the Row and Column that the labels should start printing on. If you need to start printing labels on the first row, third column, you would select the options shown in the figure.

It would be nice if the layout of the sheet of labels was displayed on the dialog box so that you could make sure that you selected the correct row and column before you previewed the labels. If you selected the options shown in Figure 8-20 and previewed the labels, they would look like the ones shown in Figure 8-21. Notice the location difference when compared to the labels shown above in Figure 8-19.

**Figure 8-20** Position tab options

**Figure 8-21** Labels with Position tab options changed

## Exercise 8.6: How To Print Envelopes

In this exercise you will learn how to print envelopes using an envelope template.

1. File ⇒ Print.

2. Select the **ENVELOPES** Printout type, then select the envelope size in the Paper type list shown in Figure 8-22. The options in the **PAPER TYPE** section are the envelope sizes.

 The **ENABLE PREVIEW** option on the Print dialog box, shown in Figure 8-22, may not always work for labels, envelopes and reports. Some people claim that updating their printer drivers allowed this option to work. I did not have this problem. I found that this option can take a while to display the address book.

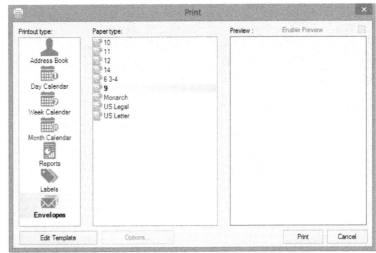

**Figure 8-22** Envelope options

3. Click the Print button.

4. Select the appropriate **CREATE REPORT FOR** option, then click OK. The envelope should look like the one shown in Figure 8-23. Notice that the return address information has been filled in.

   You may have a different addressee on the envelope, depending on which record was displayed before you started this exercise.

**Figure 8-23** Envelope in print preview

5. Close the Print Preview window.

## Exercise 8.7: Using The Quick Print Options

The **QUICK PRINT CURRENT WINDOW** and **QUICK PRINT SELECTED** options are useful if you just want to print what is on the screen. Both of these options, as well as, the Print Current Screen option in the Related Tasks section of many views, displays the dialog box shown in Figure 8-24.

The **SAME FONT IN MY LIST VIEW** option is only available when a list view is displayed. When cleared, you can select the font that you want to use to print the report, by clicking the Font button. If you are going to print the data on a tab, it is probably a good idea to resize the columns on the tab so that the data is not cut off.

The Quick Print options print data exactly as it appears. It is not perfect, but it may handle your basic printing needs.

The steps below show you how to print the data in the current window.

**Figure 8-24** Quick Print Options dialog box

1. Look up the My Record.

2. Make sure the Contact detail view is open, then click on the History tab.

3. File ⇒ Quick Print Current Window. You will see the Quick Print Options dialog box. If you click the Set Options button, you can change the printing options as needed.

If you printed the data on the History tab that is visible, it would look similar to the data shown in Figure 8-25.

| Date | Time | Result | Regarding & Details | | Record Manager | Share With |
|------|------|--------|---------------------|---|----------------|------------|
| 01/15/2018 | 7:24 PM | Contact Deleted | Contact  has been deleted. | | Chris Huffman | CH TechONE[CMP] |
| 01/15/2018 | 3:16 AM | Contact Deleted | Contact Angela Ives has been deleted. | | Chris Huffman | CH TechONE[CMP] |
| 01/15/2018 | 3:16 AM | Contact Deleted | Contact Andy Harrison has been deleted. | | Chris Huffman | CH TechONE[CMP] |

**Figure 8-25** Quick print of the current tab

# WRAP UP OF THE BASICS

In this chapter you will learn about following features in ACT!:

- ☑ Tagging records
- ☑ Copying data
- ☑ Swapping data
- ☑ Supplemental files
- ☑ Promoting secondary contacts
- ☑ Editing notes
- ☑ Filtering notes
- ☑ Record creation options
- ☑ Web Info tab
- ☑ Exporting data to Excel

**No Shame Book Plug #2**
If you have the need to export ACT! data to a file format that Excel can use (like .xls, .xlsx, or .csv), to create PivotTables, PivotCharts or reports, you may find my books on Excel's Power BI tools listed below helpful. This software will give you more control over your ACT! data, once it is in Excel.

Learning Power Pivot For Excel Made Easy
ISBN 978-1-935208-27-3

Learning Power Query And Power Pivot For Excel Made Easy
ISBN 978-1-935208-29-7

Learning Power Query, Power View and Power Map For Excel Made Easy ISBN 978-1-935208-28-0

Once the data is in Excel, it can also be used in software like Tableau and Power BI Desktop ISBN 978-1-935208-34-1. Both have a free version that doesn't expire.

**CHAPTER 9**

## Wrap Up Overview

This chapter concludes the basics of ACT!. The majority of tasks that you will use the most in ACT!, are covered in the first 8 chapters of this book. The remaining chapters contain tasks that you may use a lot when first creating a database, but may use much less frequently over time. The exceptions to this are the opportunity and dashboard functionality. The topics covered in this chapter are important to know, but in my mind were better left out of the previous chapters, because they are not essential to learning and mastering the core concepts of ACT!.

## Understanding The ID/Status And Referred By Fields

The majority of fields on the Contact detail view are pretty straight forward. The fields discussed below may not be as straight forward.

The **ID/STATUS** field is most often used to categorize contacts. This means that you can enter customers, prospects, friends and vendors in the same database. Many people would keep each of these types of contacts in different databases or spreadsheets. Using this field allows you to maintain an unlimited number of types of contacts in the same database. This field provides an informal way to group or categorize contacts. You can add to and edit the options that are in this drop-down list.

When you first enter names of potential customers in the database, you would select the "Prospects" ID/Status if the goal was to get the contact to purchase a product or service from you. If they purchase a product, you would change the value in the ID/Status field to Customer. When the value in this field is changed, an entry is automatically created on the History tab unless you change the option to not create a history record. Having this field generate a history record can be helpful if you need to know when the status of contacts change. During a marketing campaign, you could look up all of the contacts that are still "Prospects" and contact them by phone or email to see whether or not they received your mailing.

What may not be obvious is that the ID/Status field is what ACT! refers to as a **MULTI-SELECT** field. This means that the field can store more than one value. Multi-select fields look like the one shown in Figure 9-1. Open the drop-down list and check the options that you want to categorize the contact by.

The **REFERRED BY** field shown in Figure 9-2, is used as a way to know how the contact was acquired. You could have purchased a mailing list of leads from two companies and need to track which company the lead (contact) came from. You could also have acquired the contacts from a newsletter subscription service. How will you know how each contact was acquired if this field was left blank?

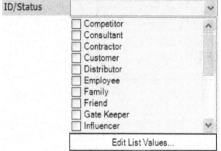

**Figure 9-1** Multi-select drop-down list field

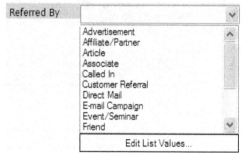

**Figure 9-2** Referred By field options

## Why Are Drop-Down Lists Important?

Drop-down lists contain the most used values that would be entered in a field. Drop-down lists are important because they help ensure that the data in a field is entered the same way for every record. Consistent data is especially helpful if the field will be used in queries, reports, filters or sorting.

For example, one user types "USA" in the Country field and another user types "United States" in the Country field. When you run a query that looks for all records with "USA" in the Country field, the query will skip records that have "United States" in the field. This means that the result of the query will not contain all of the records that it should. In Chapter 3, I had you type USA in the Country field instead of selecting United States from the Country drop-down list. [See Chapter 3, Figure 3-9] If the entries in the drop-down lists do not have the types of information that you need, you can create new entries. Later in the book you will learn how to add and delete entries in drop-down lists.

ACT! has two types of drop-down lists as shown above in Figures 9-1 and 9-2. The drop-down list shown in Figure 9-1 allows more than one option to be selected. The drop-down list shown in Figure 9-2 only allows one option to be selected. This is the more popular type of drop-down list and the one that you are probably the most familiar with. Both types of drop-down lists can be used to select or type in the value that you want. If the value that you enter is already in the list, after typing in enough characters to make the value unique, it will automatically be displayed in the field.

 Drop-down lists are used to add information to a field without typing. You can also type the first letter of the value that you are looking for. Doing this will bring you to the first entry that matches the letter that you typed in. You do not have to open the drop-down list to select an entry if you already know what you are looking for. You can type in the first few letters.

 If you enter text in a field that has a drop-down list like the City, Country or Department fields, the text that you type in may or may not be accepted. It depends on whether the **LIMIT TO LIST** option on the Define Fields dialog box, is enabled for the field. This option will force the user to select an option from the list or leave the field blank. This is done to ensure the accuracy of data in the field.

## Tagging Contacts

There may be times when you need to select contacts that do not have any data in common. Tagging records is used to create a manual lookup. If you have tried to create a lookup for contacts but can't find a common denominator, you can tag the records. To tag a record, enable the tag mode, then manually click on the records. After you tag all of the records that you need, you can create a lookup of the tagged records. With a small database like the demo database that you are using to complete the exercises in this book, manually viewing all of the records to find the ones to tag is bearable. If the database has 5,000 records, it could take a while to find the records that you need, if the records do not have common data.

### Exercise 9.1: Tagging Contacts

In this exercise, you will tag random contact records, add a note to the records and save them as a group. It is not a requirement to group tagged records.

1. Create a group named `My Tagged Record Group`.

2. Display the Contact list view ⇒ Sort the contacts by state ⇒ Check the **TAG MODE** option, illustrated in Figure 9-3.

**Figure 9-3** Tag options

The **LOOK FOR** field is used to search for a contact based on the field that the list is sorted on. If the Contact List is sorted on the Company field, you would enter the company name that you were looking for in this field.
The **EDIT MODE** option is used to modify records in the list view.
The **TAG MODE** option turns the tag functionality on and off.
The **TAG ALL** button will mark all of the contacts displayed in the list as tagged.
The **UNTAG ALL** button will remove the tag from all of the selected contacts.
The **LOOKUP SELECTED** button creates a lookup of the records that have been tagged.
The **OMIT SELECTED** button is used to remove the tagged contacts from the view. This option does not delete the records from the database.

 If you click on a record that you do not need to tag, click on the record again to remove the tag. When in tag mode, records that are tagged are highlighted, as shown in Figure 9-4.

| | | Company | Contact | Phone | Extension | Title | Address 1 | Address 2 | City | State / | ZIP Code |
|---|---|---|---|---|---|---|---|---|---|---|---|
| | | Bick's Longhorns | Jordan Benedict | 432-730-5678 | | | Two Cavalry Row | | Marfa | TX | 79843 |
| | | Making Technology | Anthony Quixno | (877) 661-5200 | | | PO Box 270514 | | Dallas | TX | 75207 |
| | | American Dreams | Hayleigh Frieda | (972) 555-8442 | | Vice President of Pr | 1113 Grainey | Suite A | Allen | TX | 75002 |
| | | Circle Photography | | (214) 555-4652 | | | 2256 Circle Lane | Suite 4 | Dallas | TX | 75214 |
| | | Making Technology | Rich Making | (877) 661-5200 | | Founder;President | PO Box 270514 | | Dallas | TX | 75207 |
| | | Bick's Longhorns | Lesley Benedict | 432-730-5678 | | | Two Cavalry Row | | Marfa | TX | 79843 |

**Figure 9-4** Tagged records

3. Tag the first record in each of the following states: AZ, CA and LA.

4. Click the **LOOKUP SELECTED** button.

At this point, you could add the same note to the contact records that are tagged, create an activity that included these records, save them as a group, subgroup, company or division.

5. Click the Note button on the Global toolbar ⇒ In the **DETAILS** field, type This contact is a tagged record that is in the Tagged Record Group.

6. Click the button at the end of the **SHARE WITH** field on the Insert Note dialog box ⇒ Click OK on the Public Note message box.

7. Select the My Tagged Record Group and add it to the list on the right ⇒ Click OK. The dialog box should have the options shown in Figure 9-5 ⇒ Click OK to close the Insert Note dialog box.

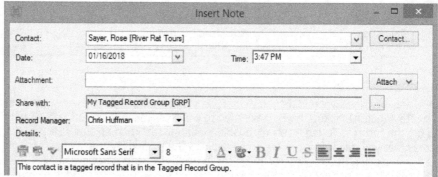

**Figure 9-5** Insert Note dialog box

8. Right-click on the tagged records and select Add Contacts to Group ⇒ Select the My Tagged Record Group option.

9. Click OK ⇒ Clear the Tag Mode option. Now when you need to access these records, you can select the group that they are in. If you view the tagged group, you will see the three contacts.

## Using The Omit Selected Option

If there are records that you do not want to view, you can remove them from the list view. Removing records from a view does not delete them from the database. Using the Omit Selected option has the same effect as creating a lookup. The difference is that the Omit Selected option does it record by record, manually. To restore the records, lookup all of the contacts.

1. On the Contact list view, display all of the contacts.

2. Click on the first record in the Contact list view. The record should now be highlighted.

3. Click the **OMIT SELECTED** button on the toolbar. The record should not be visible in the window. You will see that the record count has decreased by one.

## Copying Data From One Field To Another

You may have a need to copy data from one field to another. Instead of doing this manually, record by record, you can create a lookup for the records that you want to copy the data to, then use the **COPY FIELD** command. Not creating a lookup first means that data will be copied to every record in the database. It is not a requirement to create a lookup first.

## Exercise 9.2: How To Copy Data

In this exercise you will look up the Liberty Savings company and copy the data in the Title field to the User 6 field.

1. Create a lookup for the Liberty Savings company.

2. On the Contact detail view, Edit ⇒ Copy Field.

3. Open the **COPY CONTENTS OF** drop-down list and select the Title field, then open the **TO** drop-down list and select the User 6 field.

   You should have the options shown in Figure 9-6.

   Click OK.

**Figure 9-6** Copy Data dialog box

4. Click Yes when you see the Replace/Swap/Copy message, which indicates that all of the records in the current lookup will be modified. You will see the message shown in Figure 9-7.

   This message lets you know that the **TARGET** field (User 6) size is smaller than the **SOURCE** field (Title). If the target field is smaller, some of the data in the source field will be truncated when it is copied to the target field.

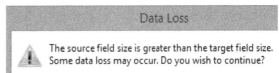

**Figure 9-7** Data Loss message

5. Click Yes on the Data Loss message window. Normally, you would not want to have data loss and would click No, if you see the message shown above in Figure 9-7.

### View The Copied Data

6. Click the Contact detail view button.

   On the User Fields tab, you will see the title in the User 6 field, as shown in Figure 9-8.

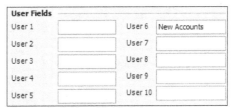

**Figure 9-8** User Fields tab

### Swapping Data

Edit ⇒ Swap Field, opens the dialog box shown in Figure 9-9. This command is used to swap the data in one field with data from another field.

Like the Copy Field command, if the target field is smaller, all of the data will not be copied to the target field. You may find that from time to time, using this feature will cause ACT! to hang (stop working).

**Figure 9-9** Swap Data dialog box

 It is recommended that you back up the database before using the **COPY FIELD** or **SWAP FIELD** command.

### What Are Supplemental Files?

Supplemental files are files that ACT! uses that are not saved in the database (**.ADF**) file. The database file only stores the data that you see in the views. Examples of supplemental files include attachments, templates, reports and layouts. Many of these supplemental files are installed when ACT! is installed. ACT! has two supplemental file types, as explained below.

① **DATABASE** This file type includes the templates, reports and layout files that you see when you first open ACT!. These files are only available when ACT! is open. They are stored in folders. The default main folder name is **NAME OF DATABASE-DATABASE FILES**. Under this folder, are folders for each type of file. [See Chapter 1, Figure 1-13] If you copy a database, these files are also copied. If the ACT! database is stored on a server, more than likely, the database supplemental files are stored on the same server.

② **PERSONAL** This file type includes files that are not associated to records in the database. The ACT! backup utility does not back up personal files, when a database is backed up. If you create a file that you do not want to share with other users of the database, save it in your personal supplemental folder. The other option is to create a folder outside of the default ACT! folders and save files that you do not want to share in that folder. An example of this would be the folder that you created for this book.

### What Are Secondary Contacts And Why Should I Use Them?

Secondary contacts are contacts that are associated to a primary contact in the database. Examples of secondary contacts include an alternate contact if the primary contact is unavailable or a primary contacts assistant. You can also create secondary contact records to store the primary contacts assistant, spouse and children. Keep the following two things in mind when creating secondary contact records.

    ① Secondary contact records cannot be used in a mail merge using the wizard.
    ② Activity, note, opportunity and history records cannot be created or associated with secondary contact records.

It would be helpful if the Secondary Contacts tab would automatically change colors as soon as one secondary contact was added to a primary contact record. That would make it easier to know if there were any secondary contacts associated to the primary contact.

### Promoting A Secondary Contact

There may be a time when a secondary contact needs to become a primary contact. Instead of creating a new primary contact record for the secondary contact (which would also leave the secondary contact record in place if you did not delete it) you can promote the secondary contact to a primary contact, by following the steps below. When a secondary contact is promoted, it is automatically deleted from the primary contact record.

1. Click on the secondary contact that you want to promote ⇒ Click the **PROMOTE** button on the Secondary Contacts tab. You will see the dialog box shown in Figure 9-10.

   The **DUPLICATE DATA** option will copy data from the primary contacts record (like the company name and address fields) to the record that you are promoting.

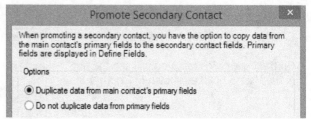

**Figure 9-10** Promote Secondary Contact dialog box

2. Select the data option that you need, then click OK. You will see that the record is no longer on the Secondary Contacts tab and has become a contact.

### Deleting A Secondary Contact

If a secondary contact should no longer be associated to the primary contact and you currently do not have a replacement contact, you should delete the secondary contact by following the steps below. For now, you can just read the steps to become familiar with the process.

1. On the Secondary Contacts tab, right-click on the secondary contact that you want to delete, then select **DELETE SECONDARY CONTACT**.

2. Click Yes to permanently delete the secondary contact.

### Notes And History Tabs

You have learned a little about these tabs and what types of data they have. You will see that they have a lot in common.

### Notes Tab

The Notes tab contains details including business and personal information about contacts, companies and groups. The goal of entering notes is to build a profile of your relationship with the contact, company or group. Notes can be edited unless the **ALLOW NOTES EDITING** option is not enabled. [See Chapter 2, Admin Tab Preferences]

The Notes tab may be under utilized because many people are use to writing messages on a note pad or on a loose piece of paper or worse, think that they will remember details of a phone call or meeting. Days later when they need this information, they cannot find the piece of paper that it was written on or they mentally draw a blank. I fall into the category of not being able to find the envelope that I wrote the information on. If you start off using the Notes tab when you first start using ACT!, the easier it will be to continue the good habit.

Whether you think that you are going to use ACT! daily or not, it may help if you open ACT! when you first turn your computer on. What I do is open the Contact list view and sort it by last name, then when I need to add a note, I do not have to wait to open ACT! and find the contact record. By the time I waited for ACT! to open, I would forget what I wanted to put in the note. <smile>

### Attaching A Document To An Existing Note

Chapter 3 covered how to add an attachment to contact records and how to attach a document on the Documents tab. Chapter 6 covered how to attach a document to a group record. Attaching a document to an existing note is similar. On the Notes tab, open the note that you want to attach a document to, then click the Attach button.

### Copy A Note From One Contact Record To Another

If you attach a note to a contact record and want to attach the note to a different contact record, you can, by following the steps below. Both records need to be displayed before you start step 1.

1. On the Notes tab, click on the note that you want to copy, then press **CTRL+C**.

2. Click on the Notes tab of the contact record that you want to copy the note to, then press **CTRL+V**.

### Editing A Shared Note

If you edit a note that is shared, you will see the Edit Shared Note dialog box, when you click OK after editing the note. The options on this dialog box are to save the changes for all contacts that are associated with the note or to create a new note for the contact record that you opened the note from, to edit. You can try this by editing the note with green text, that you created in Chapter 6 for George and Mary Bailey.

### Filtering Notes

Over time, contact, company or group records can accumulate a lot of notes. While they can be sorted, it may be more effective to filter the notes.

If you right-click in the detail section of the Notes tab on the Contact or Company detail view and select **FILTER NOTES**, you will see the dialog box shown in Figure 9-11 on the Contact detail view and Figure 9-12 on the Company detail view.

While filters narrow and reduce the number of records displayed (in this case notes), filters can be tricky and give the appearance that records are lost. If you cannot find records, check the filter options on the tabs and change them to display all of the records.

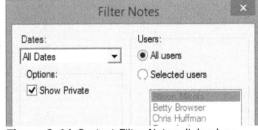

**Figure 9-11** Contact Filter Notes dialog box

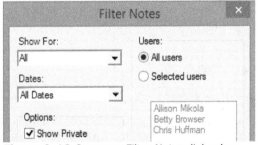

**Figure 9-12** Company Filter Notes dialog box

### History Tab

You have already viewed records on the History tab for the My Record. History records display changes that you have made to records in the database. The History tab picks up where the Notes tab leaves off. The entries on the History tab are a chronological recap of the communication and events for contacts, companies, groups and opportunities. The majority of entries on this tab come from other tabs, but you can manually create a History record.

The History tab also displays completed activities/tasks. Some entries on the History tab are created automatically when you delete a contact, when the Last Results field is updated, create a mail merge or change the value in the ID/Status field. The date and time are automatically added to each entry that is added to the History tab.

You can add an entry to the History tab from any detail view, by right-clicking in the detail section of the History tab and selecting **RECORD HISTORY**, on the shortcut menu shown in Figure 9-13. You will see the dialog box shown in Figure 9-14. It looks similar to the Schedule Activity dialog box.

The **FOLLOW-UP** button, on the New History dialog box, opens the Schedule Activity dialog box. You can also create a history record from the list views.

> **New History Dialog Box**
> In ACT! 2010 and earlier, this dialog box was called the **RECORD HISTORY DIALOG BOX**.

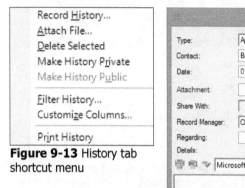

**Figure 9-13** History tab shortcut menu

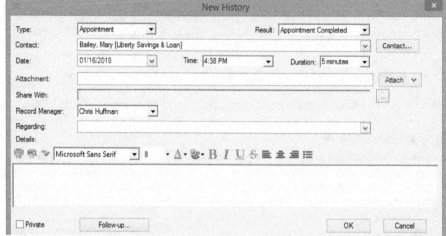

**Figure 9-14** New History dialog box

## Automatic Additions To The History Tab

As you just learned, you can manually add records to the History tab. By default, ACT! has designated the ID/Status and Last Results fields as history fields when you create a new database. When the data in a history field is changed, a record is automatically created and added to the History tab. You will learn how to designate a field as a history field. [See Chapter 14, Field Behavior Options]

## Finding Records On The History Tab

At the top of the Companies History tab shown in Figure 9-15, there are options that you can use to find specific records as explained below.

**Figure 9-15** Companies History tab

## The Dates Field

The options in this drop-down list are used to select the date range for the records that you want to view on the History tab. As time goes on, you will have more and more entries on the History tab, but you may not want to see all of them all the time.

You can reduce the number of records displayed by selecting a date range. You can also create a **CUSTOM** date range, to select history records like you can to create reports. The same Select Date Range dialog box is used.

## History Record Types

The History record type options are shown in Figure 9-16. The options include the opportunity histories and system changes options. Within each type you can select specific items to display or hide on the History tab, as illustrated. There are several types of history records that you can view, as explained in Table 9-1.

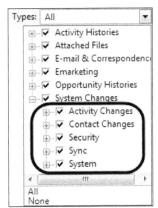

| Type | This Type Of History Record Is Created When . . . |
|---|---|
| Activity Histories | You change the value in a field that has been designated to automatically have a history record created. |
| Attached Files | A document is attached to a contact, company or group record. |
| E-mails & Correspondence | You send an email message. |
| Opportunity Histories | An opportunity or quote is created. |
| System Changes | One of the options illustrated in Figure 9-16 changes. |

**Table 9-1** History record options explained

**Figure 9-16** History record options

## Keyword Field

This field is used to search the Regarding & Details field. Type in the word or phrase that you want to search for, then click the Go button.

## Select Users Button

This option is useful if more than one person is using the database. The dialog box shown in Figure 9-17 is used to select which users entries you want to view on the History tab.

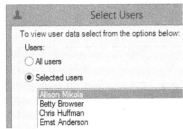

To select multiple users calendars to view, select the first user, that you want to see the calendar for, then press and hold down the Shift key ⇒ Click on the other users names. The maximum number of users that you can select is 10.

**Figure 9-17** Select Users dialog box

## Using The New History Tool

This tool is used to create a history record for tasks that you complete that do not have a scheduled activity. This is helpful when you need to remember something like an email or phone conversation that you had with a contact, that was not scheduled. History records can also be created from the company and group views.

 **Merge Documents And History Records**
Prior to ACT! 2010, a history record was automatically generated when merged documents were printed in Microsoft Word. That does not happen now. The work around is posted in the knowledge base on act.com. Search the ACT! knowledge base for Answer ID 26851, "No prompt for history recording when printing merged . . .".

## How To Open The New History Tool

Earlier in Figure 9-14, you saw the New History dialog box. You can open this dialog box by doing any of the following:

① Pressing the Ctrl+H keys.
② On the History tab of a detail view, right-click and select Record History.
③ On the History tab of a detail view, click the **NEW HISTORY** button.
④ Click the History button on the Global toolbar.

## Create A History Record For Multiple Contacts

Just like you can schedule one activity for multiple contacts at the same time, you can create a history record for multiple contacts at the same time. There are two ways to accomplish this, as explained below.

① Open the New History dialog box ⇒ Click the Contact button ⇒ Select the contacts that you want to create the history record for.

②  Tag the records that you want to create the history record for, then open the New History dialog box. Earlier in this chapter you learned how to tag records.

## Edit History Records

After viewing the history records that ACT! creates, you may decide that they need more information or that the information needs to be changed. If this is the case, double-click on the history record that you want to change. You will see the dialog box shown in Figure 9-18. Make the changes that are needed, then click OK.

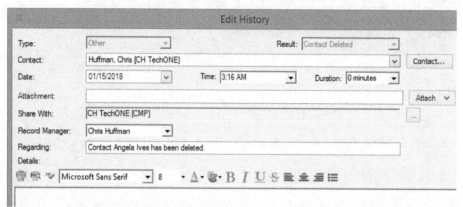

**Figure 9-18** Edit History dialog box

## Edit A History Record Associated With Multiple Contacts

After you create a history record that is associated with multiple contacts, you may have the need to change it. After you make the change, you will see the dialog box shown in Figure 9-19. These options are used to select whether to save the change for the current contact or for all contacts associated with the history record.

Select the option that fits your need, then click OK. These options are similar to the options on the Edit Shared Note dialog box.

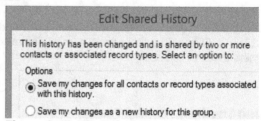

**Figure 9-19** Edit Shared History dialog box

## Preventing History Records From Being Deleted

You can delete history records. If you are the only person that is using the database, it may not be necessary to prevent history records from being deleted. If other people will be using the database, you may want to consider preventing history records from being deleted by clearing the **ALLOW HISTORY EDITING** option on the Admin tab on the Preferences dialog box.

## Documents Tab

If you will attach a lot of documents to contact, company and group records, this section will give you a better understanding of the features that the Documents tab offers. The Documents tab is the repository for attachments in the database. Unless an attachment is marked as private, all users of the database will have access it. The attachments are usually stored in the Attachments folder for the database.

Figure 9-20 shows the Documents tab with several types of attached documents. The first column displays the icon for the file type.

The **FILE TYPE** column will automatically be filled in as long as the file type is one that ACT! recognizes. Table 9-2 explains the buttons on the Documents tab.

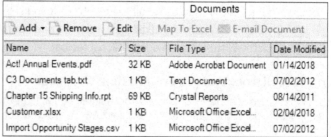

**Figure 9-20** Documents tab

| Button | Description |
|---|---|
| Add | Attach a document. If the FILE option is selected, remote database users can access the document. |
| Remove | Delete the selected attachment. This action deletes the document from the Documents folder. (1) |
| Edit | Opens the attached document so that it can be viewed or edited. To view or edit the document, you have to have the software that the document was created in, installed on your computer. For example, in Figure 9-20 above, the third document listed was created in Crystal Reports. If you do not have this software installed, you will not be able to open this document. |
| Map To Excel | Map fields in the database to fields in an Excel spreadsheet. |
| E-mail Document | Used to send the selected file via email. |

**Table 9-2** Documents tab buttons explained

(1) If you do not have another copy of the document on your hard drive, the file cannot be retrieved after it is deleted from the Database Supplemental File System. The file is only deleted from inside the ACT! environment. For example, Figure 9-20 shows the Ch3 Documents tab file. Deleting the file here, does not delete the original copy of the file that is in the ACT Book folder. Unlike many Windows applications, deleting files from inside of ACT!, does not send the deleted file to the Recycle Bin in Windows.

You can also right-click on the document (on the Documents tab) that you want to delete and select REMOVE, as shown in Figure 9-21. When you select this option you will see the message shown in Figure 9-22. Click Yes to delete the document. You can also delete an attachment from the History tab by right-clicking on the file and selecting DELETE SELECTED, as shown earlier in Figure 9-13.

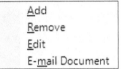

**Figure 9-21** Documents tab shortcut menu options

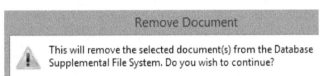

**Figure 9-22** Remove Document message

## Record Creation Options

The options shown in Figure 9-23 are used to make new contact, company, group and opportunity records default to public or private. If you know that one of these types of records needs to be private, most or all of the time, select the PRIVATE option on this dialog box.

Tools ⇒ Preferences ⇒ Startup tab ⇒ Record Creation Options button, opens this dialog box.

**Figure 9-23** Record Creation Options dialog box

## Web Info Tab

The options shown in Figure 9-24 are used to search and view web content information for a contact or company. This tab is an internal browser (to ACT!) that is used to display web pages. The options are used to display information from web sites like Yahoo™, Google™, Facebook™ and more, that the contact or company is listed on, or is a member of.

Clicking the EDIT LINKS button shown in the figure, opens the dialog box shown in Figure 9-25. You can add and edit the links that will display on the Web Info tab.

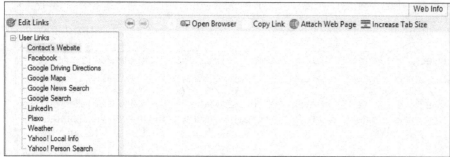

**Figure 9-24** Web Info tab

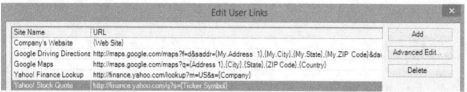

**Figure 9-25** Edit User Links dialog box

## Exporting Data To Excel

If you need to work with contact, opportunity, company or group data in a spreadsheet, you can export the data to Excel.

 The **EXPORT TO EXCEL** option is only available on the Contact, Company, Group, Task List, History List or Opportunity list views. To view the exported records, you need to have Excel installed. The only columns that are exported are the ones that are displayed on the view. If you want to export data that is not currently displayed on the view, add the columns of data that you want to export to the view before exporting data, then remove the columns that you added, if you no longer need them in the view, once the export is completed.

## Exercise 9.3: Export Contact Data To Excel

In this exercise you will export all of the contacts for a specific company to Excel.

1. Create a lookup for the `CH TechONE` company. Nine records should be displayed.

2. Click the **EXPORT CURRENT LIST TO EXCEL** button on the toolbar. The records from the lookup will be exported to Excel, which will automatically open and display the records, as shown in Figure 9-26. When you are finished viewing the spreadsheet close Excel.

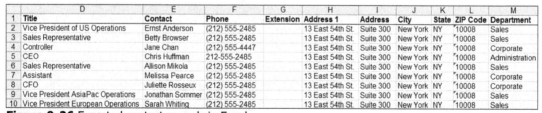

| | D | E | F | G | H | I | J | K | L | M |
|---|---|---|---|---|---|---|---|---|---|---|
| 1 | Title | Contact | Phone | Extension | Address 1 | Address | City | State | ZIP Code | Department |
| 2 | Vice President of US Operations | Ernst Anderson | (212) 555-2485 | | 13 East 54th St. | Suite 300 | New York | NY | ˹10008 | Sales |
| 3 | Sales Representative | Betty Browser | (212) 555-2485 | | 13 East 54th St. | Suite 300 | New York | NY | ˹10008 | Sales |
| 4 | Controller | Jane Chan | (212) 555-4447 | | 13 East 54th St. | Suite 300 | New York | NY | ˹10008 | Corporate |
| 5 | CEO | Chris Huffman | 212-555-2485 | | 13 East 54th St. | Suite 300 | New York | NY | ˹10008 | Administration |
| 6 | Sales Representative | Allison Mikola | (212) 555-2485 | | 13 East 54th St. | Suite 300 | New York | NY | ˹10008 | Sales |
| 7 | Assistant | Melissa Pearce | (212) 555-2485 | | 13 East 54th St. | Suite 300 | New York | NY | ˹10008 | Corporate |
| 8 | CFO | Juliette Rosseux | (212) 555-2485 | | 13 East 54th St. | Suite 300 | New York | NY | ˹10008 | Corporate |
| 9 | Vice President AsiaPac Operations | Jonathan Sommer | (212) 555-2485 | | 13 East 54th St. | Suite 300 | New York | NY | ˹10008 | Sales |
| 10 | Vice President European Operations | Sarah Whiting | (212) 555-2485 | | 13 East 54th St. | Suite 300 | New York | NY | ˹10008 | Sales |

**Figure 9-26** Exported contact records in Excel

 You can save the workbook (in .xls, .xlsx or .csv format) that has the exported data and use it in other software packages, like Tableau, Power BI Desktop and QlikView.

## Importing Data

There may be times when there is data in a file that needs to be added to an ACT! database. Data can be imported from a variety of sources including Microsoft Outlook and Excel. Keep in mind that some data sources can not be directly imported into ACT!. Previous versions of ACT! 3x-6x databases and Microsoft Access databases have to be converted before the data can be imported.

The categories of data in an ACT! database have rules about where imported data can come from. For example, contacts and companies can be imported from another ACT! database, a .txt or .csv file, while activities can only be imported from another ACT! database.

## Use The Import Wizard

This is the tool that is used to bring data into an ACT! database. The steps below show the basics of using the wizard.

1.  Open the ACT! database that you want to add data to.

2.  File ⇒ Import ⇒ On the first Import Wizard screen, click Next.

3.  On screen 2, open the drop-down list and select the type of file that has the data that you want to import.

4.  Click the Browse button and select the file that has the data to import.

5.  If necessary, enter the user login information.

    You should have the necessary fields filled in on the screen shown in Figure 9-27.

    Click Next.

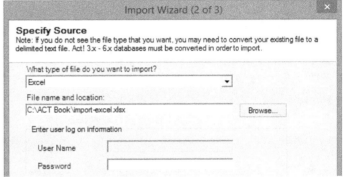

**Figure 9-27** Import Wizard Specify Source screen

6.  On the screen shown in Figure 9-28, select the type of records that you want to import, then click Next.

Only one type can be imported at a time, when using Excel. Figure 9-29 shows the options available when an ACT! database will be used to import from. As shown at the top of Figures 9-28 and 9-29, the number of wizard screens vary, depending on the file type that the data is being imported from.

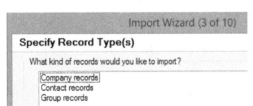

**Figure 9-28** Specify Record Type(s) screen for an Excel file

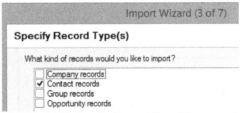

**Figure 9-29** Specify Record Type(s) screen for an ACT! Database

The screen shown in Figure 9-30 is used to select whether or not you need to customize the import. If Yes, select the **CUSTOM IMPORT** option.

Customization includes what fields to use to check for duplicate records.

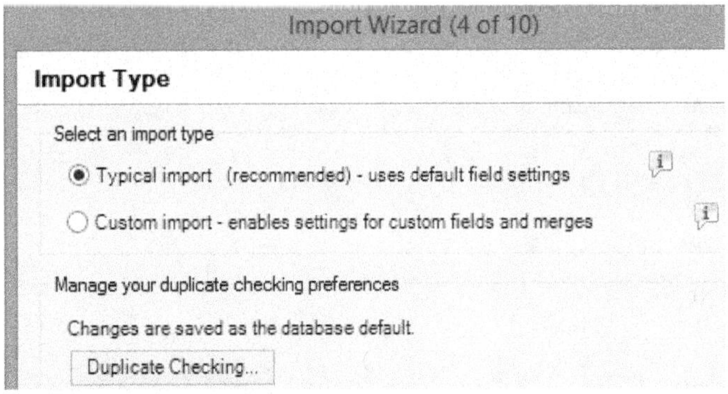

**Figure 9-30** Import Type screen

7.  Select the import type option, then click Next.

Figures 9-31 to 9-35 are only available when the Custom import option is selected on the screen shown above in Figure 9-30.

Figure 9-31 shows the import options when Excel is the data source.

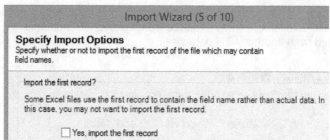

**Figure 9-31** Specify Import Options screen for Excel

The screen shown in Figure 9-32 is used to map the fields in the import file to fields in a table in the ACT! database. ACT! matches as many fields as it can. Fields that it cannot match do not have a field name in the "To this field" column.

To match an import field to a field in the ACT! database, click at the end of the column on the right to display the drop-down list, illustrated in Figure 9-32. It is not a requirement to import all of the fields in the import file.

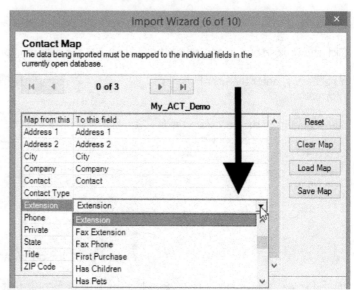

**Figure 9-32** Contact Map screen

To preview the data as illustrated in Figure 9-33, use the left and right (aka VCR buttons) arrow buttons on either side of the record count.

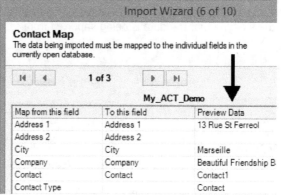

**Figure 9-33** Preview Data illustrated

8.  Map the fields as needed, then click Next.

The options shown in Figure 9-34 are used to select the merge options.

Clicking the **CONTACT** button (or the Group or Company button), opens the dialog box shown in Figure 9-35.

The options are used to select what to do when there are matching records in the import file and ACT! database.

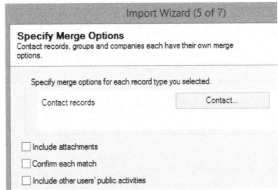

**Figure 9-34** Specify Merge Options screen

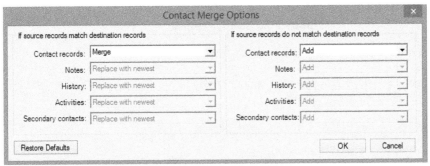

**Figure 9-35** Contact Merge Options dialog box

9. Select the merge options as needed, then click Next.

   Figure 9-36 displays the options that were selected on the wizard. If you need to change something, click the Back button.

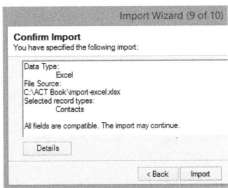

**Figure 9-36** Confirm Import screen

10. Click the Import button. When the import is finished, you will see a message letting you know that the import is complete. When you see the import is complete screen on the wizard, the results of the import are displayed.

Clicking the **VIEW IMPORT LOG** link on this screen, opens the dialog box shown in Figure 9-37.

It displays how many records were added or merged and whether or not there were any errors.

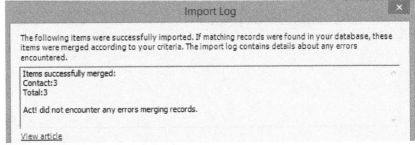

**Figure 9-37** Import Log dialog box

## Exporting Data

Earlier in this chapter, you learned how to export the data displayed on the Contact List view. File ⇒ Export, opens the wizard. The exporting option covered in this section provides a lot more control.

The Export Wizard has many of the same screens that the Import Wizard has. If you do not want to export all of the data, create a lookup to display the records that you want to export before opening the Export Wizard.

On the screen shown in Figure 9-38, select the type of file that you want to export the data to.

The destination file in the File name and location field, does not have to exist prior to opening this wizard.

You can create it by typing in the path and file name. You can also select the path and file name of an existing file, by clicking the Browse button.

Selecting the latter means that you will be over writing the existing file.

**Figure 9-38** Specify Destination screen

If **ACT! DATABASE** is selected as the Export file type, you will see the options, shown in Figure 9-39.

If **TEXT DELIMITED** is selected as the Export file type, you will see the options shown in Figure 9-40. Use this option if you want to export data to an Excel (.xls, .xlsx or .csv) or .txt file.

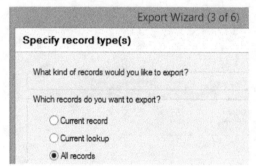

**Figure 9-39** Specify record type(s) screen for an ACT! database

**Figure 9-40** Specify record type(s) screen for a Text Delimited files

1.  Select the file type that you will export the data to ⇒ On the screen shown earlier in Figure 9-38, select an existing file or type in the location and name of the file that you want to create ⇒ Click Next.

2.  Select the records that you want to export on the Specify record type(s) screen, then click Next.

### Text Delimited File Export Options

The screens shown in this section are specifically for a text delimited export file.

Figure 9-41 shows additional export options for a text delimited file.

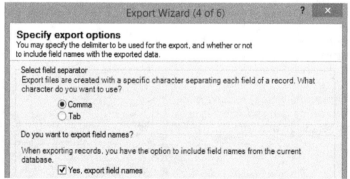

**Figure 9-41** Additional export options for text delimited files

The options shown in Figure 9-42 are used to select which fields in the ACT! database will be exported and the order that they will be exported in, to a text file. To change the order, you have to open the drop-down list for each field and select the field that you want.

For example, if you want the contact name to be the first field, open the Address 1 drop-down list and select Contact. Then repeat this process for each field that you want to use. When finished, delete (remove) the remaining fields.

By default, the fields are exported in alphabetical order. I found using this screen tiresome. I exported all of the fields, then in Excel, deleted the columns that I did not need, then rearranged the remaining columns.

**Figure 9-42** Contact Map options for a text delimited export file

### ACT! Database Export Options

The screens shown in this section are specifically for a ACT! database export file.

Figure 9-43 shows the Contact Map options for an ACT! database export file. It works the same as the Contact Map screen in the Import Wizard.

Figure 9-44 shows the merge options, which work the same as the ones on the Import Wizard.

**Figure 9-43** Contact Map options for a ACT! database export file

**Figure 9-44** Merge options

3. Select the export options based on the export file type selected.

### Review The Export Options

Figure 9-45 shows the export options that were selected on the wizard.

**Figure 9-45** Export options that were selected

4. Click Finish to export the data.

## Move Database Options

File ⇒ Move Database, displays the options shown in Figure 9-46.

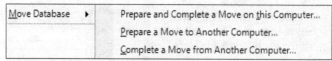

**Figure 9-46** Move Database options

The options are used to move the currently selected database to another computer. The options are explained below.

① **PREPARE AND COMPLETE A MOVE ON THIS COMPUTER** Select this option when you need to move a database from one location to another on the same hard drive.

② **PREPARE A MOVE TO ANOTHER COMPUTER** Select this option when you need to move a database on one computer to another computer.

③ **COMPLETE A MOVE FROM ANOTHER COMPUTER** Use this option after using option 2 above. This option is used on the computer that the database is being moved to.

# OPPORTUNITIES

Overview

In this chapter, you will learn about the following tasks, which will show you how to create and manage opportunities.

☑ Schedule a follow up activity for an opportunity
☑ How to edit the Product List
☑ How to view an opportunity
☑ How to associate an opportunity to a company
☑ Lookup opportunity options
☑ Export opportunities to Excel
☑ Creating quotes
☑ Change the status of an opportunity
☑ Opportunity reports
☑ Create opportunity graphs and pipelines
☑ Customize products and processes
☑ Creating process lists and stages
☑ Importing products

## What Is An Opportunity?

An opportunity is a sale in progress, meaning there is some likelihood that the contact may make a purchase. Opportunities automate the sales process. You can run reports that display what stage opportunities are in and which opportunities that you have the best chance of turning into a sale. Like activities, opportunities create history records when they are created or when certain fields like the Status or Close Date is changed.

## Tracking Potential Sales

ACT! provides a way to manage and track potential sales through opportunities. The tracking process is quite extensive. You can track opportunities through each stage of the process. There are six stages that you can monitor in the CHT1 Sales process, that comes with ACT!. You can track opportunities by dollar amount, sales rep, status and more. You can also customize the opportunity process and products that come with ACT!. You can create your own opportunity processes and import processes that you create in another software package. Opportunities can be exported, which will allow you to analyze the data in different ways.

## Opportunity Detail View

The Opportunity detail view shown in Figure 10-1 is used to create and edit sales. The options are explained in detail in Exercise 10.1, as you create an opportunity. Four of the tabs are specific to opportunities. The data types on these tabs are explained below.

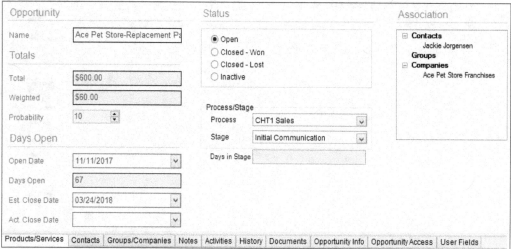

**Figure 10-1** Opportunity detail view

## Opportunity Detail View Tabs

① **PRODUCTS/SERVICES** This tab stores the basic information about the opportunity, as shown in Figure 10-2.

② **OPPORTUNITY INFO** Figure 10-3 shows the fields on this tab. The fields that you may want to fill in when creating an opportunity are the Referred By and Competitor fields. Entering data on this tab is optional.

③ **OPPORTUNITY ACCESS** The options on this tab are the same as the ones on the Contact Access tab. [See Chapter 3, Figure 3-27]

④ **USER FIELDS** Some of the fields on this tab, shown in Figure 10-4, are similar to fields on the User Fields tab on the Contact detail view because most of them have the character field type, which is free form. You can use the fields to store data that does not fit in any of the other fields on the Opportunity view. Notice that the first two fields are drop-down lists. They are explained below. You can rename these fields in the layout.

**Products/Services**

| Name | / | Item # | Quantity | Cost | Price | Adjusted Price | Discount | Subtotal |
|------|---|--------|----------|------|-------|----------------|----------|----------|
| Service Contract | | SC | 1.00 | $750.00 | $2,000.00 | $2,000.00 | 0.0000000000% | $2,000.00 |
| TechONE System | | T1SYS | 1.00 | $5,000.00 | $12,000.00 | $12,000.00 | 0.0000000000% | $12,000.00 |
| TWO Component | | TWO | 2.00 | $1,750.00 | $4,000.00 | $4,000.00 | 0.0000000000% | $8,000.00 |

**Figure 10-2** Products/Services tab

**Products/Services Tab Subtotal Field**
I am not sure why the subtotal field is so far to the right and can't be resized like the other columns on this tab can. I had to make the workspace smaller to be able to include the subtotal field in the screen shot above. The other option is to move the Subtotal field to the left, before the Discount field.

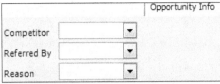

**Figure 10-3** Opportunity Info tab

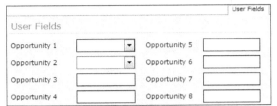

**Figure 10-4** User Fields tab

The options in the Opportunity Field 1 drop-down list, shown in Figure 10-5, are different types of payments that can be accepted to pay for the order.

The Opportunity Field 2 has the Date data type by default. Figure 10-6 shows the calendar for a date field. This field can be used for a date that you need to capture, that is not in any of the other opportunity date fields.

**Figure 10-5** Opportunity 1 field drop-down list options

**Figure 10-6** Opportunity 2 field drop-down list

## Opportunity Detail View Toolbar

Figure 10-7 shows the Opportunity detail view toolbar. Table 10-1 explains the buttons on the toolbar.

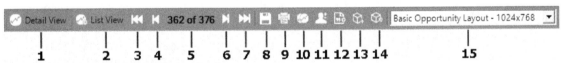

**Figure 10-7** Opportunity detail view toolbar

| Button | Description |
|--------|-------------|
| 1 | Displays the opportunities in the detail view. |
| 2 | Displays the opportunities in the list view. |
| 3 | Displays the first opportunity. |
| 4 | Displays the previous opportunity. |
| 5 | Displays the number of the record currently displayed and the total number of records. |
| 6 | Displays the next opportunity. |
| 7 | Displays the last opportunity. |
| 8 | Save the changes. |
| 9 | Opens the Quick Print Options dialog box. |
| 10 | Duplicates the current opportunity. |
| 11 | Is used to add or remove contacts for the opportunity. |
| 12 | Creates a quote for the opportunity. |
| 13 | Is used to create or edit a product that you could use in the opportunity. |
| 14 | Opens the Manage Product List dialog box. |
| 15 | Is used to select a layout. |

**Table 10-1** Opportunity detail view toolbar buttons explained

## Opportunity List View

You have the option of viewing all or some of the opportunities for contacts that you have access to. You can filter opportunities. You can also print opportunities, as well as, customize the Opportunity list view.

1. Click the Opportunities button on the Navigation Pane. Clicking on a contact name will open the Contact detail view for the contact.

## Opportunity List View Toolbar

Figure 10-8 shows the Opportunity list view toolbar. Table 10-2 explains the buttons on the toolbar, that are not on the Opportunity detail view toolbar.

**Figure 10-8** Opportunity list view toolbar

 The buttons for E-Marketing and Business Info Services that were available on the Opportunity list view toolbar in ACT! 2012 were removed in ACT! 2013.

| Button | Is Used To . . . |
|--------|------------------|
| 1 | Create an opportunity pipeline. |
| 2 | Create an opportunity graph. |
| 3 | Open the Manage Product List dialog box. |
| 4 | Create an automatic lookup of contacts associated to the opportunities that are selected. |
| 5 | Customize the columns at the bottom of the Opportunity list view. |
| 6 | Export the opportunities that are displayed in the view to Excel. |

**Table 10-2** Opportunity list view toolbar buttons explained

## Using The Opportunity List Filters

The filter options for the Opportunity list view are shown in Figure 10-9. They are helpful if there are a lot of opportunities displayed and you only need to see certain ones. Like other views, you can sort the data on the bottom half of the view by clicking on the column headings. The filter options are explained below. Any or all of the filters can be used together to filter the data.

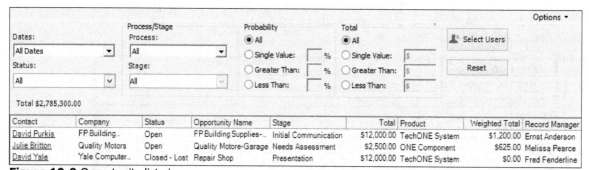

**Figure 10-9** Opportunity list view

① The **DATES** options shown in Figure 10-10 are used to select the date range that you want to see opportunities for.
② The **STATUS** options shown in Figure 10-11 are used to select the statuses that you want to see opportunities for.
③ The **PROCESS** options shown in Figure 10-12 are used to select the process that the opportunities must have in order to be displayed. The options shown are the processes in the demo database.
④ The **STAGE** options are only available once a process has been selected. The options shown in Figure 10-13 are specific to the process that is selected. The default stage is **ALL**. The stage options shown are for the CHT1 Service process.

⑤ The **PROBABILITY** options are used to select a single value and percent for opportunities that you want to see. If you only wanted to see opportunities that have a 91% or greater probability of closing (making the sale), you would select the options shown in Figure 10-14. The 90% shown in the **GREATER THAN** field will NOT return probabilities that are 90%, only probabilities that are greater. If you wanted to include 90%, you would have to enter 89% in the Greater Than field.

⑥ The **TOTAL** options are used to select the total dollar amount that the opportunity must have to be displayed. If you only wanted to see opportunities that have a total amount less than $1,000, you would select the options shown in Figure 10-15.

⑦ The **SELECT USERS** button opens a dialog box that is used to select the users that you want to see opportunities for.

⑧ The **RESET** button will clear all of the filter options that are currently selected. I tend to click this button as soon as I open the Opportunity list view so that all of the opportunities are displayed before I apply any filters.

⑨ The **OPTIONS** button is used to select whether or not private opportunities should be displayed. You can also customize the columns in the Opportunities list by selecting the **CUSTOMIZE COLUMNS** option on this button.

**Figure 10-10** Date options

**Figure 10-11** Status options

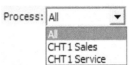

**Figure 10-12** Process options

**Figure 10-13** Stage options

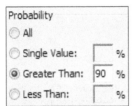

**Figure 10-14** 91% or greater probability options

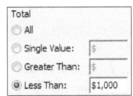

**Figure 10-15** Total amount less than $1,000 options

---

 **Additional Ways To Filter Contacts On The Opportunity List View**
① Right-click in the list of opportunities and select **CREATE LOOKUP**.
② Click the **CREATE LOOKUP FROM OPPORTUNITY** button on the toolbar.

---

## Status Bar

Figure 10-16 shows the information that is displayed in the Status bar. You will see the total number of opportunities, the weighted and grand total dollar amounts of the opportunities that are displayed. The **WEIGHTED TOTAL** field is calculated, based on the product total and the probability of closing the opportunity.

| Lookup: All Opportunities | 376 Opportunities, $1,437,875.00 Weighted Total, $2,785,300.00 Grand Total |

**Figure 10-16** Opportunity status bar

## Opportunity List View Shortcut Menu

The Opportunity list view shortcut menu is shown in Figure 10-17.

The **FILTER OPPORTUNITIES** option (on the shortcut menu) opens the dialog box shown in Figure 10-18. It is another way to filter the opportunities. It contains the same options that are at the top of the Opportunity list view.

The **PRINT OPPORTUNITY LIST** option creates the report shown in Figure 10-19. This report shows all of the opportunities that are displayed on the list view.

**Figure 10-17** Opportunity list view
shortcut menu

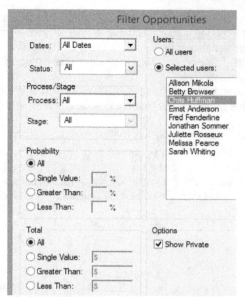

**Figure 10-18** Filter Opportunities dialog box

| Contact | Company | Status | Opportunity Name | Stage | Total | Product | Weighted Total | Record Manager |
|---------|---------|--------|------------------|-------|-------|---------|----------------|----------------|
| David Purkis | FP Building... | Open | FP Building Supplies-... | Initial Communication | $12,000.00 | TechONE System | $1,200.00 | Ernst Anderson |
| Julie Britton | Quality Motors | Open | Quality Motore-Garage | Needs Assessment | $2,500.00 | ONE Component | $625.00 | Melissa Pearce |
| David Yale | Yale Computer... | Closed - Lost | Repair Shop | Presentation | $12,000.00 | TechONE System | $0.00 | Fred Fenderline |

**Figure 10-19** Opportunity List report

## Exercise 10.1: Create An Opportunity

If you have viewed the Opportunity Tracking tour in the Help system, you may think that creating an opportunity is complicated. You can view the tour or look at the examples, but the process probably won't "click" until you create a new opportunity, which is the best way to fully understand each component of an opportunity.

> Opportunities inherit the security that the contact has.

1.  Open the contact record for Mary Wood in the Contact detail view.

2.  On the Opportunities tab, click the **NEW OPPORTUNITY** button, illustrated in Figure 10-20.

**Figure 10-20** Opportunities tab options

3.  Type `My first opportunity` in the Name field.

### Select The Probability

The probability is a percent. It signifies to what degree you think that the opportunity will result in a sale. Throughout the opportunity process, the probability can change.

4.  Type `80` in the Probability field.

### Days Open Section

The options in this section are dates for the opportunity.

**OPEN DATE** Is the date that the opportunity record was created.

**DAYS OPEN** This field is updated automatically. It displays the number of days between the Open date and the Act. Close date.

. . . . . . . . . . . . . . . . . . . . . . . . . .

The **EST. (ESTIMATED) CLOSE DATE** field is used to enter the date that you would like to have the sale closed by. Like the Probability field, the value in this field can change during the course of the opportunity process.

The **ACT. (ACTUAL) CLOSE DATE** field should be filled in when the contact buys the product or service, or when the Closed-Lost status is selected.

 The **EST. CLOSE DATE** is a field used in date range criteria for filters, lookups and reports, for open and inactive opportunities. The **ACT. CLOSE DATE** field is used in date range criteria for closed opportunities. At some point during the process, these fields need to be filled in, so that other features can capture the opportunity.

## Status Options

There are four status options, as explained below.

① **OPEN** This is the default status for a new opportunity. This status means that there is activity for the opportunity. Often, the activity is you hearing from the contact or you contacting them.

② **CLOSED-WON** Select this option when the opportunity results in a sale.

③ **CLOSED-LOST** Select this option if the opportunity did not result in a sale and there is currently no activity for the opportunity.

④ **INACTIVE** Select this option if there is currently no activity for the opportunity, but there is still a chance that a sale may happen.

## Association Section

This section displays the contacts, groups and companies that are associated with the opportunity.

5. Enter a date that is a month from today in the Est. Close Date field.

## What Is A Process List?

A Process List contains the tasks that need to be completed for a sale. If you or your company has a set of tasks for a sale or part of a sale, you should create a process list so that everyone that creates an opportunity will complete the same set of tasks for each opportunity that is created. A process list may remind you of an activity series.

For example, you or your company may have a process for new prospect contacts, like call the contact, send the contact a brochure and go see the contact. These three tasks would be a process list that you could create. You can also incorporate an existing process list into another process list.

## Select The Process

The processes shown earlier in Figure 10-12, come with ACT!. Each process has its own list of stages. Later in this chapter, you will learn how to create your own process list.

## Select The Stage

The stage options are based on the process that is selected. The stage indicates where the opportunity is in the sales process. This can be used to let you know which opportunities need your immediate attention.

6. Select the Needs Assessment stage.

   The top half of the Opportunity detail view should look like the one shown in Figure 10-21.

   The only difference should be the date in the field.

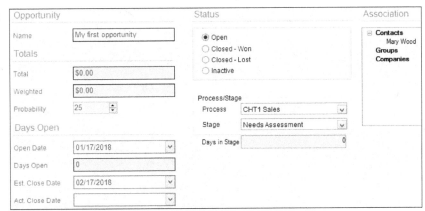

**Figure 10-21** Options for a new opportunity

## Products And Services Tab

The fields that you just filled in are the basic fields for an opportunity. The options on the Products/Services tab are the items for the opportunity that the contact will hopefully purchase.

It is not advised, but you can also enter data for a new product on this tab. Doing so means that the new product will only be available for the current opportunity. The reason that you should add the product to the list, is to help keep the products consistent for all opportunities.

The **NAME** drop-down list (on the Add/Edit Product dialog box, shown later in Figure 10-23) shown in Figure 10-22 contains all of the products and services.

When new products and services are added, they will be displayed in this drop-down list.

**Figure 10-22** Name drop-down list items

## Select The Products And Services For The Opportunity

1. On the Products/Services tab, click the Add button.

2. Open the Name drop-down list and select the service, ONE Component.

It is not a requirement that products or services have an item number. Item numbers should be set up when the product is added to the list. If the information is incorrect in the Product List you can change it in the opportunity that you are working on. Changing it here would only apply the change to the opportunity that you have open. It is best to make the changes in the product list.

3. Type 2 in the Quantity field.

## Price Considerations

The cost and price are automatically filled in because they are stored in the product list. If these values are not correct, you have two options to correct them, as explained below.

① Edit the fields on the Opportunities detail view. This option only changes the values in the current opportunity.
② Edit the data in the product list. This option will change the price throughout the database.

## Adjusted Price

Filling in this field is optional. It is used to give the contact a discount or price that is different then the default price for the product or service. If you change the price in this field, the discount percent is automatically recalculated.

4. You should have the options shown in Figure 10-23.

   The Display Fields button is used to add, remove and reorder the fields on the Products/Services tab.

   Click OK.

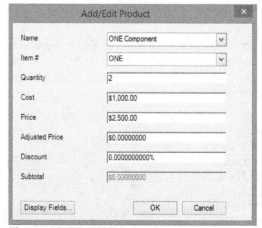

**Figure 10-23** Add/Edit Product dialog box

## Add A Service

In this part of the exercise, you will add a service product to the opportunity and learn how to set up a discount.

1. Click the Add button ⇒ Select the Service Contract product.

2. Change the discount to 20%, then click OK.

   You should have the products shown in Figure 10-24.

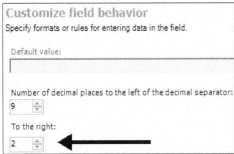

| Name | / | Item # | Quantity | Cost | Price | Adjusted Price | Discount | Subtotal |
|------|---|--------|----------|------|-------|----------------|----------|----------|
| ONE Component | | ONE | 2.00 | $1,000.00 | $2,500.00 | $2,500.00 | 0.0000000000% | $5,000.00 |
| Service Contract | | SC | 1.00 | $750.00 | $2,000.00 | $1,600.00 | 20.0000000000% | $1,600.00 |

**Figure 10-24** Products and Services added to the opportunity

> **Changing The Discount Field's Number Of Decimal Places**
> If the number of decimal places after the decimal point in the Discount column shown above in Figure 10-24 annoys you, you can edit the Discount field on the Define Fields dialog box. (Click the **MODIFY FIELDS FOR PRODUCT TAB** link in the Related Tasks section, on the left.) On the Customize field behavior screen, change the **TO THE RIGHT** field to 2, as illustrated in Figure 10-25. The Discount field will then be displayed as illustrated in Figure 10-26. If you change the field to zero, no zeroes will appear after the decimal point.

Customize field behavior
Specify formats or rules for entering data in the field.

Default value:

Number of decimal places to the left of the decimal separator:
9

To the right:
2

**Figure 10-25** Discount Field Customize Field Behavior screen options

| Name | / | Item # | Quantity | Cost | Price | Adjusted Price | Discount |
|------|---|--------|----------|------|-------|----------------|----------|
| ONE Component | | ONE | 2.00 | $1,000.00 | $2,500.00 | $2,500.00 | 0.00% |
| Service Contract | | SC | 1.00 | $750.00 | $2,000.00 | $1,600.00 | 20.00% |

**Figure 10-26** Modified discount field

> **Decimal Places**
> While the tip above for changing the number of decimal places works for the Discount field, it did not work for me on some other fields that have decimal places in ACT! v20. By this I mean that I would change the option illustrated earlier in Figure 10-25. When I entered a value in the field, more than two decimal places would be displayed. When I reopened the dialog box (shown in Figure 10-25), the value was back to what it was originally. So, it appears that the code was modified (and not retested), because the changes that you make are not saved.

> **Giving A Discount For The Entire Order**
> As you just learned, you can discount each item on the opportunity. It would be nice if we could also give a discount off of the entire order. For example, "Spend $100, get $20 off". I could not find a way to create this type of discount.

## Add A Note

1. On the Notes tab, click the Insert New Note button.

2. Type This is my first opportunity in the field at the bottom of the dialog box, then click OK.

3. Click the Save Changes button. Leave the opportunity open.

### Exercise 10.2: Schedule A Follow Up Activity For The Opportunity

The default follow up opportunity activity is a phone call. The default value for the Regarding field is the opportunity name. If there is a stage, it is automatically included in the Regarding field, as illustrated at the bottom of Figure 10-27.

Scheduling an activity for an opportunity is the same as scheduling other activities. In this exercise, you will schedule a phone call activity for tomorrow for the opportunity.

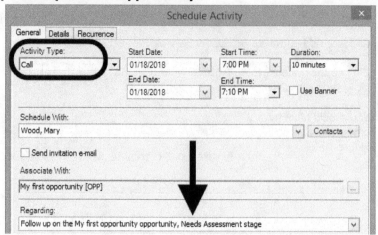

**Figure 10-27** Opportunity follow up activity

1. On the Contacts tab, click the **FOLLOW UP** button.

2. Change the Start Date to tomorrow ⇒ Change the Start time to 7 PM ⇒ Click OK to close the Schedule Activity dialog box.

### Exercise 10.3: Edit The Product List

In this exercise you will learn how to add a new product to the Product list.

1. Tools ⇒ Define Fields ⇒ Click on the **MANAGE PRODUCT LIST** link.

> **Other Ways To Open The Manage Product List Dialog Box**
> ① Click the Manage Product List button on the Opportunity list view toolbar.
> ② Opportunities ⇒ Manage Product List.
> ③ Click the Modify Fields for Product Tab link in the Related Tasks section of the Opportunity detail view.

2. Click the Add button ⇒ In the Name field, type ACT! Book.

3. Press the Tab key ⇒ In the Item Number field, type BK-0001 ⇒ In the Cost field, type 10.

4. Type 39.95 in the Price field.

The item should look like the one shown in Figure 10-28.

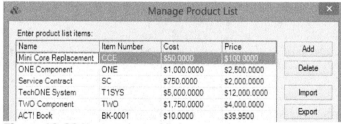

**Figure 10-28** New product added

5. Click OK ⇒ Click Close on the Define Fields dialog box.

### Exercise 10.4: How To Associate An Opportunity To A Company

In this exercise you will associate the opportunity that you created in Exercise 10.1 to a company.

1. On the Activities tab of the opportunity, double-click on the opportunity that is scheduled with Mary Wood.

2. Click the button at the end of the **ASSOCIATE WITH** field ⇒ Open the View drop-down list and select Companies ⇒ Select My New Company, then click the Add button.

3.   Click OK. You will see the company in the Associate With field ⇒ Click OK to close the Schedule Activity dialog box.

---

**Opportunity Linking Issue**
As you have learned in previous chapters, linked contacts that are marked as private can still have data from various tabs displayed under the company record that it is linked to. Opportunity records of linked contacts will not be visible from the company record, but opportunity history records will be visible from a company record. If you do not want the opportunity history records of private contacts visible, you have to clear the **AUTOMATICALLY RECORD HISTORY WHEN CONTACTS ARE LINKED OR UNLINKED** option on the Company Preferences dialog box. [See Chapter 5, Figure 5-11]

---

### Exercise 10.5: Lookup Opportunities

The Lookup Opportunity options are similar to the opportunity filter options because they are used to narrow down the opportunities that will be displayed on the screen. By default, the opportunities that are displayed from the lookup are the ones for the current user (you). If you want to view opportunities for all users or specific users, you have to select the users. In this exercise you will perform three opportunity lookups.

Figure 10-29 shows the Opportunity lookup menu options. Most of the options shown were explained earlier, in the Using The Opportunity List Filters section. The other options are explained below.

The **NAME** option uses the name of the opportunity that you want to search for.

The **PRODUCT** option uses the Name field on the Products/Services tab for the product that you want to search for.

**Figure 10-29** Opportunity lookup menu options

### Lookup Opportunity #1

In this lookup exercise you will find opportunities for all users that are in the Initial Communication stage of the CHT1 Sales process.

1.   From the Opportunity detail view, Lookup ⇒ Other Fields.

2.   Select the **PROCESS** field to search on.

3.   Type CHT1 Sales in the Value field.

     You should have the options shown in Figure 10-30.

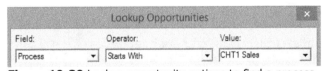

**Figure 10-30** Lookup opportunity options to find a process

4.   Click OK. You will see fewer opportunities on the list view because all of the opportunities are not in the process that you selected in the lookup.

### Lookup Opportunity #2

In this lookup exercise you will find opportunities that have been open for more than 30 days. This requires two lookups: one to find opportunities with the number of days greater than 30 and one to narrow down the opportunities to only those that are open. When the lookup requires searching on more than one field, the efficient lookup rule of thumb is to select the field that will eliminate the most records first. In databases with thousands of records, this will greatly speed up the search process. Being able to see a list of opportunities that have been open for over 30 days, will allow you to follow up to see what you can do to close the sale.

1.   Lookup ⇒ Other Fields ⇒ Select the **DAYS OPEN** field to search on.

2. Select the **GREATER THAN** operator ⇒ Type 30 in the Value field.
   You should have the options selected that are shown in Figure 10-31 ⇒ Click OK.

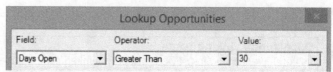

**Figure 10-31** Lookup Opportunity options to find opportunities greater than 30 days

> **Status Field Lookup**
>
> When you need to create a lookup for the Status field, you cannot type in the status name. If you do, you will see an error message that says "The value you typed is greater than the maximum field length". This did not happen in ACT! 2009 and earlier versions. Back then, you could type in the name. I suspect that the developers hooked the Status field up to the ID field, which by default is a numeric field, instead of a text field.
>
> I suspect that the developers have no intention on putting this back to the way that it was. Instead, you have to enter a number for the status, as shown below. You will see these options at the top of the Lookup dialog box, as shown in Figure 10-32. 0 (zero) = Open, 1 = Closed Won, 2 = Closed Lost, 3 = Inactive.

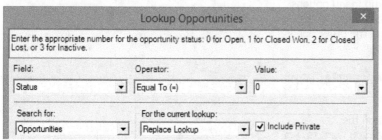

**Figure 10-32** Lookup Opportunities dialog box with Status field options

3. Lookup ⇒ Status ⇒ In the Value field, type 0 (for the Open status)

4. Change the Current lookup option to Narrow Lookup ⇒ Click OK. You will see the opportunities that have been open for more than 30 days.

## Table Names

As shown in Figure 10-33, the table name (in brackets) is visible for fields that are not in the main table for the lookup.

The fields at the bottom of the drop-down list, that do not display the table name, are from the Opportunity table, which is the main table for this lookup.

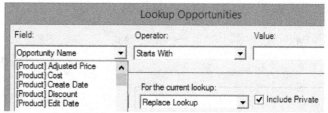

**Figure 10-33** Table name as part of the field

## Add Columns To The Opportunity List View

Like other tabs that you have read about, you can also customize the layout of the Opportunities tab. To complete the next lookup, you may need to add columns to the Opportunity list view. If the Product and Weighted Total columns are not displayed after the Total column, follow the steps below to add them.

1. Right-click in the column section and select **CUSTOMIZE COLUMNS**.

2. Add the Product and Weighted Total fields after the Total field.

## Lookup Opportunity #3

In this lookup exercise you will find opportunities that have a specific product.

1. Lookup ⇒ Product.

2. Type `Two Component` in the Value field, then click OK. As shown in Figure 10-34, you cannot see all of the products for the opportunity. To see the products, you have to double-click on an opportunity.

The way to tell if an opportunity has more than one product is when you see an ellipsis (three periods) at the end of the field, as illustrated in the figure.

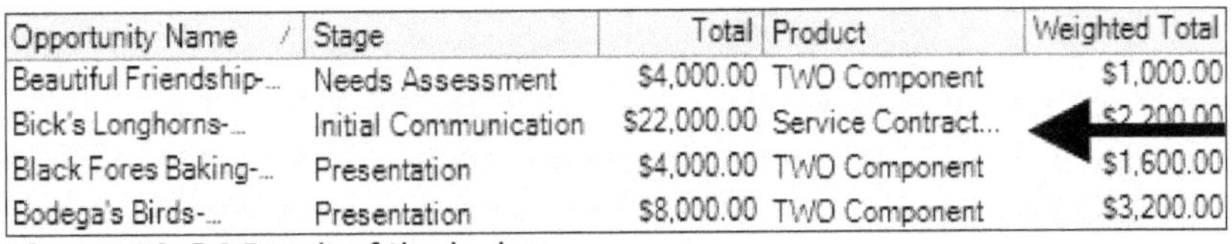

| Opportunity Name / | Stage | Total | Product | Weighted Total |
|---|---|---|---|---|
| Beautiful Friendship-... | Needs Assessment | $4,000.00 | TWO Component | $1,000.00 |
| Bick's Longhorns-... | Initial Communication | $22,000.00 | Service Contract... | $2,200.00 |
| Black Fores Baking-... | Presentation | $4,000.00 | TWO Component | $1,600.00 |
| Bodega's Birds-... | Presentation | $8,000.00 | TWO Component | $3,200.00 |

**Figure 10-34** Result of the lookup

### How To Close An Opportunity

This is the part of the opportunity process that will probably make you happy. When a contact makes a purchase, they become a customer and their opportunity needs to be closed. If a contact does not make a purchase for whatever reason, the opportunity should be closed indicating that. When you have the need, the steps below show you how to close an opportunity. These steps are also used to change the status of an opportunity.

1. Display the opportunity that you want to close.

2. Select the appropriate closed status. [See Status Options, earlier in this chapter]

3. On the Opportunity Info tab, select or type in a **REASON**, if applicable.

4. You can also add comments on the **NOTES** tab. Once a closed status is selected and you click the Save Changes button, a history record similar to the first one shown in Figure 10-35, will be created for the opportunity.

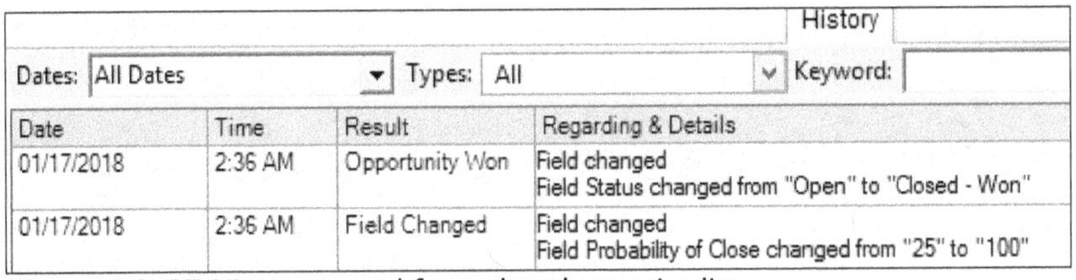

| | | History | |
|---|---|---|---|
| Dates: All Dates ▼ | Types: All v | Keyword: | |

| Date | Time | Result | Regarding & Details |
|---|---|---|---|
| 01/17/2018 | 2:36 AM | Opportunity Won | Field changed<br>Field Status changed from "Open" to "Closed - Won" |
| 01/17/2018 | 2:36 AM | Field Changed | Field changed<br>Field Probability of Close changed from "25" to "100" |

**Figure 10-35** History record for a closed opportunity

### Exercise 10.6: Export Opportunities To Excel

In this exercise, you will export opportunities to Excel. Exporting the opportunity data will allow the data to be analyzed, as well as, create charts.

1. Lookup all of the opportunities.

2. Click the Export Current List To Excel button on the toolbar. The opportunity records will be exported and Excel will open automatically.

If you look at the bottom of the spreadsheet you will see three tabs. The first tab displays the data from the Opportunity list view.

The second tab on the spreadsheet displays a pivot chart of the data. My pivot chart looks like the one shown in Figure 10-36. The Pivot Table Field List dialog box shown on the right side of the figure, displays all of the fields that were exported to Excel. You can drag any of those fields to the chart.

The third tab displays the summary information in a PivotTable that is displayed on the Pivot chart. The Opportunities Pivot tab should look like the one shown in Figure 10-37. If you change the options on this tab, the chart (shown in Figure 10-36) will automatically be updated to reflect the changes. You can select different options in the drop-down lists (Status and Record Manager) to filter the data, just like you can, on the pivot chart. Doing this will cause the following to happen.

① The data will be recalculated on the Pivot Sheet tab.
② The pivot chart will change.

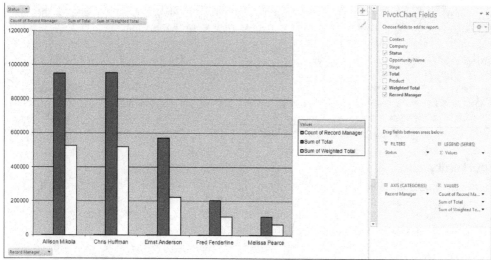

**Figure 10-36** Opportunities PivotChart

| B | C | D | E |
|---|---|---|---|
| Status | (All) | | |
| | Data | | |
| Record Manager | Count of Record Manage | Sum of Total | Sum of Weighted Total |
| Allison Mikola | 128 | $951,100.00 | $525,625.00 |
| Chris Huffman | 110 | $955,200.00 | $519,430.00 |
| Ernst Anderson | 99 | $571,500.00 | $224,395.00 |
| Fred Fenderline | 25 | $203,600.00 | $110,425.00 |
| Melissa Pearce | 15 | $110,500.00 | $64,600.00 |
| Grand Total | 377 | $2,791,900.00 | $1,444,475.00 |

**Figure 10-37** Opportunities PivotTable

3. Leave the spreadsheet open if you want to follow along in the next section. You can save the spreadsheet in your folder if you want. It is not mandatory to save it because you will not need it to complete any other exercise.

## Crash Course In Pivot Table Data

This is truly a crash course in pivot table data. Hopefully, it is enough for you to understand the basic functionality, if you have not used this tool in Excel before. The Pivot Chart tab displays the summary opportunity data graphically. ACT! displays the data in detail.

In the upper left corner of the chart is the **STATUS** drop-down list. If you select a different status, the data will be recalculated, based on the status that you select and the values displayed on the chart will change.

At the bottom of the chart is the **RECORD MANAGER** drop-down list. When you select a user from the list, the opportunities that the user created will be displayed on the chart.

Figure 10-38 shows the Pivot chart with the Status changed to **CLOSED-WON** with the record managers Allison Mikola, Chris Huffman and Ernest Anderson selected.

The **VALUES** button is used to filter the following total fields: Count of Record Manager, Sum of Total (the Grand total) and the Sum of Weighted Total.

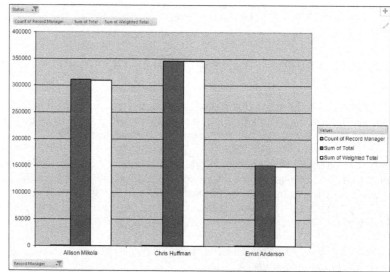

**Figure 10-38** Status changed and three record managers selected

You can move the buttons around on the Opportunities Pivot tab, as shown in Figure 10-39.

Compare this to Figure 10-37, shown earlier.

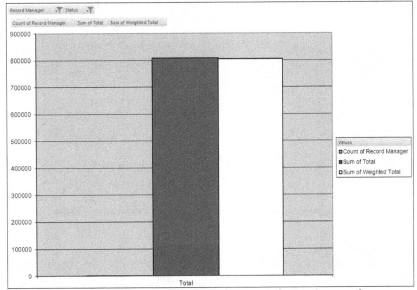

| B | C | | D | E |
|---|---|---|---|---|
| Record Manager | (All) | ⊽ | | |
| Status | Closed - Won | ⊽ | | |
| | Data | | | |
| | **Count of Record Manager** | | **Sum of Total** | **Sum of Weighted Total** |
| Total | 107 | | $807,900.00 | $804,900.00 |

**Figure 10-39** Record Manager button moved on the Opportunities Pivot tab

If you move the Record Manager button before the Status button, on the Opportunities Pivot tab, and then view the chart, it will look like the one shown in Figure 10-40.

**Figure 10-40** Pivot chart after the Record Manager button is moved

## Generating Printable Quotes

Often, you may need to send the opportunity that you create to a contact, when they request a quote. To generate a printable quote in ACT! you have to have Microsoft Word and Excel installed.

## Quote Preferences

There are preferences for quotes that you can set. Tools ⇒ Preferences ⇒ General Tab ⇒ Quote Preferences button, will open the Quote Preferences dialog box.

If the option **PROMPT FOR QUOTE NUMBER WHEN GENERATING** is checked, you can select a prefix for quote numbers, as shown in Figure 10-41.

Adding a quote prefix means that all quotes that you create will start with the same characters and numbers that you enter in the **QUOTE PREFIX** field. You can enter the prefix of your choice or leave it blank if you want to enter a free form prefix on the quote document.

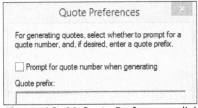

**Figure 10-41** Quote Preferences dialog box

## How To Create A Printable Quote

The steps below show you how to create a quote that can be printed.

1. On the Opportunity list view, double-click on the quote that you want to print.

2. Click the **CREATE QUOTE** button on the toolbar. The document shown in Figure 10-42 will open in Microsoft Word. If you want to save the quote, save it in your folder.

If you plan to use the quote document, you may want to customize it a little by adding fields or changing the font. To modify any of the values on the bottom half of the document, double-click in the section that has the products. The tax rate that you enter should be the tax rate for the state at the top of the quote.

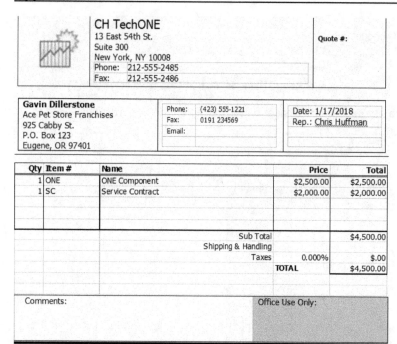

**Figure 10-42** Quote

The Excel spreadsheet shown in Figure 10-43 will appear in the Word document. It has the formulas for the calculations. If you click in the Sub Total field, you will see the formula, as shown at the top of the figure. If needed, you can change this formula or click in an empty cell and create your own formula.

This quote template is really two files, as explained below.

① The **QUOTE.ADT** file is the portion of the quote created as a Word template, which you can modify.

② The **QUOTE.XLT** file is the portion of the quote created in Excel, shown in Figure 10-43. You should not modify the structure of this file because of the formulas. You can add formulas, with the existing structure.

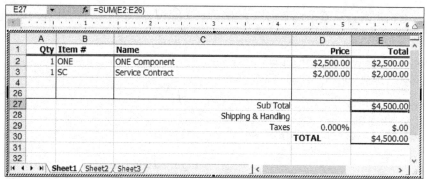

**Figure 10-43** Spreadsheet in the Word document

 Since ACT! 2012, some people have reported that they do not see the portion of the quote shown above in Figure 10-43. Make sure that the Quote.xlt spreadsheet is the only spreadsheet in the Templates folder for the database. Any other spreadsheets in that folder need to be moved or deleted.

## Viewing Opportunities From The Contacts Opportunities Tab

You have created opportunities, viewed them and learned how to filter them from the Opportunities list view. In addition to being able to view opportunities from the Opportunities list view, you can view opportunities from the Opportunities tab on detail views.

As shown in Figure 10-44, some of the filter options that are available on the Opportunities list view [See Figure 10-9] are also available on the Opportunities tab. If you need more filter options, on the Opportunities tab on the Contact detail view, right-click on a blank space on the Opportunity tab and select **FILTER OPPORTUNITIES**. You will see the dialog box shown in Figure 10-45. This dialog box is a scaled down version of the one that you saw earlier in Figure 10-18.

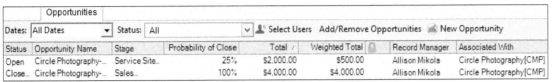

| Opportunities | | | | | | | | |
| Dates: All Dates ▼ | Status: All ▼ | | | Select Users | Add/Remove Opportunities | New Opportunity | | |

| Status | Opportunity Name | Stage | Probability of Close | Total | Weighted Total | Record Manager | Associated With |
|--------|-----------------|-------|---------------------|-------|----------------|----------------|-----------------|
| Open | Circle Photography-... | Service Site... | 25% | $2,000.00 | $500.00 | Allison Mikola | Circle Photography[CMP] |
| Close... | Circle Photography-... | Sales... | 100% | $4,000.00 | $4,000.00 | Allison Mikola | Circle Photography[CMP] |

**Figure 10-44** Opportunities tab on the Contact detail view

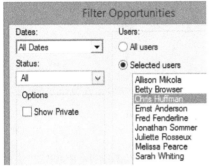

**Figure 10-45** Filter Opportunities dialog box

## Opportunity Reports

ACT! comes with reports that are specifically for opportunities. In addition to being able to preview and print the reports, there are five other output options that you can select from. You can save the reports and send them as an attachment in an email. You can also save them as a PDF file. The benefit of saving the report in PDF format is that anyone with the free Adobe Reader can view or print the report without having ACT! installed.

## Report Options

 After running some of the reports on the Opportunity Reports submenu, I noticed that the Define Filters dialog box for some opportunity reports have the options on the General tab that are usually on the Opportunity tab, on the Define Filters dialog box. For example, the Company Comprehensive report has an Opportunity tab. The following reports have the opportunity options on the General tab: Sales Analysis by Record Manager, Total By Status, Adjusted for Probability, Pipeline Report and Opportunities By Record Manager.

## Exercise 10.7: Sales Analysis By Record Manager Report

This report will display any or all of the available status categories, as well as the number and percent for each category selected. It also has a Closed-Won analysis that provides the average and total amounts, for the date range and users (record managers) that you select.

1.  Reports ⇒ Opportunity Reports ⇒ Sales Analysis By Record Manager.

2.  Select **PAST** as the Date Range. The filter options for this report are used to select opportunities based on the status and date range.

3. Click OK.

   Your report will look similar to the one shown in Figure 10-46.

   Your report will have more records because you are running the report after I did.

### Sales Analysis by Record Manager

**Date Range:** Before 01/17/2018

**Record Manager**         Allison Mikola

| | | | | |
|---|---|---|---|---|
| **Total Sales:** | | $310,800.00 | **Closed/Won Analysis:** | |
| **Total Number of Opportunities:** | | 68 | Avg. Sales Amount | $7,969.23 |
| **Status:** | **#** | **%** | Avg. Discount | 0.00% |
| Open | 10 | 14.71 | Total Gross Margin | $181,150.00 |
| Closed/Won | 39 | 57.35 | Avg. Gross Margin | $4,644.87 |
| Closed/Lost | 19 | 27.94 | Avg. # Products per Sale | 1.33 |
| Inactive | 0 | 0.00 | Avg. Days Open | 6 |

**Figure 10-46** Sales Analysis By Record Manager report

## Opportunity Graphs And Pipelines

In addition to opportunity reports, ACT! has the ability to create graphs and pipelines for opportunity data. These options are accessed from the Opportunity list view. Graphs and pipelines can be printed and saved in different file formats.

## Exercise 10.8: Creating Graphs

The graphs for opportunities that you can create, have several options that you can use to customize the graph. This includes the type of graph and date range of data displayed on the graph. On your own, depending on the data that is needed to create the graph, you may need to create a lookup first.

## Create A Bar Graph

In this part of the exercise you will create a bar graph for opportunities created in the second half of 2018.

1. On the Opportunity list view, click the **OPPORTUNITY GRAPH** button.

2. On the General tab, select the options below.

   - Display data for all users
   - Graph by month
   - Starting 06/01/2018
   - Ending 12/31/2018

   Your dialog box should have the options shown in Figure 10-47.

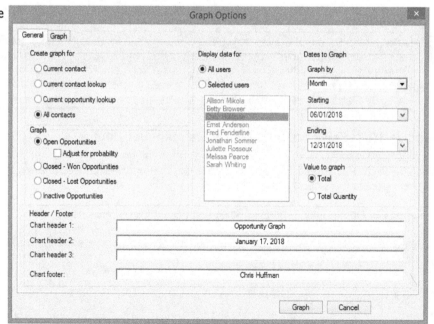

**Figure 10-47** General tab (bar) graph options

3. On the Graph tab, select the following options.
   - Allow graph to scroll
   - Show horizontal grid lines
   - 3-D Style

4. Click the button at the end of the **GRAPH** color option and select a different color.

   Your dialog box should have the options shown in Figure 10-48.

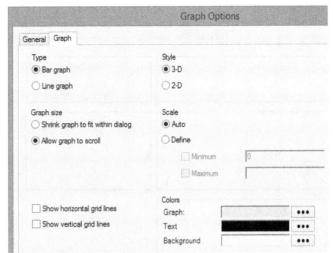

**Figure 10-48** Graph tab options

5. Click the **GRAPH** button at the bottom of the dialog box.

   The Graph button creates a graph based on the options that are selected on the dialog box.

   Your graph should look like the one shown in Figure 10-49.

   You may have to use the scroll bar below the graph to see the charted data.

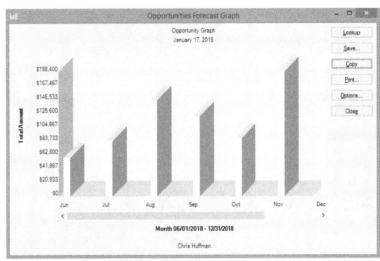

**Figure 10-49** Bar graph

## Opportunities Forecast Graph Dialog Box Options

The **LOOKUP** button will open the Opportunity list view and display the opportunities that are depicted in the graph.

The **SAVE** button is used to save the graph in .BMP or .JPG graphic file format. Save all of the graphs and pipelines that you create in this chapter in your folder, in .JPG format, as illustrated below in Figure 10-50.

The **COPY** button sends a copy of the graph to the clipboard in Windows. This allows you to paste a copy of the graph into a document like the ACT! Word Processor or a Power Point™ presentation slide.

The **PRINT** button will print the graph.

The **OPTIONS** button opens the Graph Options dialog box shown earlier in Figure 10-47, so that you can make changes and recreate the graph.

6. Save the graph as `Bar Graph`, as illustrated in Figure 10-50 ⇒ Close the Opportunities Forecast Graph dialog box.

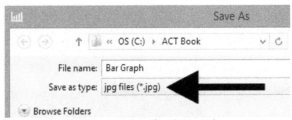

**Figure 10-50** Save options for the graph

### Create A Line Graph

In this part of the exercise you will create a line graph for opportunities in a specific date range.

1. On the Opportunity list view, click the Opportunity Graph button on the toolbar.

2. On the General tab, select the following options.

   - Display data for all users
   - Graph by week
   - Starting 09/01/2018
   - Ending 12/31/2018
   - Chart header 1 `Opportunity Line Graph`

   When finished, your dialog box should have the options shown in Figure 10-51.

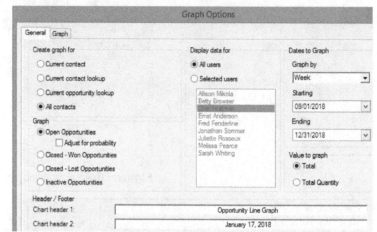

**Figure 10-51** General tab (line) graph options

3. On the Graph tab, select the following options. When finished, your dialog box should have the options shown in Figure 10-52.

   - Line graph
   - Allow graph to scroll
   - Show horizontal grid lines
   - Show vertical grid lines
   - 3-D Style
   - Change the background color to light yellow

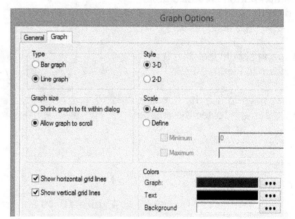

**Figure 10-52** Graph tab options

4. Click the Graph button.

   Your graph should look like the one shown in Figure 10-53, if you scroll to the right.

   Save the graph as `Line Graph`, in .jpg format.

   Close the Opportunities Forecast Graph dialog box.

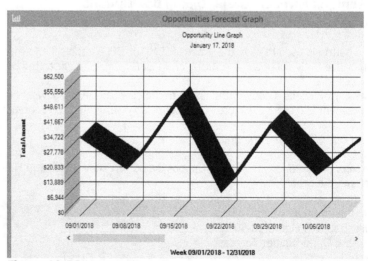

**Figure 10-53** Line graph

## Pipelines

Pipelines graphically display opportunities that have an "Open" status for a specific process at each stage. The options to create a pipeline graph are similar to the ones to create a bar or line graph.

### Exercise 10.9: Create A Pipeline Graph

1. On the Opportunity list view, click the Opportunity Pipeline button.

2. Select the options below.
   - All contacts
   - All users
   - Graph header 3, type My First Pipeline

   Your dialog box should have the options shown in Figure 10-54.

   If the opportunity has more than one process that you want to change the colors of, after you make the color changes for the first process, open the **PROCESS** drop-down list and select the next process that you want to change colors for.

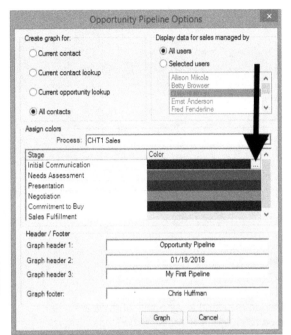

 To change a color on the pipeline graph for a stage in the process, click the ellipsis button at the end of the stage in the **COLOR** column, as illustrated in Figure 10-54.

**Figure 10-54** Opportunity Pipeline Options dialog box

I noticed that in ACT! v20, that the default date in the Graph header 2 field is tomorrows date. I did not notice this in previous versions of the software. It is possible that I missed this in the past.

3. Click the Graph button.

   You should see the pipeline graph shown in Figure 10-55.

   Save the graph as Pipeline Graph, in the file format of your choice, then close the Opportunity Pipeline dialog box.

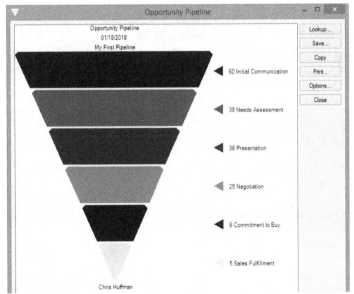

**Figure 10-55** Pipeline graph

### How To Create And Customize Product And Process Lists

Like the drop-down lists on the Contact detail view, the Opportunity products and processes drop-down lists can be customized. Earlier in Exercise 10.3, you learned how to add a new product.

### Exercise 10.10: Creating Process Lists And Stages

In this exercise you will create a process list and the stages for the process.

1. On an Opportunity view, Opportunities ⇒ Manage Process List.

2. Click on the CREATE NEW OPPORTUNITY PROCESS link.

3. In the Opportunity Process field, type My first process ⇒

   In the Description field, type This process has 3 stages, as shown in Figure 10-56.

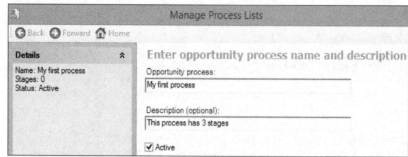

**Figure 10-56** Manage Process Lists screen

4. Click Next ⇒ In the Name field, type First Stage.

5. Press the Tab key twice ⇒ Type 80 in the Probability field.

6. Click the Add button ⇒ Add the two other stages shown in Figure 10-57.

   The MOVE UP and MOVE DOWN buttons are used to change the order of the stages.

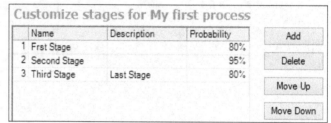

**Figure 10-57** Stages for the process

7. Click Finish. You will see the process that you created. In the PROCESS TASKS section, notice that there are options to edit and delete processes ⇒ Click Close.

### Exercise 10.11: Importing Products

If you need to add a lot of products to the database or have the products in an existing file, you can import them into the database. This means that you can create the product list in Excel, save it in .csv format, then import it into your ACT! database. In this exercise you will learn how to import data into the Products table.

1. On the Opportunity list view, click the MANAGE PRODUCT LIST button on the toolbar.

2. Click the IMPORT button ⇒ Click the BROWSE button on the Import Products dialog box.

3. Double-click on the Products To Import file in your folder. If you cannot see it, change the File type option to CSV FILES (*.CSV).

4. Check the Source file has column headers option, shown in Figure 10-58 ⇒ Click the Import button.

**Figure 10-58** Import Products dialog box

If checked, the **REPLACE PRODUCTS WITH THE SAME NAME** option will overwrite products that are already in the Product list with the changes in the file that you import. This is how you can update existing product information.

If checked, the **SOURCE FILE HAS COLUMN HEADERS** option will not import the first row of data in the file. Check this option if the file that you are importing from has column headings. If you are not sure, open the file before importing the data. You can also view the products on the Manage Product List dialog box and delete the product that has the column headings.

5. Click OK when prompted that the products have been successfully imported.

   You should see the three products illustrated at the bottom of Figure 10-59.

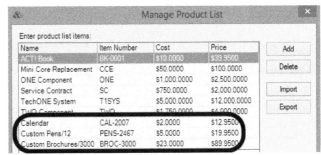

**Figure 10-59** Manage Product List dialog box

### How To Create A Product List In Excel
If the need arises, the steps below show you how to create a product list in Excel.

1. Create four columns: Name, Item Number, Cost and Price. Typing in the column names is optional. If you type them in, make sure that you do not import the first row of the spreadsheet.
2. Enter the information for each product.
3. Change the Save as type to **CSV (COMMA DELIMITED) (\*.CSV)**, as illustrated in Figure 10-60, then save the file.

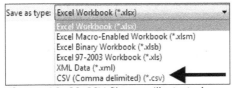

**Figure 10-60** CSV file type illustrated

## Opportunity Detail View Related Tasks

The related tasks options shown in Figure 10-61 are primarily on the detail view. Some options are also on the list view. The options are explained below.

**Figure 10-61** Opportunity detail view related tasks

**DUPLICATE OPPORTUNITY** Opens the dialog box shown in Figure 10-62.

It is used to select which opportunity fields will be duplicated on the new opportunity record.

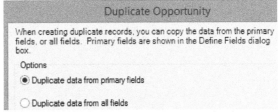

**Figure 10-62** Duplicate Opportunity dialog box

**CREATE QUOTE** [See How To Create A Printable Quote, earlier in this chapter]

**SCHEDULE FOLLOW-UP ACTIVITY** Opens the Schedule Activity dialog box. Information from the opportunity record is automatically filled in, on the activity record.

**SCHEDULE ACTIVITY SERIES** [See Chapter 3, below Figure 3-32]

**MODIFY LAYOUT** [See Chapter 3, below Figure 3-32]

**MODIFY FIELDS FOR PRODUCT TAB** Opens the Define Fields dialog box so that you can modify the fields on the Products/Services tab, as well as, other tabs on the Opportunity detail view.

**VIEW ALL OPPORTUNITIES** Displays all of the opportunities in the Opportunity list view.

**MANAGE SMART TASKS** [See Chapter 3, below Figure 3-33]

## Opportunity List View Related Tasks

The options shown in Figure 10-63 are for the Opportunity list view. The options that are only on the list view are explained below.

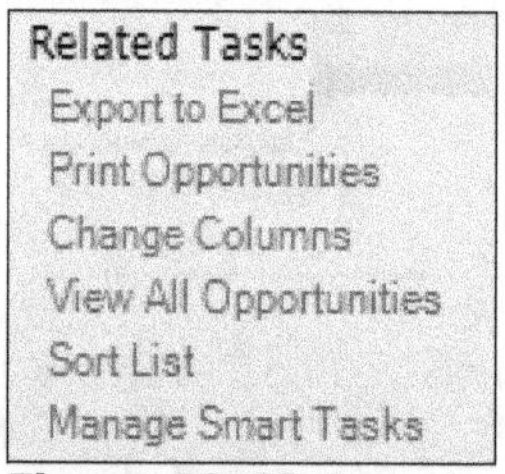

Related Tasks
Export to Excel
Print Opportunities
Change Columns
View All Opportunities
Sort List
Manage Smart Tasks

**Figure 10-63** Opportunity list view related tasks

**EXPORT TO EXCEL** Exports the opportunities that are displayed in the view to Excel.

**PRINT OPPORTUNITIES** Opens the Quick Print Options dialog box so that you can select options for how the screen will be printed.

**CHANGE COLUMNS** [See Chapter 3, below Figure 3-35]

**SORT LIST** Opens the Sort dialog box to sort the opportunities displayed in the view.

Overview

In this chapter you will learn about the following features:

☑ How to use the Task List view to work with activities
☑ How to use the calendar views
☑ How to filter activities in a calendar view
☑ Granting calendar access
☑ How to use the History List view to display and filter completed activities

CHAPTER 11

## Task List View

You have learned how to create activities and view them. You have also learned how to view several contacts at the same time using the Contact list view. If you need to view activities (tasks or open items that you need to complete) for several contacts at the same time, you can use the Task List view. The entries displayed in the Task List are linked to the current My Record. This means that by default, each person that uses the database has their own Task List and calendar, that only displays activities that they scheduled and activities that are assigned to them.

In the Task List view you can add and delete columns, sort by column headings and change the order of the column headings, just like you can with the Contact list view. In addition to being able to view activities for several contacts in the Task List view, you can also modify, filter, clear, schedule and delete activities, the same way that you can on the Activities tab.

## Task List Toolbar

Figure 11-1 shows the Task List toolbar.

Table 11-1 explains the buttons on the toolbar.

**Figure 11-1** Task List toolbar

| Button | Description |
|--------|-------------|
| 1 | Prints the current view. |
| 2 | Create a lookup. |
| 3 | Opens the Customize Columns dialog box, which is used to add, remove and change the order of the columns on the Task List. |
| 4 | Exports the Task List to Excel. |

**Table 11-1** Task List toolbar buttons explained

## Status Bar

At the bottom of the Task List window is the status bar shown in Figure 11-2. It displays the date range and totals for each type of activity that is displayed on the Task List view.

All Dates: 230 Activities - 6 Calls, 118 Meetings, 71 To-do's, 35 Custom Activities

**Figure 11-2** Task List status bar

When you click the Task List button on the Navigation Pane, you will see the view shown in Figure 11-3.

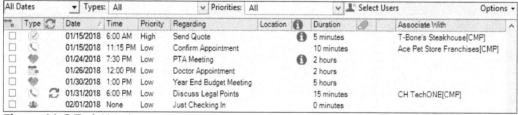

**Figure 11-3** Task List view

 If you double-click on an activity in the Task List, you can edit it or see more information about the activity.

## Filter Options

The filter options for the Task List are explained in Table 11-2.

| Filter | Is Used To . . . |
|---|---|
| Dates | Select the date or date range that you want to see activities for, as shown in Figure 11-4. If none of the options shown fit your needs, select the **CUSTOM** option at the bottom of the drop-down list. |
| Types | Select the activity types that you want to see and clear the check mark of the types that you do not want to see, as shown in Figure 11-5. |
| Priorities | Select the priority of the activity types that you want to see. Clear the check mark of the options that you do not want to see, as shown in Figure 11-6. |
| Select Users | View the public activities of other users in the database. If you select other users, keep in mind that their activities will continue to be displayed in your Task List until you remove the user from your view. |

**Table 11-2** Task List filter options explained

**Figure 11-4** Date filter options

**Figure 11-5** Activity Types options

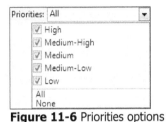

**Figure 11-6** Priorities options

## Options Button

The options shown in Figure 11-7 are other options that can be selected to filter activities on the Task List view. They are explained below.

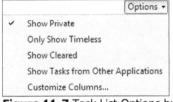

**Figure 11-7** Task List Options button options

① **SHOW PRIVATE** Displays or hides private activities.

② **ONLY SHOW TIMELESS** Hides tasks that have a time.

③ **SHOW CLEARED** Displays tasks that have been cleared, but not deleted. Cleared tasks have a line through them, as illustrated in Figure 11-8.

④ **SHOW TASKS FROM OTHER APPLICATIONS** Displays tasks that were imported or synched from Microsoft Outlook or Google.

⑤ **CUSTOMIZE COLUMNS** Opens the Customize Columns dialog box.

**Figure 11-8** Cleared tasks illustrated

## Exercise 11.1: Create A Task List Lookup Using Filters

By default, the activities are in ascending order by date. If you have hundreds of activities, you will probably not want to see all of them. You can create a lookup to only display certain activities.

1. On the Task List, open the Dates drop-down list and select the **CUSTOM** option at the bottom of the list. You will see the Select Date Range dialog box.

2. Select the range 01/01/2018 to 09/19/2018, then click OK. You should only see activities that have a date in the range that you selected ⇒ Select the All Dates option.

3. If you want to see activities for other users, click the **SELECT USERS** button ⇒ Highlight the first two users, then click OK.

4. View all of the activities and all users.

If you prefer to see all of the Task List filter options in one place, use the dialog box shown in Figure 11-9. Click the **FILTER LIST** link in the Related Tasks list, to display this dialog box.

**Figure 11-9** Filter Activities dialog box (for the Task List)

## Clearing Tasks From The Task List View

Once you have completed a task or no longer need it, you can clear the activity, by following the steps below. You can also create a follow up task.

1. Click on the **CLEARED** check box (of a activity that is not already checked) next to the activity that you want to clear. You will see the Clear Activity dialog box.

2. As needed, change the options, including adding a note stating why the activity is being cleared, in the Details field, as illustrated in Figure 11-10.

   Click OK.

   You will not see the task in the list, unless the **SHOW CLEARED** option is selected on the Options button, shown earlier in Figure 11-7.

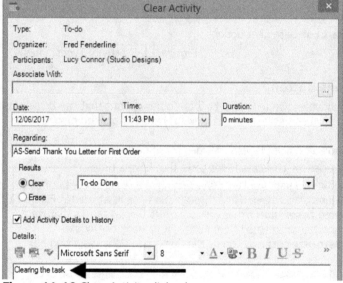

**Figure 11-10** Clear Activity dialog box

## How To Print The Task List

The Task List can be printed by following the steps below.

1. From the Task List view, click on the Print Current Screen link in the Related Tasks list.

2. Select any options that are needed on the Quick Print Options dialog box, then click OK.

## Looking Up Records On The Task List View

If you like working from the Task List view, you can accomplish the same tasks that you can from other views, by using the options on the shortcut menu shown in Figure 11-11.

Like other views, you can look up contacts from the Task List view. If you do, the contacts will open in the Contact list view.

There are two ways to create a lookup from the Task List view, as explained below.

① Use the options on the Lookup menu.
② Right-click in the Task List view and select Create Lookup, as shown in Figure 11-11.

**Figure 11-11** Task List shortcut menu

## Customizing The Task List View

The columns on the Task List view can be customized by following the steps below.

1. Open the Task List view.

2. Right-click in the view and select **CUSTOMIZE COLUMNS**. You will see the Customize Columns dialog box.

Adding the **SCHEDULED BY FIELD** to the Task List will display who created the activity. Adding the **SCHEDULED FOR FIELD** will display who the activity has been assigned to.

These two fields are useful to see on the Task List view, if you view other users activities on a regular basis. Figure 11-12 shows these two fields.

| Regarding | Scheduled By | Scheduled For |
|---|---|---|
| Industry Trade Show | Chris Huffman | Allison Mikola |
| Year End Budget Meeting | Chris Huffman | Fred Fenderline |
| Presentation | Chris Huffman | Chris Huffman |

**Figure 11-12** Modified Task List view

## Task List View Related Tasks

The options shown in Figure 11-13 are for the Task List view. The options are explained below.

**SCHEDULE ACTIVITY SERIES** [See Chapter 3, below Figure 3-32]

**EXPORT TO EXCEL** Exports the tasks that are displayed on the Task List view to Excel, as shown in Figure 11-14.

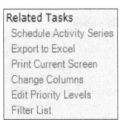

**Figure 11-13** Task List view related tasks

| | A | B | C | D | E | F | G | H | I | J | K | L | M |
|---|---|---|---|---|---|---|---|---|---|---|---|---|---|
| 1 | Cleared | Type | Recurring | Date | Time | Priority | Regarding | Location | Details | Duration | Attachment | Private | Associate With |
| 2 | False | Meeting | | 09/19/2015 | 8:00 PM | Low | Presentation | | | 2 hours | | | Ace Pet Store |
| 3 | True | Marketing Call | | 10/14/2017 | None | Low | Follow up per email | | | 0 minutes | | | |
| 4 | True | Meeting | | 10/17/2017 | 2:00 PM | Low | Presentation | | | 1 hour | | | |
| 5 | True | Personal Activity | | 10/18/2017 | 9:30 PM | Low | Rock Climbing | | | 1 hour 30 minutes | | | |

**Figure 11-14** Tasks exported to Excel

**PRINT CURRENT SCREEN** Opens the Quick Print Options dialog box so that you can select options for how the screen will be printed.

**CHANGE COLUMNS** Opens the Customize Columns dialog box.

**EDIT PRIORITY LEVELS** [See Chapter 14, Managing Priority Types]

**FILTER LIST** [See Figure 11-9, earlier in this chapter]

## Calendar Preferences

Chapter 2 covered preferences that you can set for the calendar views. ACT! has calendar options that you can customize, as needed.

## Calendar Views

The default date when you open any calendar is today's date. Each calendar view has a daily check list and date selector. Like the Task List view, the Calendar views display activities, tasks or open items that need to be completed.

**TIMELESS** activities are not displayed on calendars. They are displayed under the calendar on the right side of the workspace with the rest of the activities. There is also a mini calendar that you can use. The calendar can also be used to schedule and modify activities.

## Calendar Toolbar

Figure 11-15 shows the Calendar toolbar.

Table 11-3 explains the buttons on the toolbar.

**Figure 11-15** Calendar toolbar

| Button | Description |
|--------|-------------|
| 1 | Highlights today in any calendar view except the daily calendar. |
| 2 | Displays the daily calendar. |
| 3 | Displays the work week calendar. |
| 4 | Displays the weekly calendar. |
| 5 | Displays the monthly calendar. |
| 6 | Displays the previous day, week or month, depending on which calendar view is open. |
| 7 | Displays the next day, week or month, depending on which calendar view is open. |
| 8 | Prints the calendar. |
| 9 | Displays the contacts from the current calendar view in the contact list view. |

**Table 11-3** Calendar toolbar buttons explained

## Mini-Calendar

This calendar is used to view calendars for the previous month, current month and next month. This is a quick way to display activities from previous or future months. The single arrows will move to the previous and next month. The double arrows will move to the previous and next year. You can use this calendar to navigate to a day, week or month, by clicking on it.

1.  Click the Calendar button on the Navigator Pane.

2.  View ⇒ Mini-calendar, or press F4. You will see the calendar shown in Figure 11-16.

If you click on a date and the weekly calendar view is open, you will see the weekly calendar that includes the date that you click on.

If necessary, close the mini calendar by clicking on the X in the upper right corner of the calendar.

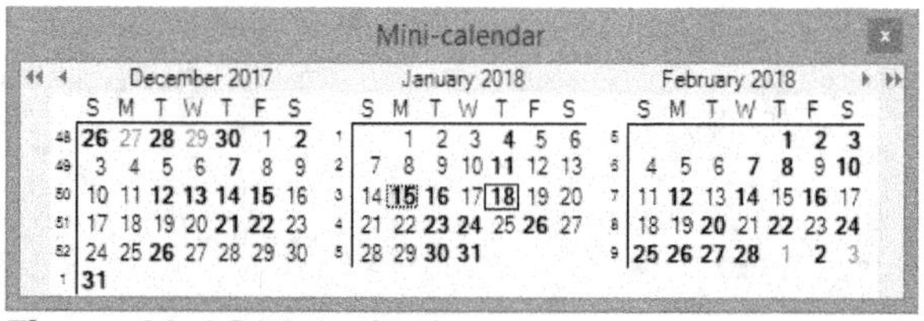

**Figure 11-16** Mini-calendar

## Calendar Tips

**MINI-CALENDAR** If you right-click on the month name in the mini calendar shown above in Figure 11-16, you will see the pop up calendar shown in Figure 11-17. Select the month that you want to view the calendar of. The dates in bold on the mini-calendar have activities. If you have a calendar view displayed and click on a date that is bold on the mini-calendar, you will see all of the activities for that day, below the calendar, on the right side of the window, as shown in Figure 11-18.

**SHORTCUT MENU** If you right-click on an activity in the calendar, you will see the shortcut menu shown in Figure 11-19. Many of the options that you will use the most are on this shortcut menu.

The **FILTER CALENDAR** option on the Calendar shortcut menu, opens the dialog box shown in Figure 11-20. This dialog box contains all of the filter options that are at the top of a calendar view.

**DROP AND DRAG AN ACTIVITY** You can move an activity from one day or time to another day or time by dragging the activity to a new location. If you select an activity to move, that is part of a recurring activity, you will be prompted to change all occurrences of the activity or only the current occurrence. If you click OK to move the activity, it will no longer be part of the recurring activities, as shown by the message in Figure 11-21.

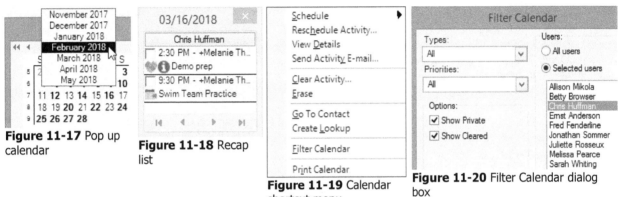

**Figure 11-17** Pop up calendar

**Figure 11-18** Recap list

**Figure 11-19** Calendar shortcut menu

**Figure 11-20** Filter Calendar dialog box

**Figure 11-21** Remove Instance message

## Daily Calendar

The daily calendar displays activities and tasks for one day. By default, the day is divided into 30 minute intervals. You can change the time interval on the Preferences dialog box.

1.  Display the My Record ⇒ Click on the Calendar button on the Navigation Pane.

2.  View the daily calendar for the date that you used in Exercise 7.1, by clicking the **DAILY** button and then selecting the day in the mini calendar, on the right side of the workspace.

The top of the calendar should look similar to the one shown in Figure 11-22.

Notice that all of the activities in the **RECAP LIST** (which is below the calendar on the right) are for one day, as illustrated in Figure 11-23. The items in this section are from the Task List. This list is helpful when there are activities that you can't see without scrolling. Timeless activities are displayed in the Recap List.

When you click on a different day on the calendar shown in Figure 11-23, the activities in the Recap list will change. When you need to view a different date in the daily calendar, click on the date in the calendar.

Figure 11-22 Daily calendar view

**Figure 11-23** Recap list

## Banner Option

The banner option will display a single line entry at the top of the daily calendar. This lets you see more information about the activity. The banner option can be disabled on the Schedule Activity dialog box. Double-clicking on a banner, like the ones shown above in Figure 11-22, will open the Schedule Activity dialog box for the activity.

## Calendar Pop-Ups

If you hold the mouse pointer over an activity on a calendar, you will see a pop-up like the one shown in Figure 11-24. This allows you to see some of the information about the activity.

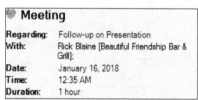

**Figure 11-24** Calendar pop-up illustrated

## Today (Calendar) Button

When clicked, this button will display today's date in the calendar view that you are in, except for the daily calendar view. For example, if today is September 19, 2017 and you are viewing the monthly calendar for June 2018, if you click the **TODAY** button, the September 2017 monthly calendar will be displayed and September 19th, will be highlighted.

## Work Week Calendar

The work week calendar view shown in Figure 11-25 displays all activities and tasks that have a start time between Monday and Friday or the work days that are selected in the calendar preferences. If you double-click on the day of the week at the top of the calendar, that day will open in the daily calendar. Double-clicking on an activity will open the Schedule Activity dialog box.

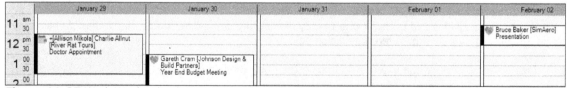

**Figure 11-25** Work Week calendar view

## Weekly Calendar

The weekly calendar view shown in Figure 11-26, displays all activities and tasks for the week. The activities under the calendar, on the right are for the day that is selected in the calendar.

 If you double-click on a date header on the weekly calendar, you will open the daily calendar for the day that you double-click on.

**Figure 11-26** Weekly calendar view

## Monthly Calendar

The monthly calendar displays all activities and tasks that have a start time in the month selected. If you double-click on a blank space in a day on the calendar, the daily calendar will be displayed.

 **Cool Calendar Tip**

I stumbled across this by accident, with the slip of the mouse. By default, the calendar on the right side of the calendar view only displays one month. The border to the left of this calendar moves. Who knew? Place the mouse pointer in the position illustrated in Figure 11-27, then drag the mouse to the left until you see as many months as you need, as shown in Figure 11-28. You can also display more calendars below, by dragging the bottom of the calendar down.

**Figure 11-27** Mouse pointer in position to display more calendars

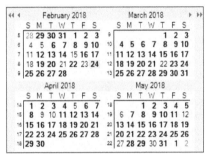

**Figure 11-28** Multiple calendars displayed

 The numbers to the left of the calendar represent the week of the year.

## Status Bar

At the bottom of each calendar view is a status bar, as shown in Figure 11-29.

14 Activities - 1 Call, 10 Meetings, 1 To-do, 2 Custom Activities

**Figure 11-29** Status bar for the weekly calendar

The status bar displays a count of the activities that are scheduled, based on the view that is displayed.

## Filtering Activities In A Calendar View

Some calendar views are better able to handle a lot of activities then others. You may only want to view a certain type of activity on a calendar. If either of these options is what you want to do, you can filter the activities that appear on calendars. Activities are filtered on a calendar the same way that you filter activities on the Activities tab. The filter that you select will be applied to each calendar view until you remove or change the filter. You can select which activity types and priorities to display.

## Calendar Filter Options

Figure 11-30 shows the calendar filter options. They are explained below the figure. They are similar to the Task List view filters that you learned about earlier in this chapter.

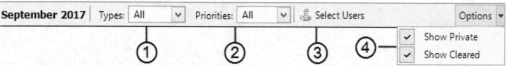

**Figure 11-30** Calendar filter options

① **TYPES** The options in this drop-down list are used to select the activity types that you want to display. The default is to display all activity types. Clear the check box of the activities that you do not want to display.

② **PRIORITIES** This option is used to select the priority of the activity types that you want to display.

③ **SELECT USERS** This button opens the Select Users dialog box.

④ **OPTIONS** This button is used to display private and cleared activities.

## How To Filter Activities On The Calendar

1. Select a month that has a lot of activities, like December 2018.

2. Only display the scheduled meetings that have a low priority. You will see fewer activities.

## Using The Calendar To Schedule Activities

In addition to being able to schedule activities from a contact view, activities can also be scheduled from any calendar view. A benefit of scheduling activities from a calendar view is that you are able to see if the start date and time are already booked. I find the daily calendar the easiest to use to schedule activities because you can select the start and end times before opening the Schedule Activity dialog box.

1. Display the start date of the activity that you want to create on a calendar.

2. If you are using the daily or work week calendar, double-click on the time that you want the activity to start.
   If you are using the weekly or monthly calendar, right-click on the day that you want to schedule the activity on, then select the schedule option and the type of activity that you want to create.

> If you highlight the start and end time for the activity that you want to create in the daily calendar, as illustrated in Figure 11-31, before you double-click on a time, you will not have to type this information in on the Schedule Activity dialog box.

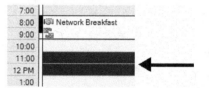

**Figure 11-31** Activity time range selected

3. Enter the remaining information for the activity, then click OK.

## Exercise 11.2: Granting Calendar Access

This tool is used to give another user access to your calendar. Granting access is helpful when you need to allow someone to schedule or manage your appointments or activities.

> All users of the database can view everyone's calendar. By default, only administrators and managers have the security level to schedule activities for other users.

1. Schedule ⇒ Grant Calendar Access.

   The names that you see in Figure 11-32 are the people that currently have rights to use the database.

**Figure 11-32** Calendar Access dialog box

2.  Select the people that you want to have access to your calendar. For this exercise select the five Standard users by holding down the Ctrl key and clicking on the names.

3.  Click the **ACCESS** button ⇒
    Click OK to grant access to **VIEW AND SCHEDULE** activities
    for the users that you selected, as shown in Figure 11-33 ⇒
    Click OK again to close the Calendar Access dialog box.

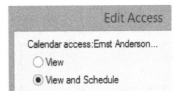

**Figure 11-33** Edit Access dialog box

 **Another Way To View Other Users Calendars**
On a calendar view, click the Select Users button, shown earlier in Figure 11-30.

On the dialog box shown in Figure 11-34, select the users that you want to view the calendar of.

**Figure 11-34** Select Users dialog box

## Viewing Other Users Calendars

When you have the access to view other users calendars and have selected users on the Select Users dialog box, one day on a weekly calendar will look similar to the one shown in Figure 11-35. Activities for other users will have their name in brackets after the time.

If you look under the calendar on the right side of the window, you will see a button for each users activities that you have access to, as shown at the bottom of Figure 11-36. If you click on one of these buttons, you will see the activities for the user below the button.

**Figure 11-35** Calendar with multiple users

**Figure 11-36** Buttons to select a user

## Exercise 11.3: Printing Calendars

ACT! provides several options to print calendars. If you already use Day Runner or Day-Timer products, you can print calendars in these formats in addition to printing calendars on plain paper. ACT! has three types of calendars that you can print: Daily, Weekly and Monthly.

1.  Open the daily calendar.

2.  File ⇒ Print. The Day Calendar option should be selected in the **PRINTOUT TYPE** section of the Print dialog box.

3. Select the **PLAIN LETTER FULL PAGE (P) (2 COL)** option in the Paper Type section, as shown at the bottom of Figure 11-37.

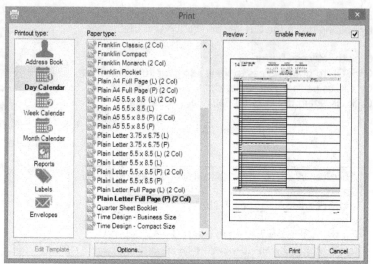

**Figure 11-37** Calendar print options

4. Click the Options button. The options shown in Figure 11-38 are used to customize how the calendar will print.

   If you want to print the Activity Details or Column for Priorities for each calendar entry, check the option.

   The **START HOUR** field is the hour of the day that you want the calendar to start printing from.

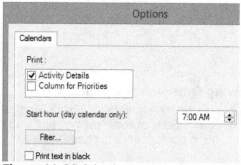

**Figure 11-38** Calendar options

The **FILTER** button opens the Filter Calendar Printout dialog box, shown in Figure 11-39. These options are used to filter the activities that will print on the calendar. You can select which users activities, the date range and activity options, including the type and priority that you want to print on the calendar. By default, the users calendars that you have access to are selected when this dialog box is opened.

**PRINT TEXT IN BLACK** This option is for color text items on the calendar that you want to print in black.

5. Check the Activity Details **PRINT** option ⇒ Clear the Column for Priorities option, if it is checked.

6. Select 7 AM in the **START HOUR** field. You should have the options selected, that are shown above in Figure 11-38.

7. Click the **FILTER** button and change the Date Range to 09/19/2018 to 09/22/2018.

8. Clear the **SHOW CLEARED** option.

   You should have the options selected, that are shown in Figure 11-39.

   Click OK.

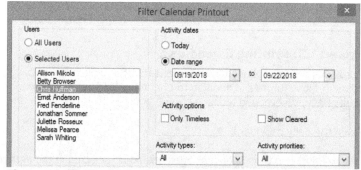

**Figure 11-39** Filter Calendar Printout dialog box

9. Click OK to close the Options dialog box.

   If you want to print the calendar, click the Print button on the Print dialog box.

   The calendar will look like the one shown in Figure 11-40.

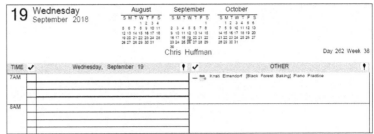

**Figure 11-40** ACT! daily calendar

## Calendar View Related Tasks

The options shown in Figure 11-41 are for the Calendar views.

**Figure 11-41** Calendar view related tasks

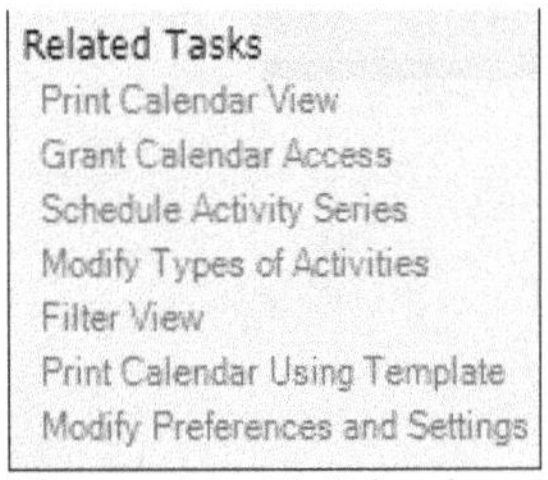

**PRINT CALENDAR VIEW** [See Chapter 8, Exercise 8.7]

**GRANT CALENDAR ACCESS** [See Exercise 11.2, earlier in this chapter]

**SCHEDULE ACTIVITY SERIES** [See Chapter 3, below Figure 3-32]

**MODIFY TYPES OF ACTIVITIES** [See Chapter 14, Exercise 14.10]

**FILTER VIEW** [See Calendar Tips box - Filter Calendar, earlier in this chapter]

**PRINT CALENDAR USING TEMPLATE** [See Exercise 11.3 earlier in this chapter]

**MODIFY PREFERENCES AND SETTINGS** Opens the Calendar & Activities tab on the Preferences dialog box. [See Chapter 2, Calendar & Activities Tab Preferences]

## History List View

As you have learned in this chapter, the Task List and calendar can be used to display what you have to do. The Activities tab displays open tasks for the contact, company, opportunity or group that is selected. The History tab displays completed activities/tasks.

The History List view displays the records from the History tab of the Contact, Company, Opportunity and Group views, all in one place. Figure 11-42 shows the History List view.

The buttons on the toolbar are the same as the ones on the Task List. [See Table 11-1].

The Filter options are the same as the ones on the History tab. The only difference is that the Regarding & Details column on the History tab, is named Regarding, on the History List view. [See Chapter 9, Finding Records On The History Tab]

| Date | Contact | Company | Result | Regarding | Record Manager | Share With |
|---|---|---|---|---|---|---|
| 01/09/2018 | Ernst Anderson | CH TechONE | Meeting Not Held | Breakfast Networking Group | Ernst Anderson | CH TechONE[CMP] |
| 01/08/2018 | Melissa Pearce | CH TechONE | Meeting Held | Staff Meeting | Chris Huffman | CH TechONE[CMP] |
| 01/08/2018 | Allison Mikola | CH TechONE | Meeting Held | Networking Breakfast | Allison Mikola | |
| 01/07/2018 | Chris Huffman | CH TechONE | Meeting Held | Network Breakfast | Chris Huffman | CH TechONE[CMP] |

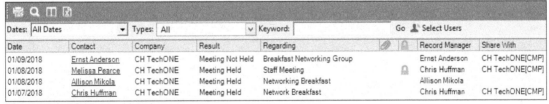

**Figure 11-42** History List view

# DASHBOARDS

In this chapter you will learn how to use dashboards and how to modify them, by exploring the following topics:

- ☑ What is a dashboard?
- ☑ Dashboard layouts
- ☑ Dashboard Designer window
- ☑ Components
- ☑ Filtering data in a dashboard
- ☑ Modifying dashboard layouts
- ☑ Modifying dashboard components

**No Shame Book Plug #3**
If you find that your dashboard needs have out grown the dashboard features in ACT!, you may find my book, Learning Tableau Made Easy ISBN 978-1-935208-37-2 helpful. Once you export your ACT! data to Excel, you will have more functionality available to you, to create the dashboards that you need.

**CHAPTER 12**

## What Is A Dashboard?

A dashboard displays a snapshot of data in a graphical format. So far in this book you have created, viewed and edited different types of data, including contacts, activities and opportunities. While it is easy to switch between views to see all of these types of data, you cannot view more than one of these types of data at the same time. You also cannot get a feel for the big picture of your data, as they say.

This is where dashboards come into play. Like other features in ACT!, the data that is displayed in a dashboard can be filtered. You can create, view and edit data from a dashboard. You can edit the default dashboard layouts by adding, modifying and removing components in a dashboard. To create a dashboard from scratch involves selecting the components that are needed, adding them to the layout, then selecting the options to customize the components.

## Dashboard Layouts

ACT! comes with five layouts, as shown in Figures 12-1 to 12-5. Each layout can be customized. The layouts contain components that display data in different formats. Components also have filters that have default values. These filters work like the other filters that you have used in ACT!. Later in this chapter, you will learn how to customize the layouts and how to change the filter preset default values. The data that is displayed on each dashboard is explained below.

The **ACTIVITIES DASHBOARD** displays the contacts schedule and activities. The Activities by User component was replaced with the Activities by Type component in ACT! Pro 2011.

The **ADMINISTRATIVE DASHBOARD** displays user status and remote database information.

The **CONTACTS DASHBOARD** displays contact records that you have created or edited and a count of history records.

The **DEFAULT DASHBOARD** displays your schedule, activities, history and opportunity information.

The **OPPORTUNITY DASHBOARD** displays opportunity sales information in several formats.

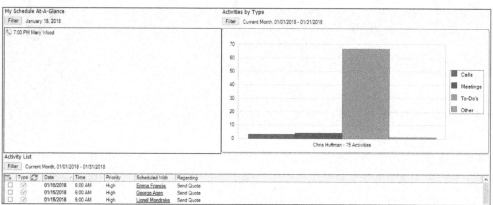

**Figure 12-1** Activities dashboard

| User Name | User Status | Role | Logon Date | Logoff Date | Logon Status | Client Machine |
|---|---|---|---|---|---|---|
| Allison Mikola | Inactive | Manager | | | ? | |
| Betty Browser | Inactive | Browse | | | ? | |
| Chris Huffman | Active | Administrator | 01/18/2018 12:16 AM | | Successful | |
| Ernst Anderson | Inactive | Standard | | | ? | |
| Fred Fenderline | Inactive | Standard | | | ? | |
| Jonathan Sommer | Inactive | Standard | | | ? | |
| Juliette Rosseux | Inactive | Restricted | | | ? | |

**Figure 12-2** Administrative dashboard

Recently Created Contacts

Filter

| Contact | Company | ID/Status | Phone | Create Date | Record Creator | Record Manager | Days Since Creation |
|---|---|---|---|---|---|---|---|
| Dan Day | Circle Photography | | (214) 555-2215 | 01/14/2018 3:13 AM | Chris Huffman | Chris Huffman | 2 |
| Jennifer Doe | | | | 01/15/2018 3:35 AM | Chris Huffman | Chris Huffman | 3 |
| Jane Doe | My Company | | | 01/15/2018 1:43 PM | Chris Huffman | Chris Huffman | 3 |
| Mary Wood | | | | 01/15/2018 3:35 AM | Chris Huffman | Chris Huffman | 3 |
| Bill Grant | | | | 01/15/2018 3:35 AM | Chris Huffman | Chris Huffman | 3 |
| Suzie Lee | AVB Enterprises | Customer;Friend | (623) 898-1022 | 12/10/2018 5:59 PM | Chris Huffman | Chris Huffman | -326 |
| Keifer Sacquoci | MI Business Plan, Inc. | Customer | (610) 898-3333 | 12/10/2018 6:05 PM | Chris Huffman | Chris Huffman | -326 |

Recently Edited Contacts

Filter

| Contact | Company | ID/Status | Phone | Edit Date | Last Edited By | Record Manager | Days Since Edited |
|---|---|---|---|---|---|---|---|
| James Jayson | HAL's Consulting Corp | Customer | (503) 555-2252 | 01/16/2018 9:11 PM | Chris Huffman | Chris Huffman | |
| Allison Mikola | CH TechONE | Employee | (212) 555-2485 | 01/16/2018 1:54 AM | Chris Huffman | Allison Mikola | 3 |
| Mary Bailey | Liberty Savings & Loan | Prospect | 315-988-6700 | 01/16/2018 3:57 PM | Chris Huffman | Chris Huffman | 2 |
| Dan Minnick | Django Consulting | Customer | | 01/15/2018 8:11 PM | Chris Huffman | Chris Huffman | 2 |
| Morty Manicotti | Corleone's Pasta Company | Friend;Customer | (480) 555-4512 | 01/15/2018 8:11 PM | Chris Huffman | Chris Huffman | 2 |
| Dan Day | Circle Photography | | (214) 555-2215 | 01/14/2018 3:17 AM | Chris Huffman | Chris Huffman | 4 |
| Sean Duffy | Circle Photography | Prospect | 0164 262546 | 01/15/2018 8:11 PM | Chris Huffman | Chris Huffman | 2 |

Contact History Count by History Type

Filter

**Figure 12-3** Contacts dashboard

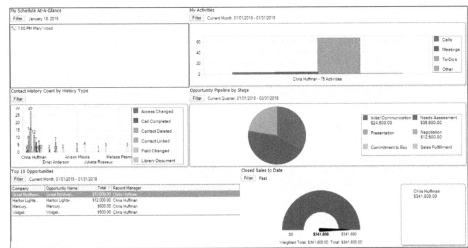

**Figure 12-4** Default dashboard

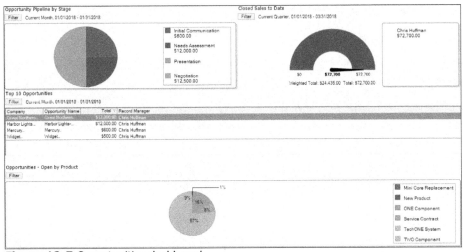

**Figure 12-5** Opportunities dashboard

### Dashboard Toolbar

Figure 12-6 shows the Dashboard toolbar. Table 12-1 explains the buttons on the toolbar.

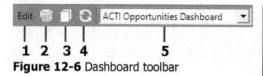

**Figure 12-6** Dashboard toolbar

| Button | Description |
|--------|-------------|
| 1 | Is used to edit the dashboard that is displayed. |
| 2 | Prints the dashboard that is displayed. |
| 3 | Copies the dashboard that is displayed to the clipboard. |
| 4 | Refreshes the data in the dashboard. |
| 5 | Is used to select a different dashboard layout. |

**Table 12-1** Dashboard toolbar buttons explained

### Exercise 12.1: Selecting A Dashboard Layout

The steps below show you how to select a dashboard.

1. Click the **DASHBOARD** button on the Navigation Pane.

2. To select a different dashboard, open the Dashboard drop-down list and select one of the options shown in Figure 12-7.

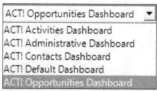

**Figure 12-7** Default dashboard layouts

### Dashboard Components

Components display different types of data from the database. There are six components in two categories that can be added to a layout, as explained below. The options shown are the defaults for the component, which can be modified. For example, the Closed sales to date component, shown in the upper right corner of Figure 12-5, displays opportunities in the CHT1 Sales process. If you created a process, you can modify this component to display your process by default, instead of the CHT1 Sales process.

### Activity Components

The two activity components that come with ACT! are explained below.

① **MY ACTIVITIES** Displays a chart with your activities for the current month.
② **MY SCHEDULE AT-A-GLANCE** Displays your scheduled activities for today.

### Opportunity Components

The four opportunity components that come with ACT! are explained below. The opportunity data that each component displays is from the CHT1 Sales process.

① **CLOSED SALES TO DATE** Displays opportunities that have the Closed-Won status for the current month.
② **MY OPPORTUNITIES** Displays a bar chart that represents the open opportunities for the current month.
③ **OPPORTUNITY PIPELINE BY STAGE** Displays a pie chart that represents the open opportunities for the current month.
④ **TOP OPPORTUNITIES** Displays a list of your top 10 opportunities for the current month that have the Closed-Won status.

### Getting Things Done From A Dashboard

Yes, the dashboard provides a great way to view a lot of data in a graphical format, but you still need to be able to get work done. Many of the components have a shortcut menu. This is in addition to the menu and toolbar options on the dashboard workspace.

### Activity Component Shortcut Menu Options

The activity shortcut menu options explained in this section are available, regardless of the dashboard that they are on.

1. Open the ACT! Activities Dashboard.

2. Right-click in the
   My Schedule At-A-Glance component.

   You should see the shortcut menu
   shown in Figure 12-8.

   These are the activity options that
   you can use.

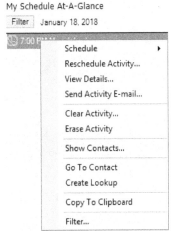

**Figure 12-8** My Schedule At-A-Glance shortcut menu

3. If you right-click in the Activity List component, you will see the shortcut menu shown above in Figure 12-8. The Activity List shortcut menu also has the **CUSTOMIZE COLUMNS** option at the bottom of the menu.

4. If you right-click in the Activities by Type component on the Default Dashboard, you will see that the options shown in Figure 12-9 are the only ones available.

**Figure 12-9** Activities by Type shortcut menu

The **COPY TO CLIPBOARD** option creates an image of the component. This image can be pasted into a document.

The **VIEW ALL DATA IN LIST** option displays the Task List view.

## Opportunity Component Shortcut Menu Options

The opportunity shortcut menu options explained in this section are available in dashboards that have an opportunity component.

1. Open the ACT! Opportunities Dashboard.

2. Right-click in the grid in the Top 10 Opportunities component. You should see the shortcut menu shown in Figure 12-10.

   The majority of the other opportunity components only have the shortcut menu options shown above in Figure 12-9.

   The Opportunities - Open by Product component has the shortcut menu options shown in Figure 12-11.

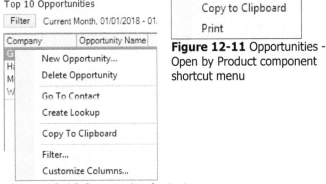

**Figure 12-11** Opportunities - Open by Product component shortcut menu

**Figure 12-10** Opportunity shortcut menu

## Filtering Data In A Dashboard

As you have seen, each activity component has a filter button. The filter button is used to change the data that is displayed in the component. The options that you will see on the Filter dialog boxes are the default options that were set for the component.

If you select different options on a filter dialog box, the next time that you open a dashboard, those options will still be selected. The exception to this is if you or another administrator or manager of the database modifies the default filter options for the component.

### Exercise 12.2: Filtering Activity Component Data

In this exercise you will learn how to filter the activity component data.

### My Schedule At-A-Glance Filter Component Options

1. Open the ACT! Activities Dashboard.

2. Click the **FILTER** button in the My Schedule At-A-Glance component. You will see the dialog box shown in Figure 12-12.

   The filter options on this dialog box are a subset of the filter options that are on the Activities tab.

   If the My Schedule At-A-Glance component displays a lot of activities, you can change some of the options on this dialog box to reduce the number of activities that appear in the component.

**Figure 12-12** My Schedule At-A-Glance component filter options

### Activities By Type Filter Component Options

1. Click the **FILTER** button in the Activities By Type component.

   You will see the dialog box shown in Figure 12-13.

   The filter options on this dialog box are the same filter options that are on the Activities tab of the Contact detail view.

   The **SHOW TASKS FROM OTHER APPLICATIONS** option is helpful if you want to display tasks that were created in Outlook or Google.

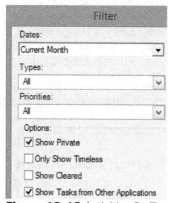

**Figure 12-13** Activities By Type component filter options

### Activity List Filter Options

The Activity List filter is the list view display type of the My Activities component.

1. Click the **FILTER** button in the Activity List component. As you see, the Filter dialog box has the same options as the one shown above in Figure 12-13.

2. Clear the Call and To-Do **TYPES**, then click OK. You will see fewer activities in this component on the dashboard.

### Administrative Dashboard

The components on this dashboard display users of the database. The filter buttons in both remote database sections open the dialog box shown in Figure 12-14.

This dialog box is used to enter the name of the remote database(s) that you want to view the status of, as shown in Figure 12-15. (This figure is from a previous version of this book, because I no longer have any remote databases, set up.)

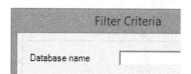

**Figure 12-14** Filter Criteria dialog box

| User Status | | | | | | |
|---|---|---|---|---|---|---|
| Filter | | | | | | |
| User Name | User Status | Role | Logon Date | Logoff Date | Logon Status | Client Machine |
| Allison Mikola | Inactive | Manager | 4/16/2008 11:19 AM | | Successful | ACTDIVA |
| Betty Browser | Inactive | Browse | | | | |
| Chris Huffman | Active | Administrator | 10/4/2009 2:34 PM | | Successful | INDERA |
| Ernst Anderson | Inactive | Standard | 4/18/2008 1:59 PM | | Successful | ACTDIVA |
| Fred Fenderline | Inactive | Standard | | | | |

| Remote Database Synch Status by User | | | | | | | | | |
|---|---|---|---|---|---|---|---|---|---|
| Filter | | | | | | | | | |
| Database Name | Last Attempt | Last Complete | Last Success | Last Status | RECV Attempt | RECV Complete | RECV Result | RECV Success | Last Edited By |
| MyRemoteDB_1 | 10/4/2009 2:03 PM | | 10/4/2009 2:03 PM | 0 | | | | | |
| MyRemoteDB_2 | 10/4/2009 2:04 PM | | 10/4/2009 2:04 PM | 0 | | | | | |
| MyRemoteDB_3 | 10/4/2009 2:05 PM | | 10/4/2009 2:05 PM | 0 | | | | | |
| MyRemoteDB_4 | 10/4/2009 2:06 PM | | 10/4/2009 2:06 PM | 0 | | | | | |

| Remote Database Information by User | | | | | | | |
|---|---|---|---|---|---|---|---|
| Filter | | | | | | | |
| Created On | Database Name | Edited On | Expire Days | Expired | Include Attachments | Last Edited By | Server Name |
| 10/4/2009 1:22 PM | My_ACTDemo | | 30 | No | Yes | | INDERA\ACT7 |
| 10/4/2009 2:03 PM | MyRemoteDB_1 | | 30 | No | No | | INDERA\ACT7 |
| 10/4/2009 2:04 PM | MyRemoteDB_2 | | 30 | No | No | | INDERA\ACT7 |

**Figure 12-15** Remote database dashboard information

## Dashboard Designer

The Dashboard Designer is used to create new dashboards and modify the dashboards that come with ACT!. It has the two functions explained below.

① **CREATE OR MODIFY THE LAYOUT** Select this option when you want to create a new dashboard layout or modify an existing layout.

② **MODIFY A DASHBOARD COMPONENT** Select this option when you want to modify a component, like changing the default filter options.

## Dashboard Designer Window

When you open the Dashboard Designer in Edit mode, you will see the window shown in Figure 12-16.

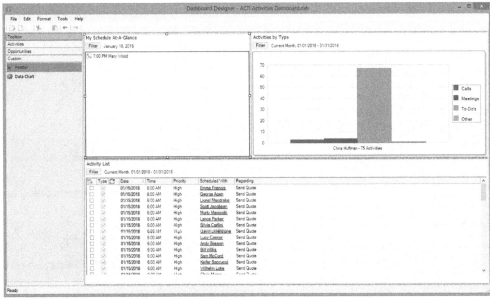

**Figure 12-16** Dashboard Designer window

### Dashboard Designer Toolbar

Not to be out done, the Dashboard Designer has its own toolbar, as shown in Figure 12-17. Table 12-2 explains the buttons on the toolbar.

**Figure 12-17** Dashboard Designer toolbar

| Button | Description |
|---|---|
| 1 | Creates a new dashboard. |
| 2 | Opens an existing dashboard. |
| 3 | Saves the changes. |
| 4 | Deletes the selected component. |
| 5 | Copies the selected component. |
| 6 | Pastes the selected component. |
| 7 | Undoes the last action. |
| 8 | Redoes the previous action. |

**Table 12-2** Dashboard Designer toolbar buttons explained

### Dashboard Designer Menu Options

The Dashboard Designer has some menu options that are unique. They are explained in Table 12-3.

| Menu | Option | Description |
|---|---|---|
| File | Layout Settings | Opens the dialog box shown in Figure 12-18. These options are used to change the size of the dashboard. |
| Format | Insert/Delete | Both options have the submenu shown in Figure 12-19. |
| Tools | Add Component | This option is only available when a dashboard layout has an empty section. It opens the submenu shown in Figure 12-20. This is one way to add a component to the dashboard. The components are divided into the activity, opportunity and custom categories that you read about earlier in this chapter. |
| Tools | Component Configuration | Opens the **COMPONENT CONFIGURATION WIZARD**, which is covered later in this chapter. |

**Table 12-3** Dashboard Designer menu options explained

The dimensions shown in the **TARGET SIZE** drop-down list are the same size as computer screen resolutions.

This means that if you are creating or modifying a dashboard and all of the people that will use it have the same screen size resolution, you can select that size instead of using the smaller default size.

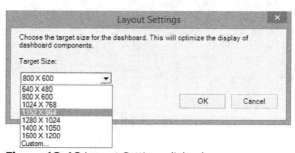

**Figure 12-18** Layout Settings dialog box

### Format Menu

The **COLUMN ON THE FAR RIGHT** option will add/delete a column on the right side of the dashboard.

The **ROW AT THE BOTTOM** option will add/delete a row at the bottom of the dashboard.

The **CELL AT END OF THE ROW** option will add/delete a cell at the end of the row that is selected.

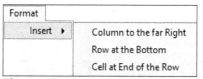

**Figure 12-19** Insert and Delete layout options

### Tools Menu

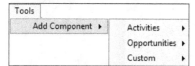

**Figure 12-20** Add Component options

## Dashboard Designer Toolbox

The Dashboard Designer toolbox options are shown in Figures 12-21 to 12-23. Each component was explained earlier in the Dashboard Components section. These are the components that you can add to a dashboard.

**Figure 12-21** Activity components

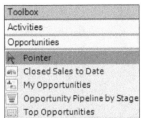

**Figure 12-22** Opportunity components

**Figure 12-23** Custom component

## Dashboard Layout Overview

By default, a new layout has six sections that you can add a component to. It is not a requirement that all six sections be used in a layout. Each section can be resized. Figures 12-1 to 12-5 display the dashboards that come with ACT!. What may not be obvious is that you can create a layout from scratch and add components of different types. For example, you could add the Activities type component shown in Figure 12-1, the Recently created contacts component shown in Figure 12-3 and the Opportunity pipeline by stage component from Figure 12-4, to a new layout, to create your own custom dashboard.

I think the Dashboard Designer is a good first step in being able to modify dashboards. It has some quirks that I hope will be worked out. It is not as user friendly as the other designers in ACT!. For example, in the exercise below, the goal is to move the component that is at the bottom of the dashboard to the top of the dashboard. Sounds easy right? As you will see, it requires several steps.

### Exercise 12.3: Modify The ACT! Activities Dashboard Layout

In this exercise you will modify the Activities dashboard layout to put the Activity List component at the top of the layout.

1. Open the ACT! Activities Dashboard ⇒ Click the **EDIT CURRENT DASHBOARD** button on the Dashboard toolbar. You will see the Dashboard Designer window.

2. File ⇒ Save As.

    You will see the dialog box shown in Figure 12-24.

    The folder shown at the top of the figure is where the dashboard layouts are stored, that appear in the drop-down list at the top of the dashboard. If you want the dashboard layouts that you create to appear in the drop-down list, you have to save them in this folder.

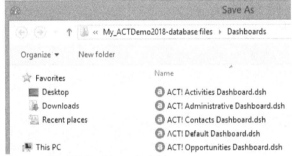

**Figure 12-24** Dashboards folder

3. Type My Activities Dashboard in the File name field, then press Enter.

4.  The My Schedule component should be selected in the layout.

    Format ⇒ Insert ⇒ Row at the bottom.

    You should see a new row at the bottom of the window, as illustrated in Figure 12-25.

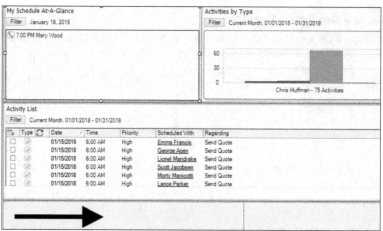

**Figure 12-25** New row added to the dashboard layout

5.  Drag the Activity List component in the layout to the bottom row.

6.  Right-click in the middle row ⇒ Insert ⇒ Cell at End of the Row.

7.  One by one, move the two components in the first row to the cells in the middle row.

8.  Right-click in the first row and select Delete ⇒ Cell at End of the Row.

9.  Move the Activity List component in the third row to the first row.

10. Format ⇒ Delete ⇒ Row at the Bottom.

11. File ⇒ Exit ⇒ Click Yes, when prompted to save the changes to the dashboard. Wasn't that a lot of steps to rearrange the components on the layout? <smile> The reason is because there is no option to add a row above an existing row. Truthfully, it is easier to delete some components and re-add them, then it is to move them.

## View The Changes

1.  On the Dashboard view, open the Dashboard drop-down list.

    You should see your dashboard at the bottom of the list, as shown in Figure 12-26.

**Figure 12-26** Dashboard added to the list

2.  Select your dashboard.

    It should look like the one shown in Figure 12-27.

    Compare it to the one shown earlier in Figure 12-1.

    If a component is not displaying data, change the filter options.

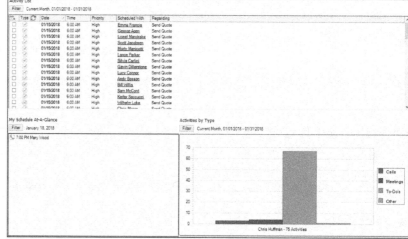

**Figure 12-27** Modified Activities dashboard

## Component Configuration Wizard

This wizard is used to add components to a dashboard. It is accessed from the Tools menu in the Dashboard Designer. Once you select an option on a component wizard screen, you can preview the change by clicking the **PREVIEW** button. The following seven steps are available on the Component Configuration Wizard once a component has been added to a layout. All steps are not available for each component. The options available for some steps vary, depending on the component.

### Step 1: Select Display Type

This step is used to select the chart type, as shown in Figure 12-28.

All chart types are not available for all components.

You can also select where to place the filter button, by changing the **FILTER BAR PLACEMENT OPTION**, illustrated at the bottom of the figure.

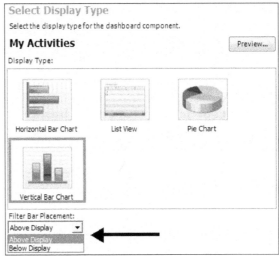

**Figure 12-28** Component display type options

### Step 2: Edit Default Filters

This step displays the current default filter options for the component and is used to select new default filter options. The filter options change, depending on the display type (chart) that is selected.

Figure 12-29 shows the filter options for the My Activities component.
Figure 12-30 shows the filter options for the Opportunity Pipeline by Stage component.

**Figure 12-29** Filter options for the My Activities component

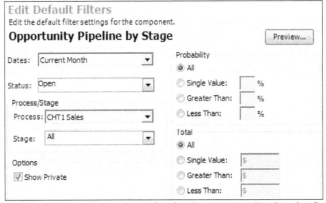

**Figure 12-30** Filter options for the Opportunity Pipeline by Stage component

### Step 3: Edit Header/Footer

This step is used to add or edit the header and footer information for the component, as shown in Figure 12-31.

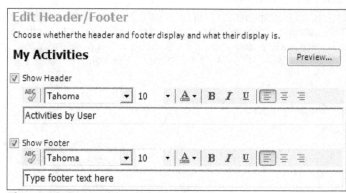

**Figure 12-31** Header and footer options

### Step 4: Change Legend

This step is used to select whether or not the component displays a legend and where the legend should be placed, as shown in Figure 12-32.

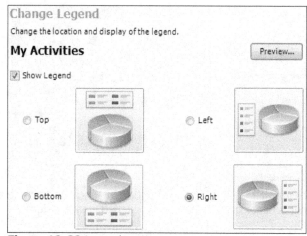

**Figure 12-32** Legend options

### Step 5: Change Totals

This step is used to select whether or not the component displays totals. The totals for each component type are pre-determined, which means that you can only select whether or not to display totals. Figure 12-33 shows the totals for the Closed Sales to Date component. Figure 12-34 shows the totals for the My Activities component.

**Figure 12-33** Total options for the Closed Sales to Date component

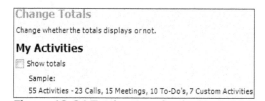

**Figure 12-34** Total options for the My Activities component

### Step 6: Specify Targets

This step is used to select whether or not the component displays the minimum acceptable amount or value that will reach the expected goal. Figure 12-35 shows the target options. Figure 12-36 illustrates the target option applied to a chart. The line illustrated in Figure 12-36 across the chart, represents the target. This allows the user to see which items meet the goal and which ones do not.

As illustrated in Figure 12-37, the target is $30,000. The target is indicated by a triangle pointer on the chart. In this example, the target has not been met. In Figure 12-38, the target is $17,500, which means that the target has been met and exceeded.

Figure 12-35 Target options

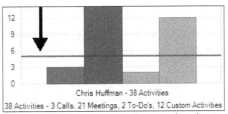

**Figure 12-36** Target option on the chart

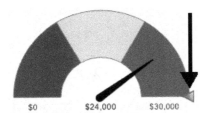

**Figure 12-37** Target has not been met

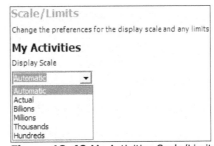

**Figure 12-38** Target has been met

## Step 7: Scale/Limits

This step is used to select the range of numeric data displayed on the chart. The scale and limits change, depending on the display type that is selected. Figures 12-39 to 12-41 show different types of scale/limits. The BREAKPOINT options are used to measure progress.

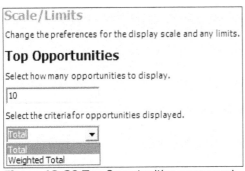

**Figure 12-39** Top Opportunities component Scale/Limits options

**Figure 12-40** My Activities Scale/Limits component options

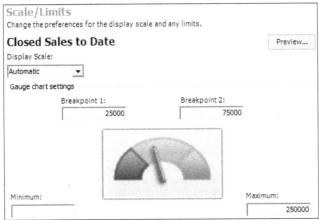

**Figure 12-41** Closed Sales to Date Scale/Limits component options

### Top Opportunities Component

This component has an additional step, as shown in Figure 12-42.

The options shown are used to change the columns that are displayed in the grid and how the opportunity records are sorted.

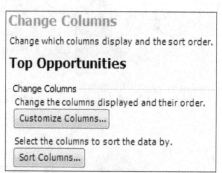

Change Columns

Change which columns display and the sort order.

**Top Opportunities**

Change Columns

Change the columns displayed and their order.

Customize Columns...

Select the columns to sort the data by.

Sort Columns...

**Figure 12-42** Change Columns options for the Top Opportunities component

### Exercise 12.4: Modify The Components Of The Default Dashboard

In this exercise you will modify the default filter options for the Default Dashboard. The default date range filter is the current month.

1. Open the ACT! Default Dashboard ⇒ Click the **EDIT CURRENT DASHBOARD** button on the Dashboard toolbar.

2. File ⇒ Save As ⇒ Type `My New Filter Dashboard` as the file name, then press Enter.

### Modify The My Activities Component Filter Options

 In ACT! 2009 and earlier, by default, the My Activities component (formerly called the **ACTIVITIES BY USER COMPONENT**) displayed totals of the activities, for the user by category, at the bottom of the component.

In this part of the exercise, you will learn how to change the location of the legend and filter button, as well as, add totals to the Activities component.

1. Right-click on the My Activities component and select **COMPONENT CONFIGURATION**.

2. Click on the Select Display Type link ⇒ Select the **HORIZONTAL BAR CHART** display type ⇒ Open the **FILTER BAR PLACEMENT** drop-down list and select Below Display ⇒ Click Next.

3. On the Edit Default Filters screen, open the Dates drop-down list and select Today and Future ⇒ Click Next twice.

4. On the Change Legend screen, select Top ⇒ Click Next.

5. On the Change Totals screen, check the Show totals option ⇒ Click Finish.

6. Click Yes, when prompted that the changes will affect all users.

   As shown in Figure 12-43, the Details section on the Configuration Wizard screen shows the options that have been selected for the component.

   Click Close to close the Component Configuration dialog box.

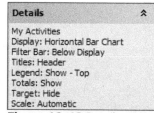

**Details** ⌃

My Activities
Display: Horizontal Bar Chart
Filter Bar: Below Display
Titles: Header
Legend: Show - Top
Totals: Show
Target: Hide
Scale: Automatic

**Figure 12-43** Details section

### Modify The Closed Sales To Date Component Filter Options

1. Right-click on the Closed Sales to Date component and select Component Configuration.

2. On the Edit Default Filters screen, open the Dates drop-down list and select Today and Future.

3. On the Edit Header/Footer screen, type `Pending Sales` in the Header field ⇒ Change the font size to 14 ⇒ Change the color to red.

4. On the Specify Targets screen, display the target and change the Target value to $100,000.00.

5. On the Scale/Limits screen, make the changes below. You should have the options shown earlier in Figure 12-41.
   - Breakpoint 1 25000
   - Breakpoint 2 75000
   - Maximum 250000

6. Click Finish ⇒ Click Yes to continue with changes, then click Close.

7. Delete the My Schedule at a glance component ⇒ Move the My Activities component to the left cell.

8. Delete the cell at the end of the row. Close the Dashboard Designer.

9. Select the My New Filter Dashboard ⇒ Change the filter options below.
   - Change the Opportunity Pipeline by Stage date filter to Past.
   - Change the Pending Sales date filter to Past and the Status to Open.

The dashboard should look similar to the one shown in Figure 12-44.

Compare this to the ACT! Default Dashboard, shown earlier in figure 12-4.

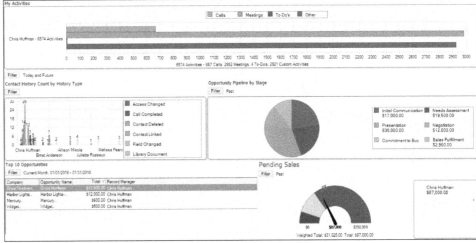

**Figure 12-44** Modified dashboard components

## Create A New Dashboard

When you need to create a dashboard from scratch, you can follow the steps below.

1. Click the **NEW DASHBOARD** link in the Related Tasks section on the Navigation Pane. You will see an empty layout in the Dashboard Designer.

2. Drag a component from the Toolbox to the layout. The Component Configuration Wizard will automatically open ⇒ Select the default options that you need, for the component.

3. Repeat step 2 for each component that you want to add to the dashboard layout.

4. Remove any sections from the layout that are not needed.

5. Save the dashboard and give it a descriptive name.

## Data Chart Component

This component is on the Dashboard Designer [See Figure 12-23]. It is used to create a custom component.

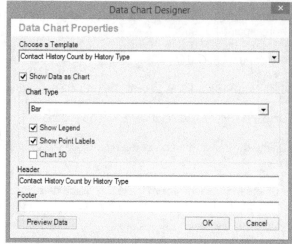

**Figure 12-45** Data Chart Designer dialog box

When you add the Custom Data Chart component to a section of the layout, you will see the dialog box shown in Figure 12-45.

The options on this dialog box are used to configure the component. The options are explained below.

**CHOOSE A TEMPLATE** The options shown in Figure 12-46 are the layouts that you can select from to create your custom component. You have seen many of these layouts earlier in this chapter. Some of these templates will disable other options on the dialog box.

**SHOW DATA AS CHART** If checked, the data will be displayed as a chart in the component instead of in grid format.

**CHART TYPE** The options shown in Figure 12-47 are the chart types that can be created.

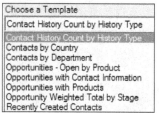

**Figure 12-46** Choose a Template drop-down list options

**Figure 12-47** Chart Type options

**SHOW LEGEND** If checked, a legend for the charts data will be displayed on the component.

**SHOW POINT LABELS** If checked, the value that each part of the chart represents will be displayed on the component, as shown in Figure 12-48.

Depending on the size of the chart, the lines may not be displayed. The lines are displayed when the chart size is small.

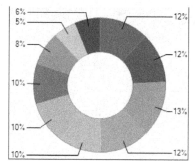

**Figure 12-48** Show Point Labels option

**CHART 3D** If checked, the chart will be displayed in 3D format, as shown in Figure 12-49.

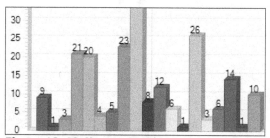

**Figure 12-49** Chart in 3D format

**HEADER** Is used to type in information that you want to appear at the top of the component. By default, the template name is added to this field.

**FOOTER** Is used to type in information that you want to appear at the bottom of the component.

**PREVIEW DATA BUTTON** Depending on the template selected on the dialog box, shown earlier in Figure 12-45, a different Filter Criteria dialog box will appear. The options are used to set up the default filter criteria and to view the data. Some of the filters are explained and shown below.

Figure 12-50 shows the filter criteria options for the Contact History Count By History Type component.
Figure 12-51 shows the filter criteria options for the Contacts By Department component.
Figure 12-52 shows the filter criteria options for the Opportunities with Products component.

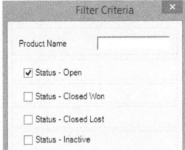

**Figure 12-52** Opportunities with Products component Filter Criteria dialog box

**Figure 12-50** Contact History Count By History Type component Filter Criteria dialog box

**Figure 12-51** Contacts By Department component Filter Criteria dialog box

## Dashboard View Related Tasks

The options shown in Figure 12-53 are for the Dashboard view. The options are explained below.

**NEW DASHBOARD** Opens the Dashboard Designer to create a new dashboard.

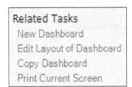

**Figure 12-53** Dashboard view related tasks

**EDIT LAYOUT OF DASHBOARD** Opens the current dashboard layout in the Dashboard Designer, so that it can be modified.

**COPY DASHBOARD** Is used to create a screen shot (image file) of the entire dashboard, so that it can be pasted into a document.

For example, if you click on this link, then open Microsoft Word, right-click and select Paste, you will see a copy of the dashboard in the document, as shown in Figure 12-54.

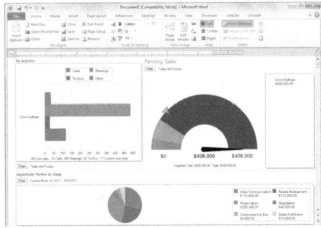

**Figure 12-54** Image of dashboard pasted in a document

**PRINT CURRENT SCREEN** Opens the Quick Print Options dialog box so that you can select options for how the screen, in this case the dashboard, will be printed. The options are similar to those shown in Chapter 8, Exercise 8.7.

# CREATING QUERIES

Overview

In this chapter you will learn about the following query techniques:

- ☑ Create queries using the Lookup By Example tool
- ☑ Query operators
- ☑ Running and saving queries
- ☑ Advanced queries
- ☑ Creating dynamic groups
- ☑ Sorting records retrieved from a query

CHAPTER 13

## Queries Overview

Queries and lookups for that matter, are used to get answers to questions like "Which contacts are in a particular state and were referred by Agency 1 or Agency 2?". Another question a query could answer would be "Which customers have not been contacted in the last 60 days?". You have learned how to use the Lookup command to find contacts. Depending on the types of contacts that you are trying to find, you will have to perform several lookups. If you needed to find contacts in two cities, you would have to perform two lookups and add the results of the second lookup to the results of the first lookup.

The Lookup By Example dialog box resembles the Contact detail view. It contains all of the fields that are on the layout. If you add a field to the top of a layout or to a tab, it will also appear on the Lookup By Example dialog box.

Queries have several advantages over lookups. Queries are used to find contacts based on multiple values in the same field or find contacts that match criteria in more than one field at the same time. Another advantage of using queries is that you can save them and use them again. You can create contact, company, group and opportunity lookups on the Lookup By Example dialog box. If you need to lookup data in a range of values, you have to use the Advanced Query tool.

Like other features in ACT!, there is more than one way to create a query. You can use the Lookup By Example dialog box or the Advanced Query tool. In this chapter you will learn how to create queries using both options.

> **Saved Query File Extensions**
> Saved queries have one of the file extensions listed below.
> **.QRY** are contact queries.
> **.CRY** are company queries.
> **.GRY** are group queries.
> **.ORY** are opportunity queries.

### Exercise 13.1: Creating Queries Using The Lookup By Example Tool

The primary reason to use the Lookup By Example tool is to save a query without having to create all of the syntax that is required when using the Advanced Query tool. Another reason to use the Lookup By Example tool is if you need to find records that requires using more than one field, to look up the data. As you know, the Lookup dialog box does not support using multiple criteria. In this exercise you will create a query to find all customers in Arizona.

1.  Make sure that all of the contacts are displayed. Lookup ⇒ By Example. You should see the Lookup By Example dialog box.

2.  Select AZ in the State field.

3.  Check the Customer option in the **ID/STATUS** field drop-down list. You should have the options selected, that are shown in Figure 13-1.

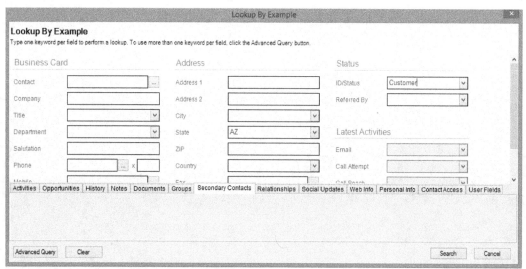

**Figure 13-1** Lookup By Example search criteria

Some of the tabs like Personal Info, Contact Access, and User Fields, display fields and some do not, like the History and Notes tabs. The tabs that have fields displayed can be used in the lookup.

 The bottom half of the **LOOKUP BY EXAMPLE DIALOG BOX** cannot be moved down. I find this problematic.

### Saving Lookup By Example Queries

If you create a query that you will want to run again, you should save it. If you save the query, you can also edit and use it as the basis for another query. Actually, you should save the query before you run it. If you do not save the query before it is run and discover that you did not select the correct options, you will have to start over. You cannot save the query on the Lookup By Example dialog box. You have to save it using the Advanced Query tool.

1. Click the Advanced Query button ⇒ Click the **SAVE** button (last button at the top) on the Contact Criteria dialog box. The default folder for saving queries that ACT! uses, is automatically displayed.

2. Navigate to and select your folder ⇒ Type `Customers in AZ` as the query name.

3. You should see the query name in the Title bar, at the top of the Contact Criteria dialog box.

   Click the Preview button. The contact records that meet the query criteria, will be displayed at the bottom of the dialog box, as shown in Figure 13-2.

   There should be nine customers in AZ.

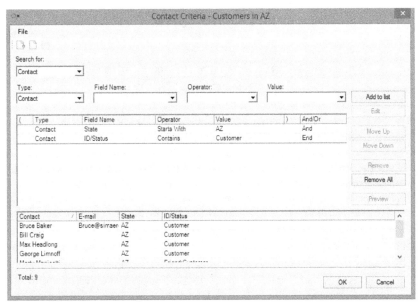

**Figure 13-2** Query results

The **ADD TO LIST** button adds the criteria from the Type, Field Name, Operator and Value fields to the grid in the middle of the dialog box.

The **EDIT** button opens the Edit dialog box, which is used to modify the selected row of criteria in the grid.

The **MOVE UP** and **MOVE DOWN** buttons are used to change the order of the criteria in the grid.

The **REMOVE** button will delete the criteria on the row that is selected.

The **REMOVE ALL** button deletes all of the criteria.

The **PREVIEW** button runs the query and displays the results at the bottom of the dialog box.

4. Click OK. You will see the dialog box shown in Figure 13-3 ⇒ Click OK.

   If you scroll through the records in the Contact detail view, you will see that each record has **CUSTOMER** in the ID/Status field and **AZ** in the State field.

**Figure 13-3** ACT! Run Query Options dialog box

## Wildcards

The Lookup By Example tool has two wildcard characters that are used to search for characters in a field. They are discussed below. The default search method will only search for the characters that you enter.

① The **%** (percent sign). This wildcard character is used to find characters any place in the field. If you wanted to find all companies that had a specific word or character, you would type the percent sign followed by the characters that you want to search for like this, %Toys. If you entered this in the Company field, all of the records with "Toys" any place in the Company field would be retrieved.

② The **_** (underscore). Use this wildcard character to replace one character in the string of characters that you are searching for. If you entered t_n as the search criteria, the search would return records that have ten, tan and ton in the field, but not toon.

> If you used a version prior to ACT! 2007 and used the asterisk (*) in a lookup or query and tried it in ACT! 2009 or higher, you saw that it did not work. I do not know why, but the functionality of the asterisk has been changed to the percent sign (%), as discussed above.

## Exercise 13.2: How To Run A Saved Query

There are two ways that you can run a saved query, as discussed below.

① From the Advanced Query window (Lookup ⇒ Advanced ⇒ Advanced Query).

② Add it to the Lookup menu and run it from there.

## How To Run A Query From The Advanced Query Window

1. Lookup ⇒ Advanced ⇒ Advanced Query.

2. Click the Open button ⇒ Double-click on the query, Customers in AZ, in your folder.

3. Click OK ⇒ Select **REPLACE LOOKUP**. You will see the same nine contacts. If more records were added to the database that met the criteria, they would appear at the bottom of the dialog box. Lookup ⇒ All Contacts.

## Advanced Queries

You will need to create an advanced query when the Lookup command and Lookup By Example query options will not retrieve the records that you need. This is usually the case when you need to search for two or more values in the same field. An example of when you would need to create an advanced query is if you need to find all customers and prospects in AZ. Advanced queries are a little harder to create then Lookup By Example queries because syntax is required, but it is not as difficult as you may think. Some conditions must be enclosed in parentheses as shown below.

**(ID/STATUS = CUSTOMER OR ID/STATUS = PROSPECT) AND STATE = AZ**

The equation above will find all contacts that have "Customer" or "Prospect" in the ID/Status field and AZ in the State field. There is a syntax checker to help you fix syntax errors. You can convert a Lookup By Example query to an advanced query. This may save you some time when creating an advanced query.

Earlier, you created a query to find all customers that are in AZ. You can recreate this query on the Lookup By Example dialog box and then open the **ADVANCED QUERY** dialog box to add the prospect criteria to the query.

Even though the Advanced Query dialog box was designed to create the entire query, some people feel more comfortable creating as much of an advanced query using the Lookup By Example dialog box as possible, and then open the Advanced Query dialog box to finish creating the query.

## Query Options

There are four options (drop-down lists) on the Advanced Query dialog box that are used to create the criteria for a query, as explained below. They are similar to the options on the Lookup dialog box.

① **TYPE** Is used to select the record type (Contact, Company, Opportunity, etc) for the field that you need to create criteria for. The option selected in this field controls the fields that are displayed in the Field Name drop-down list. For example, if you select Company in the Type field, the fields in the Field Name drop-down list will be Company fields.

② **FIELD NAME** Is used to select the field that you will create the criteria for.

③ **OPERATOR** They are used to describe the relationship between the criteria in the query. This relationship is a comparison of the data in the database to the value selected in the query. "Starts With" is the default operator. Table 13-1 explains the query operators. You will only see operators that the selected field can use.

④ **VALUE** This field contains the data that you want to use in the comparison. If the field selected has a drop-down list, the options in the Value drop-down list come from the data in the field in the database. If the field does not have a drop-down list, you have to type in the value.

## Query Operators

| This Operator | Will Find Records That . . . |
|---|---|
| After Next [days] | Have a date in the future that is at least the number of days from today that you enter in the Value field. (1) (2) |
| Contains | Have the criteria that you enter any place in the field. |
| Contains Data | Have data in the field, meaning the field is not empty. (3) (4) |
| Day Equals [number] | Have the day of the month that you enter. (1) |
| Does Not Contain | Do not have the value entered in the Value field. |
| Does Not Contain Data | Do not have any data in the field, meaning that the field is empty. (3) (4) |
| Ends With | Have data in the field that ends with the criteria that you enter. (3) |
| Equal To (=) | Are equal to the criteria that you enter. (3) |
| Greater Than | Have an amount larger than the amount that you specify in the Value field. If you want to see all orders with an order amount over $500, enter $500 in the Value field and the query will display records with an order amount of $500.01 or more. (5) |
| Greater Than or Equal To | (Works similar to "Greater than"). The difference is that this operator will also select records that have the amount that you specify. In the greater than example above, the query would not retrieve records with an order amount of exactly $500. The greater than or equal to operator will. (5) |
| Less Than | Have an amount less than the amount that you specify in the Value field. If you want to see products that have a reorder level of less than 10 items in stock, enter 10 in the Value field and the query will display products with a reorder level of nine or less. (5) |
| Less Than or Equal To | (Works similar to "Less than"). The difference is that this operator will also select records that have the value that you specify. In the less than example above, the query would not retrieve records with a reorder level of 10 items. The less than or equal to operator will. (5) |
| Month Equals [number] | Have the month that you enter. (1) |
| Not Equal To (!=) | Do not have data that matches the criteria that you enter. (3) |
| Starts With | Have data in the field that starts with the criteria that you enter. (3) |
| Older Than [days] | Have a date that is more than the number (of days) that you enter. (1) (2) |
| On or After | Have a date that is greater than or equal to the date that you enter. (1) |
| On or Before | Have a date that is equal to or less than the date that you enter. (1) |
| Within Last [days] | Have a date that is within the previous number of days that you specify. (1) |
| Within Next [days] | Have a date that is within the next number of days that you specify. (1) |
| Year Equals [number] | Have the year that you enter. (1) |

**Table 13-1** Query operators explained

(1) This operator is only for date fields.
(2) This operator is not available for the Birth date field in the Contact table.
(3) This operator is for text fields.
(4) The Value field is not enabled when this operator is selected.
(5) This operator is only for numeric fields.

## Exercise 13.3: How To Create An Advanced Query

1. Lookup ⇒ Advanced ⇒ Advanced Query ⇒ Open the Customers in AZ query.

2. Select the criteria in the Field Name, Operator and Value fields shown at the top of Figure 13-4. The criteria shown at the bottom of the figure is from the Customers in AZ query.

| Type: | | Field Name: | | Operator: | | Value: | |
|---|---|---|---|---|---|---|---|
| Contact | ▼ | ID/Status | ▼ | Starts With | ▼ | Prospect | ▼ |

| ( | Type | Field Name | Operator | Value | ) | And/Or |
|---|---|---|---|---|---|---|
| | Contact | State | Starts With | AZ | | And |
| | Contact | ID/Status | Contains | Customer | | End |

**Figure 13-4** Criteria options to select

If you look in the **AND/OR** column in the grid, you will see that contacts must meet the criteria of the State starting with AZ and the ID/Status field starting with Customer. Changing the value of the And/Or field in the first ID/Status criteria row to **OR** will retrieve contacts if the value in the ID/Status field is Customer or Prospect, which is what you want in this exercise.

If you previewed the contacts now, based on the criteria shown in Figure 13-5, the query would not retrieve any records.

That is because the query needs to enclose the two ID/Status rows of criteria in parentheses so that if a contact has the status of Customer or Prospect, the state still has to be equal to AZ.

| ( | Type | Field Name | Operator | Value | ) | And/Or |
|---|---|---|---|---|---|---|
| | Contact | State | Starts With | AZ | | And |
| | Contact | ID/Status | Contains | Customer | | And |
| | Contact | ID/Status | Starts With | Prospect | | End |

**Figure 13-5** Incomplete query criteria

Using **AND** means that you want both conditions to be met: The condition on the first row with the And condition (in the And/Or column) and the condition on the row below it.

For example, if you want to find all customer and prospect records in AZ that were edited between 1/1/2010 and 5/21/2011, you would create the criteria shown in Figure 13-6.

| ( | Type | Field Name | Operator | Value | ) | And/Or |
|---|---|---|---|---|---|---|
| ( | Contact | ID/Status | Starts With | Customer | | Or |
| | Contact | ID/Status | Starts With | Prospect | ) | And |
| | Contact | State | Starts With | AZ | | And |
| ( | Contact | Edit Date | On or After | 1/1/2010 | | And |
| | Contact | Edit Date | On or Befor | 5/21/2011 | ) | End |

**Figure 13-6** Status, State and Date range criteria

**Starts With Operator**

I am not sure why "Starts With" is used as the default operator on the Lookup By Example and Lookup Opportunities dialog boxes when most people really want to use **EQUAL TO**. The "Starts With" operator does just that. The operator will look for all records that have the value that you enter at the beginning of the field. Using the Starts With operator can return unexpected results. The problem that I have with using the Starts With operator is that if there are other values that "Start with" the same characters as those in the Value field, those records will also be retrieved when the query is run.

I personally do not use the Starts With operator for this reason. From a programmers perspective, the query criteria shown earlier in Figure 13-5 is not what most users want. The criteria shown in Figure 13-7 is what should be used. You will find out how to correct this query later in the chapter when you learn how to edit a query.

| ( | Type | Field Name | Operator | Value | ) | And/Or |
|---|---|---|---|---|---|---|
| | Contact | State | Equal To (=) | AZ | | And |
| (( | Contact | ID/Status | Equal To (=) | Customer | | Or |
| | Contact | ID/Status | Equal To (=) | Prospect | )) | And |

**Figure 13-7** Equal to criteria

3.  Click the **ADD TO LIST** button.

4. Click in the **(** column of the first ID/Status criteria row, as shown in Figure 13-8, then select **((.**

**Figure 13-8** Left parenthesis criteria options

5. Open the And/Or drop-down list for the first ID/Status criteria row and select **OR,** as shown in Figure 13-9.

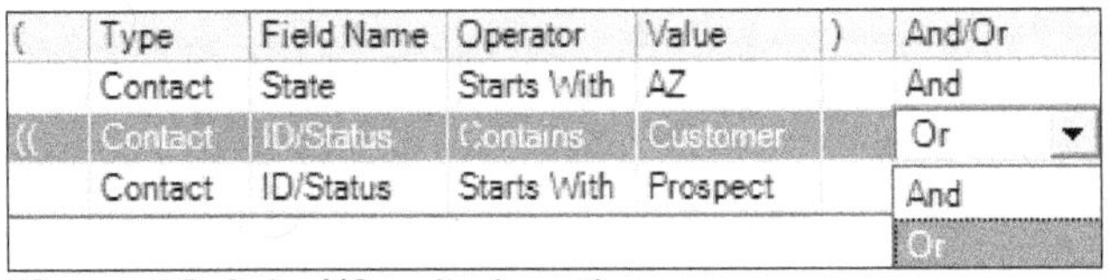

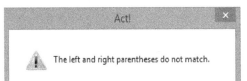

**Figure 13-9** And/Or criteria options

## Check The Query Syntax

If you preview a query and see a message similar to the one shown in Figure 13-10, it means that there is something wrong with the syntax (code) of the query.

**Figure 13-10** Query syntax error message

In this example, the message is telling you that there is something wrong with the parentheses. Look at the parentheses in the query. There should be an equal number of each type of parentheses that you select and the corresponding parentheses should be on different lines.

1. If you see the message shown above in Figure 13-10, click OK and fix the query criteria based on what the message indicates.

2. Click in the **)** column on the last criteria row and select **)),** as shown in Figure 13-11.

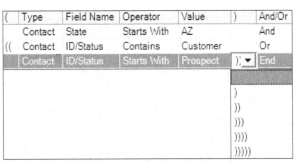

**Figure 13-11** Right parenthesis criteria options

## Save And Run The Query

1. File ⇒ Save As ⇒ Select your folder ⇒ Type Customers & Prospects in AZ in the File name field.

2. Click OK on the Criteria dialog box ⇒ Select Replace Lookup, then click OK. There should be 14 contacts displayed in the Contact list view.

## Exercise 13.4: Find Records Created In The Last 30 Days Query

You may have the need to know which contacts you added to the database or modified in the past. An example would be if you wanted to review all of the contacts that you added to the database in the last 30 days. The field that stores when a contact record is added to the database is the **CREATE DATE** field.

1. Lookup ⇒ Advanced ⇒ Advanced Query.

2. Select the Create Date field.

3. Select the **WITHIN LAST [DAYS]** operator ⇒ Type 30 in the Value field.

4. Click the Add to list button. You should have the criteria shown in Figure 13-12.

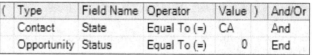

| ( | Type | Field Name | Operator | Value | ) | And/Or |
|---|------|-----------|----------|-------|---|--------|
| | Contact | Create Date | Within Last [days] | 30 | | End |

**Figure 13-12** Last 30 days criteria

5. Save the query in your folder as New contacts in last 30 days.

6. Preview the results. You will see the contact records that you have added in the last 30 days.

 If you edit the criteria shown above in Figure 13-12 and change the Field Name to **EDIT DATE**, you will see all of the contact records that you have edited in the last 30 days.

## Exercise 13.5: Find Contacts In CA With Open Opportunities

In this exercise you will create a query that finds contacts in California that have opportunities with an open status.

1. If the Contact Criteria dialog box is still open, click the New button, otherwise, Lookup ⇒ Advanced ⇒ Advanced Query.

2. Select the State field, Equal To operator and CA from the Value drop-down list ⇒ Click the Add to list button.

3. Open the Type drop-down list and select Opportunity.

4. Select the Status field and Equal To operator ⇒ Type 0 in the Value field.

5. Click the Add to list button. You should have the options shown in Figure 13-13.

   Click the Preview button.

| ( | Type | Field Name | Operator | Value | ) | And/Or |
|---|------|-----------|----------|-------|---|--------|
| | Contact | State | Equal To (=) | CA | | And |
| | Opportunity | Status | Equal To (=) | 0 | | End |

**Figure 13-13** Contacts in CA with open opportunities criteria

6. Save the query as Open opportunities in CA.

7. Run the query. You will see the contacts in CA that have open opportunities. If you double-click on a contact, on the Opportunities tab, you will see at least one open opportunity for the contact.

 **Opening Existing Queries From The Advanced Query Dialog Box**
Before you open an existing query, you have to select the type of query that you want to open in the Search for drop-down list at the top of the dialog box.

## How To Edit A Query

If you need to edit a query you can follow the steps below. For now, you can just read this section. If you want to practice editing a query you can change the operator on each criteria row to Equal To (=) in the Customers & Prospects in AZ query.

1. Open the query that you want to edit, on the Advanced Query dialog box.

2. Click on the criteria row that needs to be changed, then click the Edit button.

   You will see the dialog box shown in Figure 13-14.

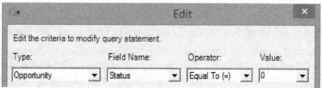

**Figure 13-14** Edit dialog box

3. Make the criteria changes that you need, then click OK. Save the changes to the query.

## Exercise 13.6: Sorting Records Retrieved From A Query

You can sort the records that the query retrieves. This will be useful if you will do a bulk mailing and need the records sorted in order by zip code when you print the mailing labels. You can sort the records from the query in the detail or list view by following the steps below. To complete this exercise, the records retrieved from the Open opportunities in CA query, should be displayed, or any query that uses a field in the Contact table.

1.  Edit ⇒ Sort ⇒ Open the **SORT BY** drop-down list and select Zip Code.

2.  Change the **AND THEN BY** option to <None>.

    You should have the options selected that are shown in Figure 13-15.

    Click OK. The records in the Contact list view will now be sorted by zip code.

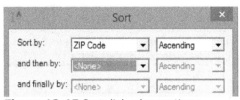

**Figure 13-15** Sort dialog box options

## Exercise 13.7: Find Prospects Query

In this exercise you will create a query to find prospect contacts in the US that do not have an email address. You can use the Lookup By Example and Advanced Query dialog boxes to get the contacts that meet the criteria. Using the Lookup By Example dialog box to create as much of the query as possible and then use the <Type> Criteria dialog box to complete the query is a good idea. (Type is a contact, company, group or opportunity.) This will keep you from having to create the entire query manually.

1.  Create a query to display all contacts with a Prospect ID Status in the United States that do not have an email address.

2.  Save the query in your folder as
    US Prospects with no email
    address.

    Figure 13-16 shows the query syntax.

| ( | Type | Field Name | Operator | Value | ) | And/Or |
|---|------|-----------|----------|-------|---|--------|
| | Contact | ID/Status | Contains | Prospect | | And |
| | Contact | Country | Equal To (=) | United States | | And |
| | Contact | E-mail | Does Not Contain Data | Nothing | | End |

**Figure 13-16** Prospects without an email address query

 The Country field operator could be Starts With or Equal To.

## Dynamically Linking Contacts To Companies

Chapter 5 covered how to manually link contacts to companies. If you want to have contacts automatically linked to a company, you have to create a query.

An example of when this would be useful is when you want to have certain fields filled in for the contact. This is one way to make sure that the data is being maintained. If you needed to make sure that every contact record has a company name, you could create a query that looks for records that do not have data in the Company field.

This works for the Company field, but not for other types of linked fields. For example, if you wanted to put all contact records that do not have a zip code into a company. If the Zip Code field is a linked field, this would not work. You would have to put the records in a group instead of a company.

## Exercise 13.8: How To Create A Dynamic Group

In Exercise 6.6, you created a Sales Reps group and added contacts to it. As time goes on, more contacts will be added to the database and some of them will be sales reps. You could create a lookup to find the new contacts that are sales reps, but you would have to do that on a regular basis, so that all of the contacts with this title will be in the group.

ACT! has a dynamic option that can be used to create criteria to automatically add records to a group. The dynamic option also causes records to automatically be removed from a group, if they no longer meet the criteria. This is done by creating a query. In this exercise, you will modify the Sales Reps group so that it is dynamic. You can add as much criteria as needed to create a dynamic group.

1.  On the Group detail view, click on the Sales Reps group in the tree ⇒ Click the Add/Remove Contacts button on the Contacts tab.

2.  Click the Edit Criteria button on the Add/Remove Contacts dialog box.

3.  Open the Field Name drop-down list and select TITLE ⇒
    Open the Operator drop-down list and select EQUAL TO (=) ⇒
    Open the Value drop-down list and select SALES REPRESENTATIVE.

4.  Click the Add to list button. You should have the criteria shown in Figure 13-17.

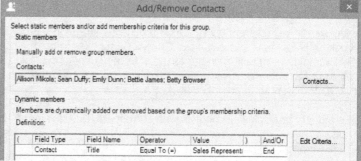

| ( | Type | Field Name | Operator | Value | ) | And/Or |
|---|------|-----------|----------|-------|---|--------|
| | Contact | Title | Equal To (=) | Sales Representative | | End |

**Figure 13-17** Sales rep group criteria

 If you make a mistake, click on the criteria under the drop-down lists that needs to be changed, then click the EDIT button to correct the mistake.

5.  Click the PREVIEW button. You should see five contacts at the bottom of the dialog box ⇒ Click OK to close the Group Criteria dialog box.

6.  You should see the criteria in the DYNAMIC MEMBERS section of the Add/Remove Contacts dialog box, as shown in Figure 13-18.

    Click OK.

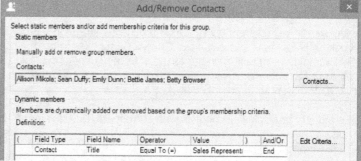

**Figure 13-18** Dynamic criteria

 Contacts that are added to the group via a query will stay in the group as long as they meet the criteria. In the exercise that you just completed, if any of the contacts that were added dynamically has a change in title, they will automatically be removed from the Sales Reps group. If you add a contact to this group manually, they will stay in the group whether or not they meet the criteria.

It is probably best to link contacts to a company on more than the Company name field. It is possible that there is more than one company with the same name in the database, meaning one company could end with "Inc" and the other one doesn't. If you also linked on the street address, the chances of linking to the wrong company is greatly reduced.

 **Creating Dynamic Companies**
To create a dynamic company, start from the Company detail view in step 1 above, instead of the group detail view.

## Test The Dynamic Group Criteria

1.  Create new records for the contacts in Table 13-2.

    The last two records in the table should automatically be added to the Sales Reps group.

| Contact | Title |
|---------|-------|
| Tim Dynamic | Sales Manager |
| Tina Dynamic | Sales Representative |
| Tom Dynamic | Sales Representative |

**Table 13-2** Test records for the dynamic group criteria

2.  Click the Groups button ⇒ Click on the Sales Reps group, in the tree. You should see the records for Tina and Tom Dynamic, on the Contacts tab, as illustrated in Figure 13-19.

The Groups/Companies tab on the Contact detail view does not automatically show dynamic groups that the contact is a member of. You have to click the SHOW DYNAMIC MEMBERSHIP button, illustrated in Figure 13-20, to see if the contact is a member of a dynamic group. When you click this button you will see the dialog box shown in Figure 13-21. This dialog box lets you know which dynamic groups the contact is a member of.

Contacts
Add/Remove Contacts...
Contact
Company
Tina Dynamic
Tom Dynamic
Emily Dunn
Boomer's Artworx
Bettie James
Boomer's Artworx
Betty Browser
CH TechONE
Allison Mikola
CH TechONE
Sean Duffy
Circle Photography

**Figure 13-19** Result of the dynamic group criteria

Groups/Companies
Show for:
Groups and Subgroups
Show Dynamic Membership
Group Name
Group Description

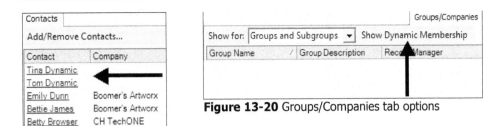

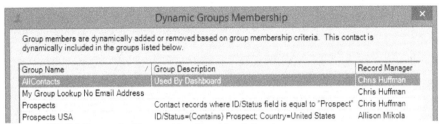

**Figure 13-20** Groups/Companies tab options

Dynamic Groups Membership
Group members are dynamically added or removed based on group membership criteria. This contact is dynamically included in the groups listed below.
Group Name
Group Description
Record Manager
AllContacts
Used By Dashboard
Chris Huffman
My Group Lookup No Email Address
Chris Huffman
Prospects
Contact records where ID/Status field is equal to "Prospect"
Chris Huffman
Prospects USA
ID/Status=(Contains) Prospect; Country=United States
Allison Mikola

**Figure 13-21** Dynamic Groups Membership dialog box

The query for the dynamic group that you just created will automatically run each time either of the following actions occur:

① The Group detail view is opened.
② The Groups/Companies tab is displayed.

# CUSTOMIZING ACT!

In this chapter you will learn several ways to customize ACT!, including how to:

- ☑ Modify preferences
- ☑ Create and edit drop-down list fields
- ☑ Modify fields
- ☑ Customize columns
- ☑ Create new fields
- ☑ Create an annual event
- ☑ Create calculated fields

**CHAPTER 14**

## Why Waiting To Customize ACT! Is A Good Idea

I suspect that this may be the chapter that many readers are very interested in. There was a time when I wanted to customize (aka tweak) software as soon as I installed it, even if I did not know how to use the software. When you think about it, how could one customize software that they really do not know? I call it "Click Fever". We really like clicking on options to see what will happen. Depending on how well you already know the software, that may not be a problem.

If you are not very familiar with the software, waiting until you have used it for a while before customizing it is probably a good idea. If you have a question or something does not work as expected, you will not know if it is a problem with the software or if the cause is from a customization change that you made and were not aware of all of the ways that a certain customization changes the functionality of the software.

## Modifying Preferences

There are several options in ACT! that you can modify. Chapter 2 covered how to modify the General preferences. In this chapter you will learn how to modify other options on the Preferences dialog box.

## Name And Salutation Preferences

You learned how ACT! displays the contact names that you enter. [See Chapter 3, Exercise 3.1] If the default prefix and suffix options do not meet your needs, the options shown in Figures 14-1 to 14-4 should help. The options that are selected in the figures are the defaults. Tools ⇒ Preferences ⇒ General tab ⇒ Salutation Preferences button, opens this dialog box.

The options shown in the list on the right of Figure 14-2 are the prefixes that ACT! will ignore as being the contacts first name. You can add or delete items in this list. Tools ⇒ Preferences ⇒ Admin tab ⇒ Name Preferences button, opens this dialog box.

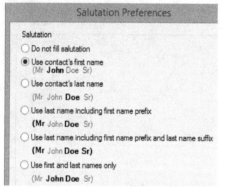

**Figure 14-1** Salutation Preferences dialog box

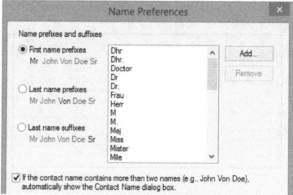

**Figure 14-2** Name Preferences dialog box

The **LAST NAME PREFIXES** options, shown in Figure 14-3, are the first part of a last name that has two words.
An example would be Dr. Van Ost. "Van" is the type of prefix that you would add to this list, if it was not already there.

The **LAST NAME SUFFIXES** options, shown in Figure 14-4, are a list of abbreviations that people use after their last name. If they are the last word entered in the Contact field, they are ignored based on the default options that ACT! uses.

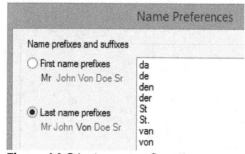

**Figure 14-3** Last name prefix options

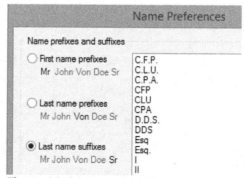

**Figure 14-4** Last name suffix options

## Exercise 14.1: Calendar Preferences

You can change some of the default calendar settings. The ones that you can change are the day that the calendar week starts on, the time slot increments on the daily and weekly calendars and whether or not you want to only show the current month in the mini-calendar.

1.  Tools ⇒ Preferences ⇒ Calendar & Activities tab ⇒ **CALENDAR PREFERENCES** button.

2.  Change the options in Table 14-1.

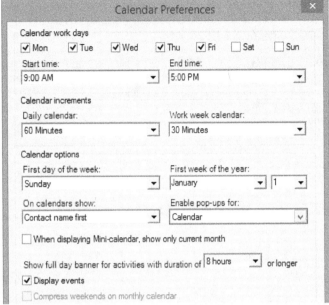

| Option | Change To |
|--------|-----------|
| Start Time | 9 AM |
| Daily Calendar | 60 minutes |

**Table 14-1** Calendar options to change

Changing these options will cause the daily calendar to display the time slots in one hour increments.

The dialog box should have the options shown in Figure 14-5.

The default starting time of the calendar will now be 9 AM.

**Figure 14-5** Calendar Preferences dialog box

### Pop-Up Options

This option is on the Calendar Preferences dialog box shown above in Figure 14-5. There are pop-ups that you may find useful. They will not slow down your computer, like the pop-ups that you may see when surfing the Internet.

Figure 14-6 shows the features that you can enable pop-ups for. By default, the calendar pop-ups are enabled. Check the options that you want and clear the check mark for the options that you do not want to see pop-ups for.

**Figure 14-6** Pop-up options

3.  Click OK to close the Calendar Preferences dialog box.

## Exercise 14.2: Activity Preferences

Chapter 7 covered creating a variety of activities. There are activity options that you can modify as needed. You can modify the following activity preferences.

① Activity type (Call, Meeting, To-Do).
② Priority levels.
③ Alarm options.
④ Have certain types of activities automatically roll over to the next day if they are not completed.
⑤ Designate how cleared activities should appear.

1.  On the Calendar & Activities tab, click the Activity Preferences button.

To change the settings, click on the activity type that you want to change (call, meeting etc.), then select the options that you want to change. If modified, the options in the **DEFAULT ACTIVITY SETTINGS TO** section will change the default values that you see when you create an activity.

2.  Change the options in Table 14-2 for the To-Do activity type. Your dialog box should have the options selected that are shown in Figure 14-7.

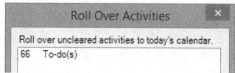

| Option | Change To |
|--------|-----------|
| Ring alarm | 15 minutes |
| Duration | 1 Hour |

**Table 14-2** To-do activity options to change

If set, the alarm will start warning you 15 minutes prior to the start time of the activity.

If checked, the **AUTOMATICALLY ROLL OVER TO TODAY** option moves activities that have not been completed to the next day. This can be used to ensure that activities do not fall through the cracks, as they say. This option is only applied to activities that have a single user.

Depending on how many activities you schedule, you may want to check the roll over option. I find this option most useful for phone calls that have not been completed. Take caution when using the roll over option because it is cumulative, meaning that all past activities that were not completed will also be rolled over. If there were 500 activities that were not completed, all of them will be rolled over. The roll over is not automatic though. When you open the database, you will be asked if you want to roll over the activities. You will see how many activities would be rolled over, as shown in Figure 14-8.

If you create activities that need to be assigned to multiple contacts and want each contact to have an activity record created automatically, check the option **CREATE SEPARATE ACTIVITIES WHEN SCHEDULING WITH MULTIPLE CONTACTS**.

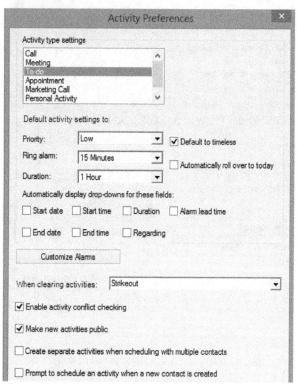

**Figure 14-7** To-Do activity preference options

**Figure 14-8** Roll Over Activities dialog box

 If you want to set or remove the same options for several or all of the activity types, select all of the activity types that you want to change, in the **ACTIVITY TYPE SETTINGS** list. This lets you make the changes to all of the selected activity types, at the same time.

 In previous versions of ACT!, the Activity Preferences dialog box was named **SCHEDULING ACTIVITIES**.

## Alarm Preferences

1. On the Activity Preferences dialog box, click the **CUSTOMIZE ALARMS** button.

   The options shown in Figure 14-9 are used to customize the sound that the alarm will make.

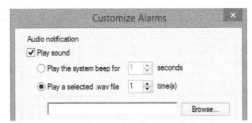

**Figure 14-9** Customize Alarms dialog box

2. Click OK to close all of the dialog boxes.

## Exercise 14.3: Customize The Contact List View

The Contact list view, as well as the Task List view, can be customized to sort records according to your needs. You can rearrange the order of the columns and make a column smaller or wider. You can also add and remove columns.

## Rearrange The Order Of Columns

 If you have used a previous version of ACT! on the same computer, you may have already customized your layout. If that is the case, you can skip the step below.

1. In the Contact list view, click on the Title column heading and drag it to the left, so that it is before the Contact column. The Contact list view should look like the one shown in Figure 14-10.

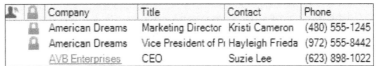

**Figure 14-10** Title column moved

## Resize A Column

1. Place the mouse pointer on the line between the Company and Title column headings. The mouse pointer is in the right place when you see a double-headed arrow, as shown in Figure 14-11.

**Figure 14-11** Mouse pointer in position to resize a column

2. Hold down the left mouse button and drag the line to the right, as shown in Figure 14-12.

   Release the mouse button. The Company column should be wider.

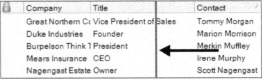

**Figure 14-12** Company column made wider

## Add A Column

1. Right-click in the list and select **CUSTOMIZE COLUMNS**.

   You should see the dialog box shown in Figure 14-13.

   The **AVAILABLE FIELDS** list contains all of the fields that have not already been added to the view.

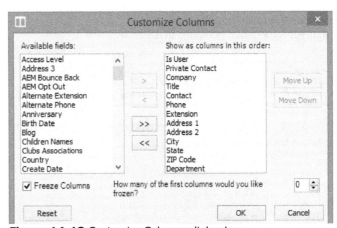

**Figure 14-13** Customize Columns dialog box

The fields in the **SHOW AS COLUMNS IN THIS ORDER** list are the order that the columns will be displayed in, on the tab, from left to right.

The **MOVE UP** and **MOVE DOWN** buttons are used to rearrange the order of the columns in the view. Click on the field that you want to move, then click on the appropriate button.

If enabled, the **FREEZE COLUMNS** options are used to select how many columns from the left, should stay visible on the list view, when you scroll to the right to see more data. The columns that you freeze will have a blue background. These options work like the freeze option in Excel.

The **RESET** button will restore the columns back to the order they were when ACT! was first installed.

 Tools ⇒ Customize ⇒ Columns, will also open the Customize Columns dialog box.

2. Click on the Department field in the **AVAILABLE FIELDS** list. Press and hold down the Ctrl key. Scroll down the list and select the Last Meeting and Last Results fields.

3. Click the Add button (the top arrow button), then click OK.

4. Scroll to the right in the Contact list view, so that you can see the three fields that you just added to the view.

 **Another Way To Add Or Remove Columns**
If you double-click on a field in the Available Fields section on the Customize Columns dialog box, you will add the field to the view. If you double-click on a field in the Show as columns in this order section, you will remove the field from the view. When you remove a column from a view, the data is still in the database. It is just not visible on the view. If you need to view the data from a field that you removed, you can add the field back.

## Delete A Column

1. Open the Customize Columns dialog box.

2. Click on the Last Meeting field in the list on the right, then click the Remove button (the second arrow button from the top) and click OK. The column will be removed from the Contact list view. Click OK.

## Customize Columns On A Tab

Customizing columns on a tab is very similar to adding a column to a view. The steps below illustrate how to customize columns.

1. On the Contacts detail view, click on the Notes tab.

2. Click the arrow on the Options button and select **CUSTOMIZE COLUMNS**, as shown in Figure 14-14.

   You will see the Customize Columns dialog box that you saw earlier in Figure 14-13.

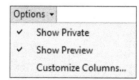

**Figure 14-14** Options drop-down list

 All tabs on a view, like the Documents and Personal Info tabs, do not have the Options button. Some tabs only have the Customize Columns option on the drop-down list and other tabs have additional options.

3. Add the fields that you want to see on the tab, then remove the fields from the list on the right that you do not want to see on the tab.

4. Rearrange the order of the fields if necessary, then click OK.

## Creating Fields

If you have the need to customize a layout, fields are probably the item that you will customize the most. Depending on your needs, the fields that come with ACT! may not be sufficient. You may have to create additional fields to store data. Administrator or Manager rights are required to create fields. Users cannot be logged into the database while you are creating new fields or editing existing fields. If anyone else is logged in, you will see a message that contains a list of who is logged in. (Tools ⇒ Define Fields, opens the dialog box, used to create new fields.)

While the process of creating fields is easy, you should have a plan for the fields that you need to create. If the database has been in use for a while or has a lot of contacts, you can still add fields. You may have to go through all of the records in the table, before the field was added and fill in the data for the new field. This could be very time consuming. At a minimum, you should have the following items in your plan for each field that you want to add:

    ①  What type of field (drop-down, date, free form, etc.) is best suited for the data that the field needs to store.

    ②  Which views should the field be placed on.

    ③  Will the field be used as a lookup field or added to a report? If so, determine if the field would be more useful if it was a drop-down list.

## Field Data Type Options

If you are creating a new field, you can use the data types that are explained in Table 14-3. When editing a field, not all of the data types in the table are available. Each field can only have one data type.

| Data Type | Description |
| --- | --- |
| Address | When you select this field type, seven fields are automatically created: Address 1, 2 and 3, City, State, Zip Code and Country. (1) |
| Annual Event | Creates a date field for events that only happen once a year. This data type is only available for the Contacts table. (2) (3) |
| Calculated | Is used to create a field that displays the result of a calculation. |
| Character | Creates a free form data field, which means that any combination of data (text and numbers) can be entered in the field. While it is tempting to use this data type for all fields, it should really only be used when none of the other data types discussed in this table are a better option. |
| Currency | Only accepts monetary values. By default, a dollar sign, commas and decimal point (for cents) are automatically filled in. If the user entered 123456 in a currency field, the number would be displayed as $1,234.56. (2) |
| Date | Allows a date to be entered in the field. (2) (3) |
| Date/Time | Allows a date and time to be entered in the same field. (2) (3) |
| Decimal | Only allows numbers and decimal points to be entered. (2) |
| Email | Used to enter an email address. This data type is only available for the Contacts and Opportunities tables. (1) |
| Initial-Caps | This data type forces the first character of each word entered in the field to be a capital letter and the remaining letters in each word to be lower case. |
| Lowercase | Converts all upper case characters to lower case. |
| Memo | Similar to the Character data type because it is free form. The difference is that a memo field allows a lot more data to be entered in the field. |
| Number | Only accepts numeric values. |
| Phone | Used to enter telephone numbers. By default, a dash is automatically filled in after the area code and after the first three digits of the phone number. (1) |
| Picture | Used to store graphic files, images or photos. (1) |
| Time | Allows a time to be entered in the field. The drop-down list shown in Figure 14-16 is added to this field type. A time can be selected from the drop-down list or the time can be typed in the field. (2) |
| Uppercase | Converts all lower case characters to capital letters. |
| URL Address | Enter a web site address. |
| Yes/No | Creates a check box field. ACT! queries do not use Yes and No values, instead they use True and False. If this field is used in a query, keep in mind that Yes equals True and No equals False. (1) |

**Table 14-3** Field data types explained

(1)   This field type is only available if you are creating a new field.

(2)   The format for this field comes from the Region dialog box shown in Figure 14-15 (which is part of the Windows operating system) or the Region and Language dialog box (the name of the dialog box in earlier versions of Windows). The currency field formats on the Opportunities view also come from this dialog box.

(3)   A calendar object is automatically added to this field type so that all dates will be entered in the same format.

 To view the dialog box shown in Figure 14-15, open the Control Panel in Windows, then double-click on the **REGION** or **REGION AND LANGUAGE** option.

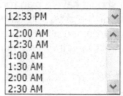

**Figure 14-16** Time data type drop-down list

**Figure 14-15** Region dialog box

## Field Behavior Options

The field behavior options discussed below are used to customize the fields that you create or modify. All of the attributes are not available for each data type.

①  **ALLOW BLANK** If checked, this option will not require data to be entered into in the field.

②  **GENERATE HISTORY** Automatically creates a history record each time the value in the field is changed. By default, several fields in the database have this option enabled.

③  **PRIMARY FIELD** Designates the field as a primary field. Fields that have this option checked will be duplicated. For example, this option is useful when you duplicate a contact record.

④  **USE DROP-DOWN LIST** Is used to select an existing drop-down list or create a new drop-down list. This option is not enabled for all data types.

## Customize Field Behavior

The options discussed below are some of the options on the Customize field behavior screen, shown in Figure 14-17.

They allow for more functionality to be added to fields.

The options on this screen change, depending on the data type that is selected.

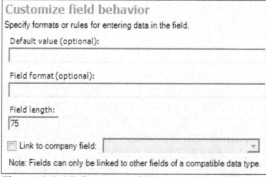

**Figure 14-17** Customize field behavior options

①  **DEFAULT VALUE** The value that you enter in this field will automatically be filled in the field for each new record added to the database. This is useful if the majority of records need to have the same value in the field.

② **FIELD FORMAT** Is used to enter symbols that will automatically appear in the field. This formatting is used to help the user enter the correct type of numeric data.

③ **FIELD LENGTH** The number entered in this field is the maximum number of characters that can be entered in the field. Try not to make the field length too long because that will waste space in the database and make the database larger than it needs to be. This will cause the database to run slower then it should.

④ **LINK TO COMPANY FIELD** Is used to link a contact field to a field in the company record. When the company field is updated, the linked field in the contact record is automatically updated. This option is only available when you edit an existing field. [See Chapter 5, Linking and Unlinking Contact And Company Fields]

## Triggers

Triggers allow an action to take place on a field in one of three ways, as shown in Figure 14-18.

The types of triggers and their options are explained below.

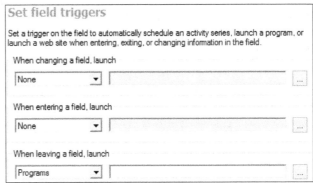

**Figure 14-18** Set field triggers screen

## Types Of Triggers

There are three types of triggers that can be set, as explained below.

① **NONE** This is the default trigger type. It means that the trigger will not have an event occur.

② **PROGRAMS** Is used to select a program (software package), file or web site to open.

③ **ACTIVITY SERIES** Is used to select a list of activities that you want to schedule.

## Trigger Options

There are three triggers that can be set for a field, as explained below.

① **WHEN CHANGING A FIELD**, an event will happen when the value in the field changes.

② **WHEN ENTERING A FIELD**, an event will happen when the cursor first enters the field.

③ **WHEN LEAVING A FIELD**, an event will happen when the cursor leaves the field.

An example of when to use the **WHEN CHANGING A FIELD** trigger would be when the data in a field changes, you want a document to automatically open. You would select the programs option from the drop-down list and add the file name in the field to the right. You could also use this trigger to open a file that provides helpful information about what type of data should be entered in the field.

An example of when to use the **WHEN ENTERING A FIELD** trigger would be when the cursor enters the field, a web site will open to display information about the data in the field or some aspect of the current record.

An example of when to use the **WHEN LEAVING A FIELD** trigger would be to set up an activity series automatically when the cursor leaves the field.

## Creating And Editing Drop-Down List Fields

You have already seen and used many of the default drop-down lists that come with ACT!. You can create drop-down lists for a field that you need. You may have a database that has all types of doctors and may want to list their specialty. You could modify a user defined field and add a drop-down list to it, that contains specialties. A list can be used by more than one field.

### Exercise 14.4: Create A Drop-Down List Field

In this exercise you will create a drop-down list field for doctor specialties. The options in the **TYPE** drop-down list were explained earlier in Table 14-3.

1. Tools ⇒ Define Fields.

2. Click the **MANAGE DROP-DOWN LISTS** link ⇒ Click the **CREATE DROP-DOWN LIST** link.

3. In the **DROP-DOWN LIST NAME** field type `Specializes In` ⇒
   In the Description field type `What the doctor specializes in` ⇒
   Clear the **AUTOMATICALLY ADD NEW ITEMS USERS ENTER TO THE LIST** option.

> You should avoid using special characters in field names because they can create problems in reports and queries.

If checked, the Automatically add new items users enter to the list option is used to allow users to type in a value that is not already in the list. When this happens, the value will automatically be added to the list. At some point, this will be a problem because typos will not be caught and the lists can get out of hand and hard to manage.

4. You should have the options shown in Figure 14-19.

   The **ALLOW USERS TO EDIT ITEMS IN THIS LIST** option has to be checked for each field that you want to let users add, delete or edit the values in the drop-down list.

   Click Next.

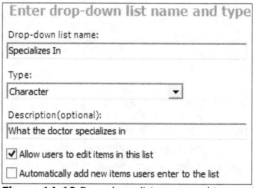
**Figure 14-19** Drop-down list name and type options

> The following options cannot be accessed when the **ALLOW USERS TO EDIT ITEMS IN THIS LIST** option is selected: **ALLOW MULTI-SELECT**, **SHOW DESCRIPTIONS** and **TYPE-AHEAD**. These options can only be enabled from the Define Fields dialog box.

5. Click the Add button ⇒ Type `Brain Surgery` in the Value column.

   Click the Add button ⇒ Type `OB-GYN` in the Value column.

   You should have the options shown in Figure 14-20.

**Figure 14-20** Drop-down list values

6. Click Finish. You should see the drop-down list that you just created on the screen shown in Figure 14-21.

   If you look in the **DETAILS** section illustrated on the left, you will see information about the drop-down list that you just created.

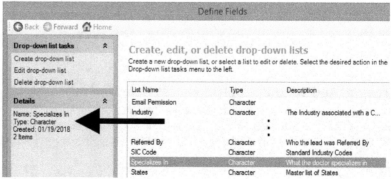
**Figure 14-21** Details for the drop-down list

7. Click the Back button in the upper left corner of the dialog box. Leave the Define Fields dialog box open to complete the next exercise.

## Managing Drop-Down List Options

If the field has a drop-down list you can decide whether users can add or delete entries in the list. If you need to change the contents of a field, like the address field, click in the field and back space out what you do not want and type in the new information. ACT! is in **INSERT** mode by default. In the next exercise you will learn several drop-down list editing techniques.

You can modify drop-down lists on the Define Fields dialog box or as you learned earlier, you can select the Edit List Values option at the bottom of a drop-down list. System fields can be modified on the Define Fields dialog box. Other fields are modified in a view. To use the Define Fields dialog box, other users cannot have the database open.

### Exercise 14.5: How To Add Items To A Drop-Down List Field

In this exercise you will add a value to the Contact ID/Status field.

1. Open the Define Fields dialog box if it is not already open ⇒ Click the Manage drop-down lists link, in the List Tasks section.

2. Select the Contact ID/Status list name, then click the **EDIT DROP-DOWN LIST** link.

3. Click Next on the Enter drop-down list name and type screen.

4. Click the Add button ⇒
   In the Value field, type `Purchased Book`.

   Press the Tab key ⇒
   In the Description field, type `Purchased the ACT! Book`.

   The entry should look like the one shown at the bottom of Figure 14-22.

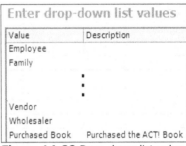

**Figure 14-22** Drop-down list values

5. Click Finish. The item will be added to the drop-down list ⇒ Close the Define Fields dialog box.

### View The New Entry

1. Switch to the Contact detail view ⇒ Open the ID/Status drop-down list on any contact record.

2. Scroll down the list. You will see the item that you created, as illustrated in Figure 14-23.

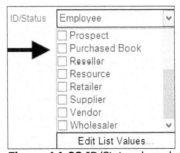

**Figure 14-23** ID/Status drop-down list options

### Exercise 14.6: How To Edit The Values In A Drop-Down List (From A View)

Many of the fields in the contact and company detail views have drop-down lists. You can add, modify or delete the entries in these lists.

### How To Add An Item To A Drop-Down List

In this part of the exercise you will learn how to add an item to a drop-down list.

1. On the Contact detail view, click on the arrow at the end of the Department field ⇒ Click the **EDIT LIST VALUES** option. You should see the Edit List dialog box. This is a list of the items that can currently be selected for the Department field.

2. Click the Add button ⇒ Type `Computer` in the Value field. If you wanted, you could type in a description to help clarify the item that you are adding.

3. Click OK to close the Edit List dialog box. The item that you just added will be available in the Department field drop-down list.

### How To Modify Or Delete An Item In A Drop-Down List

The steps below explain how to modify or delete an item in a drop-down list. Read through the steps now, but do not modify or delete anything.

### How To Modify An Item In The Drop-Down List

1. Open the Edit List dialog box for the drop-down list that you want to modify.

2. Select the value that you want to modify, then change the item to what you want it to be, as illustrated in Figure 14-24 ⇒ Click OK.

   Figure 14-24, illustrates that the Prospect value was changed to Brand Marketing.

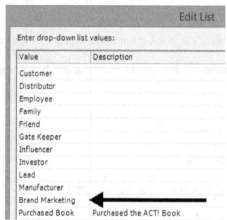

**Figure 14-24** Prospect value changed to Brand Marketing

### How To Delete An Item In A Drop-Down List Field

I do not advise deleting items from a drop-down list unless you know that the value has not been used for any record. If you delete a value and it is being used, the records that are using it will retain the value, but the value will not be available for any other records. If the value that you want to delete for example, is "Computer", I would change it to "Not in use - Computer" or something similar. That way, it is still available and if at some point in the future you need to reclassify contacts that have the value, you will be able to easily find the records.

1. To delete an item in a drop-down list, open the Edit List dialog box shown above in Figure 14-24.

2. Select the value that you want to delete, then click the **DELETE** button. Click Yes, when prompted to delete the list value, then click OK.

 You can also delete an item using the Define Fields dialog box.

### Exercise 14.7: How To Modify A User Field

There are 10 contact user fields that you can customize to store data that does not exist in the fields that come with ACT!. If you customize these fields, the name changes on the Define Fields dialog box, but not on the User Fields tab. This is because the "User 1" label on the layout has to be modified. You will not see the label change on the User Fields tab until you edit the layout (Editing layouts in detail is beyond the scope of this book). In this exercise you will modify the User 1 field.

1. Tools ⇒ Define Fields.

2. Select the **CONTACTS** field from the drop-down list, if it is not already selected.

3. Scroll down the list and click on the User 1 field, then click the **EDIT FIELD** link.

4. In the Field Name field, type `Specializes In`.

5. Open the Select a field drop-down list and select **INITIAL-CAPS**. This will cause the first letter of each word that is typed in this field to automatically be capitalized ⇒ Click Yes when prompted that data may be lost. You will see a dialog box that lets you know that your changes are being saved.

6. Check all of the options in the **CUSTOMIZE FIELD BEHAVIOR** section, except for the Use drop-down list, as illustrated in Figure 14-25 ⇒ Click Next.

**Figure 14-25** Customize field behavior options illustrated

7. In the **DEFAULT VALUE** field, type `General Practitioner`, as illustrated in Figure 14-26.

None of the triggers need to be set.

Click Finish.

The User 1 field will be renamed to Specializes In, in the database.

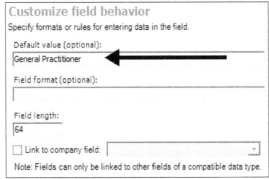

**Figure 14-26** Default value for the user field

## Exercise 14.8: How To Create A Field

So far in this chapter you have learned how to create and manage drop-down list fields and modify user fields. On your own, these are probably the types of fields that you will need to create and modify the most. It is possible though, that you may need to create a field that is not a drop-down list. You can create fields and link them to an existing drop-down list. The steps below show you how to create a drop-down list field, that will be linked to an existing field.

1. Open the Define Fields dialog box ⇒ Click the **CREATE NEW FIELD** link.

2. Type `Specialty` in the Field name field.

3. Check the **USE DROP-DOWN LIST** option ⇒ Select Specializes In from the drop-down list, as shown in Figure 14-27.

**Figure 14-27** Drop-down list options

 The options shown above in Figure 14-27 are the default fields in ACT! that have data for a drop-down list. If one of them is appropriate for a field that you are creating, you can use it.

4. Click Next ⇒ Select the **LIMIT TO LIST** option, shown in Figure 14-28.

   This option will prevent a value from being selected (in the field) that is not in the list.

**Customize field and list behavior**

☑ Limit to List - Allows users to select values from the drop-down list only

☐ Allow Multi-select - The user can select multiple values from the list

☐ Show Descriptions - Displays description text along with list values

☑ Enable Type-ahead - As user types, list values are displayed based on the entered value

**Figure 14-28** Customize field and list behavior options

5. Click Finish. The field will be created. Later, you would add this field to a layout so that it can be used.

6. Close the Define Fields dialog box. When prompted to modify the layout, click No.

As shown above in Figure 14-28, the **SHOW DESCRIPTIONS** option is not enabled by default. This description refers to the one like you created in Exercise 14.5. [See Figure 14-22]

If the Show Descriptions option is checked, the drop-down list will display the description, as shown in Figure 14-29. Notice that some options do not have a description. This figure shows the Specialty field that was created in this exercise with a few values. This is what the field would look like when it is added to a layout.

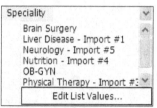

Speciality

Brain Surgery
Liver Disease - Import #1
Neurology - Import #5
Nutrition - Import #4
OB-GYN
Physical Therapy - Import #3
Edit List Values...

**Figure 14-29** Show Descriptions option enabled

## Calculated Fields

Calculated fields are used to create a formula to get a value, that will be displayed on a view. The value is not stored in the database. There are two types of calculated fields that can be created, as explained below.

① **DATE** This type of calculation displays the result in days or years.
② **NUMERIC** This type of calculation displays the result as a numeric value. It is possible that to create the calculation, you may need to create another field to use in the calculation.

## Calculated Field Tips

Below are some tips that will help you create calculated fields.

① Calculated fields can only be displayed as read only.
② Only date or numeric fields can be used in the formula.
③ When first created, a calculated field is applied to all of the records in the database.
④ Text based calculations like concatenation, cannot be created.
⑤ Constant values can be used in the formula.
⑥ If records are imported that have a field used in the calculation, the calculation is applied to the imported record.
⑦ Calculated fields are automatically updated when a value in a field used in the formula changes.
⑧ Once a numeric field (in a table in the database) is used in a calculated field, the numeric field cannot be modified, unless the calculated field is deleted.
⑨ Existing fields cannot be changed to a calculated field.
⑩ Once a calculated field is created, the only thing that can be changed is the field name. If any other change needs to be made to the calculated field, the calculated field has to be deleted and recreated. If a field that is referenced by a calculated field needs to be changed, the calculated field has to be deleted first.

## Exercise 14.9: Create Calculated Fields

In this exercise, you will learn how to create date and numeric calculated fields. You will also learn the basics of adding a field to a layout.

## Create A Date Calculated Field

In this part of the exercise you will create a calculation that counts the number of days since the last activity with the contact took place.

1. Tools ⇒ Define Fields.

2. Select the Contacts table, in the drop-down list ⇒ Click the **CREATE NEW FIELD** link.

3. In the Field Name field, type `Days Since Contacted`.

4. Open the Field data type drop-down list and select Calculated ⇒ Click Next.

5. Open the Calculated field type drop-down list and select Date.

6. Open the Field drop-down list and select Edit Date.

   You should have the options shown in Figure 14-30.

   Click Finish ⇒
   Once the field has been created, click the Close button on the Define Fields dialog box ⇒
   Go to the next section.

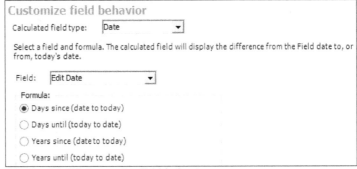

**Figure 14-30** Customize field behavior screen

## Add The Calculated Field To A Layout

Keep in mind that fields are not automatically added to a layout. Fields have to manually be added to a layout.

1. When you see the message shown in Figure 14-31, click Yes.

   You should see the Basic Contact Layout - 1024 x 768 layout. (The Contact detail view) If not, File ⇒ Open ⇒ Contact Layout.

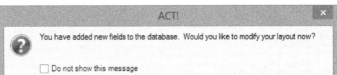

**Figure 14-31** ACT! message to modify the layout

2. On the Layout Designer, click on the tabs, then drag them down a little.

3. Click the Field button (below the pointer) on the left, in the ToolBox ⇒ Click in the layout below the Letter Sent field and draw a box.

4. On the dialog box shown in Figure 14-32, select the Days Since Contacted field ⇒ Click the Add button.

**Figure 14-32** Select Field dialog box

5. Click on a blank space in the layout ⇒ Click on the Days Since contacted field.

   You should see the field, illustrated in Figure 14-33.

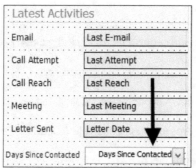

**Figure 14-33** Calculated field added to the layout

6. Open the Background color list (4th button in, from the end of the toolbar) and select the light yellow color on the second row.

7. Click the Save button. File ⇒ Exit ⇒ On the Contact Detail View, scroll through some of the records. You will see the calculated field that you created.

## Create A Numeric Calculated Field

In this part of the exercise, you will create a sales tax formula.

1. Tools ⇒ Define Fields ⇒ Open the drop-down list and select Opportunities.

2. Click the Create new field link.

3. In the Field Name field, type `Sales Tax` ⇒ Change the Field data type to Calculated ⇒ Click Next.

4. Change the Calculated field type to Numeric.

## Create The Sales Tax Calculation

The formula that you will create will multiply the Total times 6.5% to calculate the sales tax. In the real world, sales tax is calculated for each item, not the total amount of the order, because not all items are taxable.

1. In the Fields list, double-click on the Total field.

2. In the Formula section, click after the Total field ⇒ Double-click on the Product (*) function.

3. In the Formula section, click after the * and type `.065`.

4. Click the **VALIDATE FORMULA** button.

   You should see a message that says the formula is valid.

   Change the **DISPLAY CALCULATED FIELD AS** option to Currency.

   You should have the options shown in Figure 14-34.

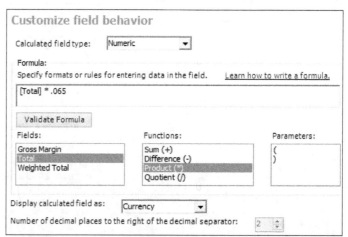

**Figure 14-34** Customize field behavior options for a calculated field

5. Click Finish to create the calculated field ⇒ Click Close to close the Define Fields dialog box. When prompted to add the field to the layout, click Yes. You should see the Opportunity layout. If not, select it now.

## Modify The Layout

It would probably make the most sense to put the sales tax field as close to the total as possible.

1.  Make the tabs section smaller.

2.  Select the Weighted field and all fields and objects below it, as shown in Figure 14-35, by drawing a box around them with the mouse ⇒
    Drag the fields down a little, so that a field can be added above the Weighted field ⇒
    Click on a blank space on the layout.

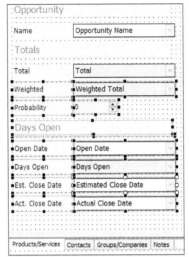

**Figure 14-35** Several fields selected to be moved

3.  On the left, click the Field button ⇒ Draw a field below the Total field.

4.  On the Select Field dialog box, add the Sales Tax field.

5.  Click on a blank space on the layout ⇒ Select the Sales Tax label (on the left) ⇒ Drag it left to line it up with the other labels in the column.

6.  Click on the Sales Tax field ⇒ Click the Left button on the toolbar.

7.  Save the changes, then close the Layout Designer.

    The Totals section of the Opportunity Layout in the Detail view should look like the one shown in Figure 14-36.

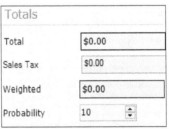

**Figure 14-36** Totals section of the Opportunity layout

## Deleting Fields

As a programmer, I do not delete fields from a database that have data, when I first come to the conclusion that the data is no longer needed. Instead, I will modify the layouts that display the field, so that the field is not visible on the layout. I will also remove the field from the queries and reports, but not from the database. If you want to delete a field right away, make a backup copy of the database, then delete the field. While deleting the field from the database is easy to do, you should also remove it from the layouts, queries and reports that it is used in. The steps below show you how to delete a field.

1.  Tools ⇒ Define Fields.

2.  Open the drop-down list and select the table, that has the field that you want to delete.

3.  Click on the field that you want to delete in the list, then click the Delete Field link on the left.

4.  Click Yes, when prompted if you are sure that you want to delete the field. Once the field is deleted, close the Define Fields dialog box.

### Managing Priority Types

Schedule ⇒ Manage ⇒ Priorities, opens the dialog box shown in Figure 14-37.

Chapter 7 covered how to schedule activities and set the priority for the activity. Renaming or disabling a priority does not effect activities that already have a priority. They will still display with the priority they had when the activity was created.

The changes that you make on this dialog box only effect new activities. There are five priority options that come with ACT!.

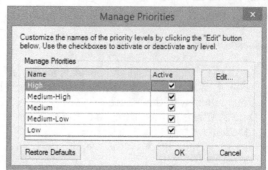

**Figure 14-37** Manage Priorities dialog box

You cannot create new entries, but you can modify the names of the existing entries to better meet your needs or to be more descriptive. If you need to rename a priority, click on it, then click the **EDIT** button and type in the new name.

If you do not need a priority, clear the check mark for it in the **ACTIVE** column. This prevents users from selecting a priority on the Schedule Activities dialog box.

The **RESTORE DEFAULTS** button will reset the priorities back to what they were when ACT! was first installed.

### Exercise 14.10: Creating Activity Types

Chapter 7 covered the activity types that come with ACT!. They cannot be deleted. Only users with administrator or manager level security rights can create new activity types. In this exercise you will learn how to create activity types.

1.  Schedule ⇒ Manage ⇒ Activity Types ⇒ Click the Add button.

2.  In the **NAME** field, type `Post Card Mailing`.

3.  If you want the activity type to have an icon, click the **BROWSE** button. Navigate to and double-click on the icon file that you want to use.

4.  Click the Add button on the Add Activity Type dialog box ⇒ Type `Post Card Mailing Completed` in the **RESULT NAME** field, then click OK.

5.  Check the option that you just created on the Add Activity Type dialog box to make it the default. You should have the options shown in Figure 14-38.

    The options on the bottom half of this dialog box are the values that will appear in the Results drop-down list field on the Schedule Activities dialog box.

    These options are also used to clear an activity on the Clear Activity dialog box. You can enter as many options as you need. When a new activity type is created, the **COMPLETED** and **NOT COMPLETED** result types shown in the figure are added automatically.

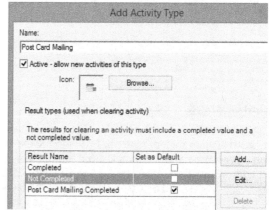

**Figure 14-38** Add Activity Type dialog box

6.  Click OK. The dialog box should have the Post Card Mailing activity shown in Figure 14-39 ⇒ Click the Close button.

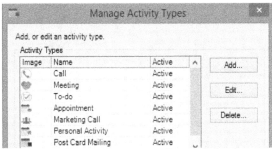

**Figure 14-39** Manage Activity Types dialog box

## Annual Events

Annual Events are activities that can be displayed on your calendar, but not on the Task List. Events can be recurring like birthdays or one-time events like a business trip. A good use of the events option is to set up holidays on your calendar. Events do not cause scheduling conflicts and do not appear on reports. Only users with an administrator or manager level account can create events.

### Exercise 14.11: Create An Annual Event Activity

In this exercise you will create an event for July 4th.

1.  Schedule ⇒ Manage ⇒ Events.

2.  Click the **ADD** button ⇒ Type `4th of July` in the **EVENT NAME** field.

3.  Select July 4th of next year in the Date field ⇒ Change the **DURATION** to 1 day, if necessary.

4.  Change the **OCCURS** option to yearly.

    You should have the options shown in Figure 14-40.

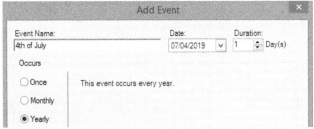

**Figure 14-40** Add Event dialog box

5.  Click OK. You will see the event on the dialog box shown in Figure 14-41.

    Click the Close button.

**Figure 14-41** Manage Events dialog box

## Add The Event To Your Calendar

In this part of the exercise, you will add the event that you just created to your calendar.

1.  Tools ⇒ Preferences.

2.  On the Calendar & Activities tab, click the Calendar Preferences button.

3. Check the **DISPLAY EVENTS** option, illustrated in Figure 14-42, if it is not already checked ⇒
Click OK twice to close both dialog boxes.

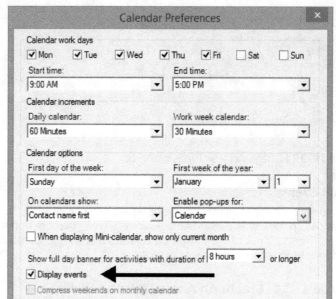

**Figure 14-42** Display events option illustrated

4. Open a calendar view and display July 4th of next year. You will see the entry illustrated in Figure 14-43. If you do not see the entry, make sure that all of the filter options are set to All.

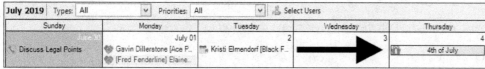

**Figure 14-43** Event added to the calendar

# INDEX

www.ingramcontent.com/pod-product-compliance
Lightning Source LLC
LaVergne TN
LVHW060138070326
832902LV00018B/2850